GEORGE R.R. MARTIN'S
DOORWAYS

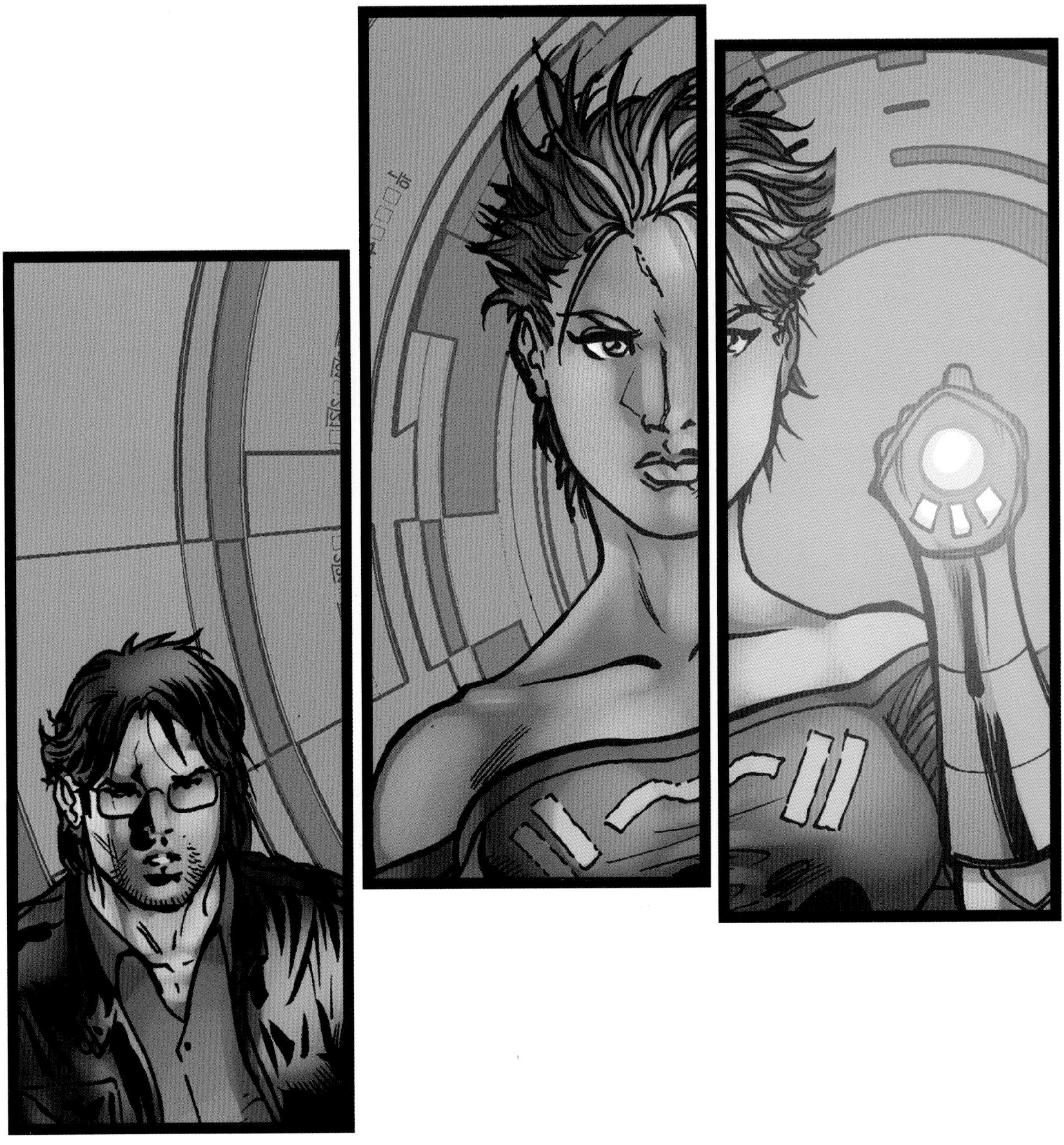

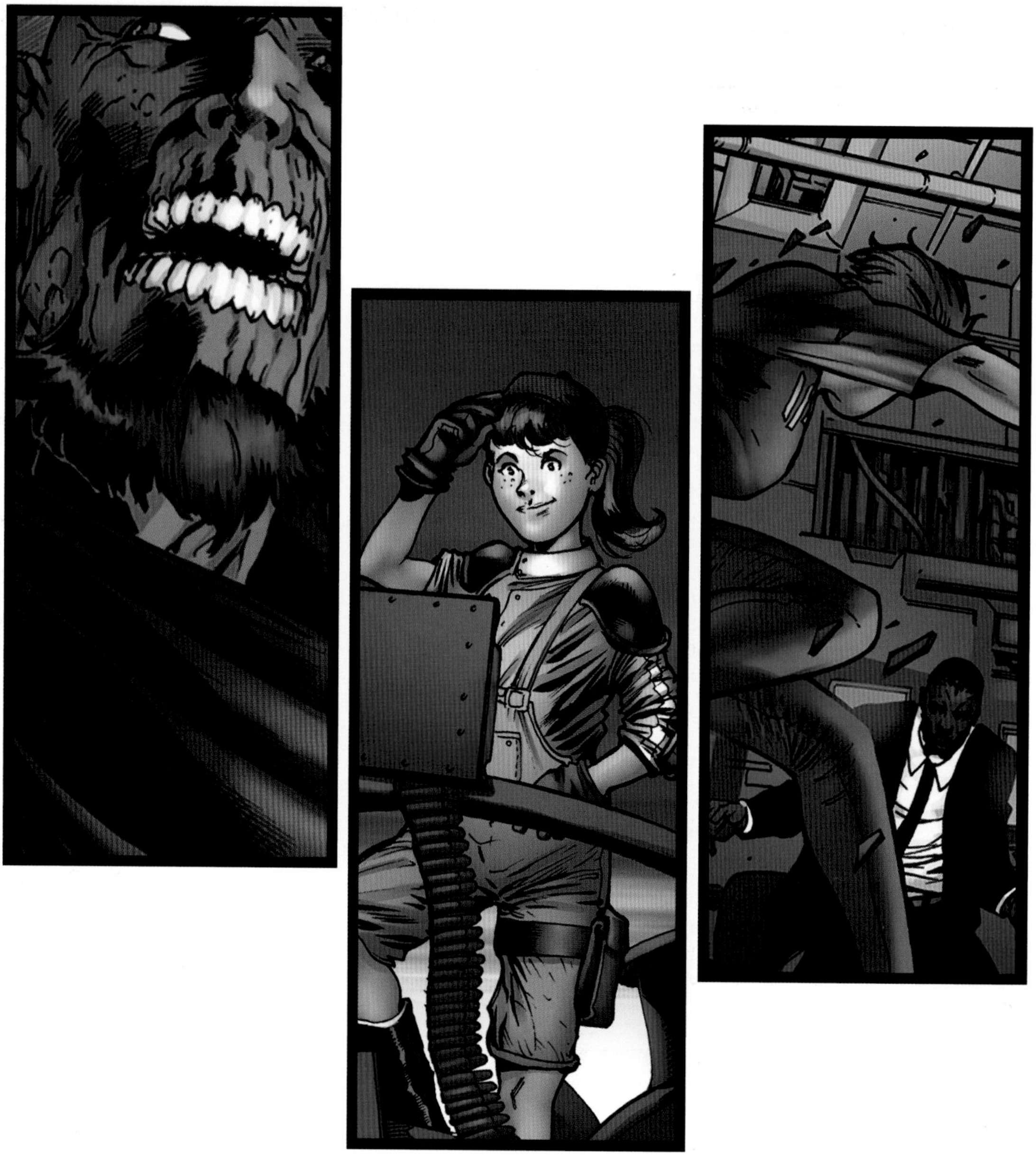

CREATED & WRITTEN BY

GEORGE R.R. MARTIN

ART BY

STEFANO MARTINO

COLORS BY CHARLIE KIRCHOFF & ALFREDO RODRIGUEZ

LETTERS BY SHAWN LEE & NEIL UYETAKE

EDITS BY MARIAH HUEHNER • ASSISTANT EDITS BY BOBBY CURNOW

COLLECTION EDITS BY JUSTIN EISINGER • COLLECTION DESIGN BY SHAWN LEE

IDW

ISBN: 978-1-60010-916-4   14 13 12 11   1 2 3 4
www.IDWPUBLISHING.com

Originally published as GEORGE R.R. MARTIN'S DOORWAYS Issues #1–4.

WHAT IF ?

BY GEORGE R.R. MARTIN

For all sad words of tongue and pen,
the saddest are these, "it might have been."
- JOHN GREENLEAF WHITTIER

Every life has its turning points, its might-have-beens, the places where the road forks, leading off in two different directions. Sometimes you choose which way to go after long deliberation, carefully weighing your options. At other times you hurry past, taking the broader path or the busiest, hardly even pausing to look down the other fork. And sometimes the choice is made for you by time or chance or other people. However you decide, life is what it is, and there is seldom any turning back… though all of us, I think, look behind us later on and wonder. "What if things had turned out differently?" we ask ourselves. "What if I had done that instead of this, gone left instead of right, bet on red instead of black? What if I had gone to the other school, taken the other job, married the other girl, what would my life have been? What if, what if, what if…"

A writing career is often full of such "what if" moments, both good and bad. What if I had been able to get an actual entry-level job on a newspaper in the spring of 1971, when I left Northwestern with my master's degree in journalism? I might still be a journalist today. Instead, unemployed, I spent that summer writing science fiction and fantasy stories, subsequently sold them all, and took another road. What if my fourth novel, *The Armageddon Rag*, had not been such a huge commercial failure? Most likely I would never have gone to Hollywood or written for television and film. What if I had not put aside the SF novel that I was working on during the summer of 1991 to write this fantasy idea I had, about some direwolf pups found in the summer snows? *Avalon* might have been a good book, even a popular one, but would it have transformed my life and career the way *A Game of Thrones* did? Not likely.

But the biggest "what if" and "might-have-been" in my career, appropriately enough, was a story about what ifs and might-have-beens, called *Doorways*.

The Armageddon Rag did flop, after all. So I found myself unable to sell my journalism novel, *Black and White and Red All Over*, when I offered it to publishers in 1985. So I did go out to L.A., where I joined the writing staff of *The Twilight Zone*, and later *Beauty and the Beast*. After both of those series had run their course, I continued to work in Hollywood, writing screenplays and pitching television pilots. In that fateful (for me) summer of 1991, finding myself back home in New Mexico and between contracts, I started that SF novel (*Avalon*), then put it aside for the fantasy that would become *A Game of Thrones*. I was only about a hundred pages into the book when my agent Jodi Levine called to tell me that she'd set pitch meetings for me at ABC, NBC, and Fox. So I hopped on a plane and flew back out to L.A. to try and sell a series of my own.

I had a great concept for a show, I thought. I wanted to base a series on "The Skin Trade," my World Fantasy Award-winning novella about a sexy female private eye and an asthmatic, hypochondriac werewolf collection agent. But you don't go into pitch meetings with only one arrow in your quiver. I needed a second idea, in case the suits did not warm to my first. On the flight to Burbank, I found one. I remembered an old fantasy story that I had written back in the '70s, called "The Lonely Songs of Laren Dorr." High fantasy romance, not what the networks wanted back then—but the first line of that story still resonated with me:

"There is a girl who goes between the worlds."

That old line from an old story was the seed that sprouted *Doorways*. The rest of "The Lonely Songs of Laren Dorr," I put aside. This was a whole new story, with new characters. Television had done plenty of shows about space travel and time travel, but there was one huge SF trope that had gone almost (not entirely, but almost) untouched: alternate worlds.

The perfect television pitch, as my old friend and partner in mayhem Michael Cassutt likes to say, goes like this: "He's the pope. She's a chimp. They fight crime." They call it "high concept," and if your idea can't be boiled down into three sentences to fit that pattern, you're probably dead before you open your mouth. My pitch went like this: "He's an emergency room doc. She's a feral slave girl fleeing her alien masters. They travel to parallel worlds."

Over the span of two days, I met with the development execs at NBC, Fox, and ABC, and pitched them my ideas. As the fates would have it, none of them showed the slightest bit of interest in "The Skin Trade," but they all went wild for the concept I was then calling simply *Doors*. Fox had seemed the most enthusiastic in the room, and for a day or two I thought we would end up there, but ABC moved the fastest, and that's where we cut the deal. I needed a studio, so I took the project to Columbia Pictures. James Crocker, a colleague and friend from my days on *The Twilight Zone*, joined me as an executive producer.

For the next year and a half, my life was *Doors*.

I spent the rest of 1991 plotting out the pilot story, revising it, expanding it when the network decided they wanted to do a ninety-minute pilot instead of just an hour, writing the first-draft teleplay, rewriting the teleplay when the network decided they wanted a completely different second half, revising again, revising again, cutting, polishing, revising, cutting…

In January of 1992, after a few suspenseful weeks, we got great news. ABC loved the script. We got the greenlight to shoot the pilot.

There were more revisions, of course. (In television, there are always more revisions.) We hired a director and a line producer, the director hired a DP and the line producer a crew. We found our Cat in Paris, in the person of a wonderful young French actress named Anne LeGuernec… but the Tom that we wanted, an actor named George Newbern, was tied up filming a movie all through the spring. We looked at a hundred other possibilities, but none of them were as good as George, so finally it was decided to push back filming until he was free. (Which had the unfortunate side effect of taking us out of contention for a slot in the fall schedule for 1992, since we would not be filming until May, when all the other pilots were in the can, and the networks were already deciding which shows to slot for fall.) Rob Knepper, another fine young actor, was cast as our third regular, Thane. The guest cast consisted of Kurtwood Smith as Trager, Carrie Ann Moss as Laura, Hoyt Axton as Jake, and the delightful and vivacious Tisha Putman as Cissy. With Peter Werner at the helm, we started shooting in May of 1992, wrapped in July, then spent a month in editing and post-production. And somewhere along the line, the title was changed to *Doorways*, after the network expressed concern that people might confuse *Doors* with Jim Morrison's band or Oliver Stone's film about the same (though in the script, and in the show, the doors are still called doors, never doorways.)

In August of 1992 we screened a rough cut for ABC.

The network loved it. The reaction could not have been more positive, despite the fact that there was still a lot of work to be done on the pilot (the special effects, in particular). If it had been May, I don't doubt we would have gotten a series order right then and there.

Alas, it was August. ABC's fall schedule was already set. "No problem," the network told us. "We will put you on in February as a mid-season replacement." And they backed up those sweet words with an immediate order for six back up scripts.

Then or now, that sort of order was very unusual, and a real sign of the network's enthusiasm for a show. A pilot that the network is lukewarm about won't get any script order whatsover. One that they think might be a strong contender might get an order for two scripts. And six scripts? Even the guys at Columbia said that was unprecedented. It was the nearest thing to a series order you could get, aside from an actual series order.

Doorways was so close to prime time that I could taste it.

I spent the rest of 1992 and the first few months of 1993 working on those six back up scripts, intended as the first six episodes of our eventual series. One episode I wrote myself. Another was scripted by Jim Crocker, my fellow executive producer and showrunner. The remaining scripts were assigned to four terrific freelance writers: Michael Cassutt, Ed Zuckerman, Steve DeJarnett, and J.D. Feigelson. We met, we plotted, we outlined, we revised, we wrote, and rewrote, and rewrote, and polished, and rewrote some more… with one eye on the calendar, waiting for that pickup. All that fall and into the winter, I went forward fully expecting to have my own show on the air Real Soon Now, and jotting down ideas about the worlds that Tom and Cat might visit, the adventures they might have.

(Meanwhile, I was also going over pattern budgets, frowning a little, then a lot, fretting, worrying, sweating, wondering how the hell we were going to do the show I wanted to do on an episodic television budget. But that's a story for another day).

But as the months passed, things happened, as things often do. Television is inexorable, and even as the new shows are debuting in the fall, pilot scripts are being ordered for the following year's schedule… even newer shows, to take the place of any of the current crop that falter. Meanwhile, one of our biggest supporters at ABC got moved to the New York office, another took a job heading a studio, a third quit when he did not get a promotion. All of them were replaced by people who did not know *Doorways*, and had no part in its development.

We did not go on the air as a mid-season replacement in 1993. Instead we were thrown back in the hopper, to compete for a fall slot with all the new

pilots. But by then we were old news, a leftover show from the previous season and the previous regime… and come May, when ABC announced its fall schedule, we were not on it. "We only had room for one SF show on the schedule," we were told, "and we thought *Lois & Clark* had more name recognition." And that pretty much was the end of *Doorways*… until now.

It was not the end of my stint in Hollywood, mind you. I wrote two more pilots, neither of which got as far as *Doorways*. As a producer, I supervised other writers on other pilots. I wrote three screenplays for the live-action division of Disney, and one for a small indie studio, none of which ever got filmed. I made wheelbarrows full of money. But eventually I got tired of it all, and dusted off that novel I'd been writing in 1991, when I was called out to Hollywood to pitch. It turned into *A Game of Thrones*, the first book in my epic fantasy series *A Song of Ice and Fire*. I'm working on the fifth book in the series now, with two more yet to come.

But I won't say that I've never looked back. We all look back. *Doorways* was a huge turning point for me. If we had not been out of sync with the inexorable timetable of network television… if we had delivered our pilot in May instead of August… if ABC had made a different call… everything might have changed. Would we have lasted ten episodes, or ten years? Would we have been a hit, a flop? Would the critics have thrown laurels or brickbats? Would Anne LeGuernec, George Newbern, and Rob Knepper have become stars (for one of them, at least, I think the answer is "yes")? Would I have gone on from *Doorways* to create more television shows, become the new Steven Bochco, the new Dick Wolf, a Joss Whedon before Joss Whedon, made dump trucks full of money instead of mere wheelbarrows?

Maybe. Maybe not. Probably not. We'll never know. That's the nature of what ifs and might-have-beens. But I will always wonder. We came so close…

One thing is pretty certain, though. If *Doorways* had gone to series, I would have remained in television much longer than I did, *A Game of Thrones* might never have been finished, and no one would be calling me "the American Tolkien" today. So all in all, I can't complain. I'm pretty pleased with the way that all worked out.

I do grieve for the untold stories, though. A writer's characters are like his children, I've often said. Tom and Cat were a huge part of my life for a year and a half, and of course I came to love

them, just as I love Tyrion and Daenerys and Jon Snow, Jay Ackroyd and the Great and Powerful Turtle, Haviland Tuf and Abner Marsh, and all the other characters that I've created over the years. It broke my heart to know that the world would never know them, or share their exploits and adventures.

Which is why this comic series is such a thrill for me. Thanks to Stefano Martino and the good folks at IDW, Tom and Cat live again, and their stories will at last be told. That pleases me more than I can say.

One thing I should make clear, however. A few of you may have seen the pilot that we filmed for ABC back in 1992. Though it was never screened on American television (ABC did schedule it in the summer of 1993, during the dog days of August when all the busted pilots are "burned off," but their bright boys forgot that it was a ninety-minute pilot and put it in a sixty-minute timeslot, so they had to scrap it at the last moment), *Doorways* was released on videotape (VHS) around the world, albeit in a bloated two-hour version.

But this comic and that video are two different animals. Tom and Cat and the other characters depicted here look nothing like the actors who portrayed them in the pilot; these versions were created by Stefano, who has never seen the video. We've changed some things as well. The great thing about a graphic novel is that you don't have the sort of budgetary limitations you do on a television show… you can afford all the special effects you want, elaborate sets, spectacular costumes, astonishing architecture… and your aliens won't need to be actors dressed up in rubber suits. Television requires hard choices and compromises, more often than not. A graphic novel gives you much more freedom. So all in all, I think, this version of *Doorways* is going to be much cooler than the television show could ever have been.

We're thirteen years late, but at last the door is opening, and…

There is a girl who goes between the worlds.

George R.R. Martin

Santa Fe, New Mexico

August 2010

(Did someone mention *Sliders? Sliders!!!* Slowly I turned. Step by step… inch by inch…)

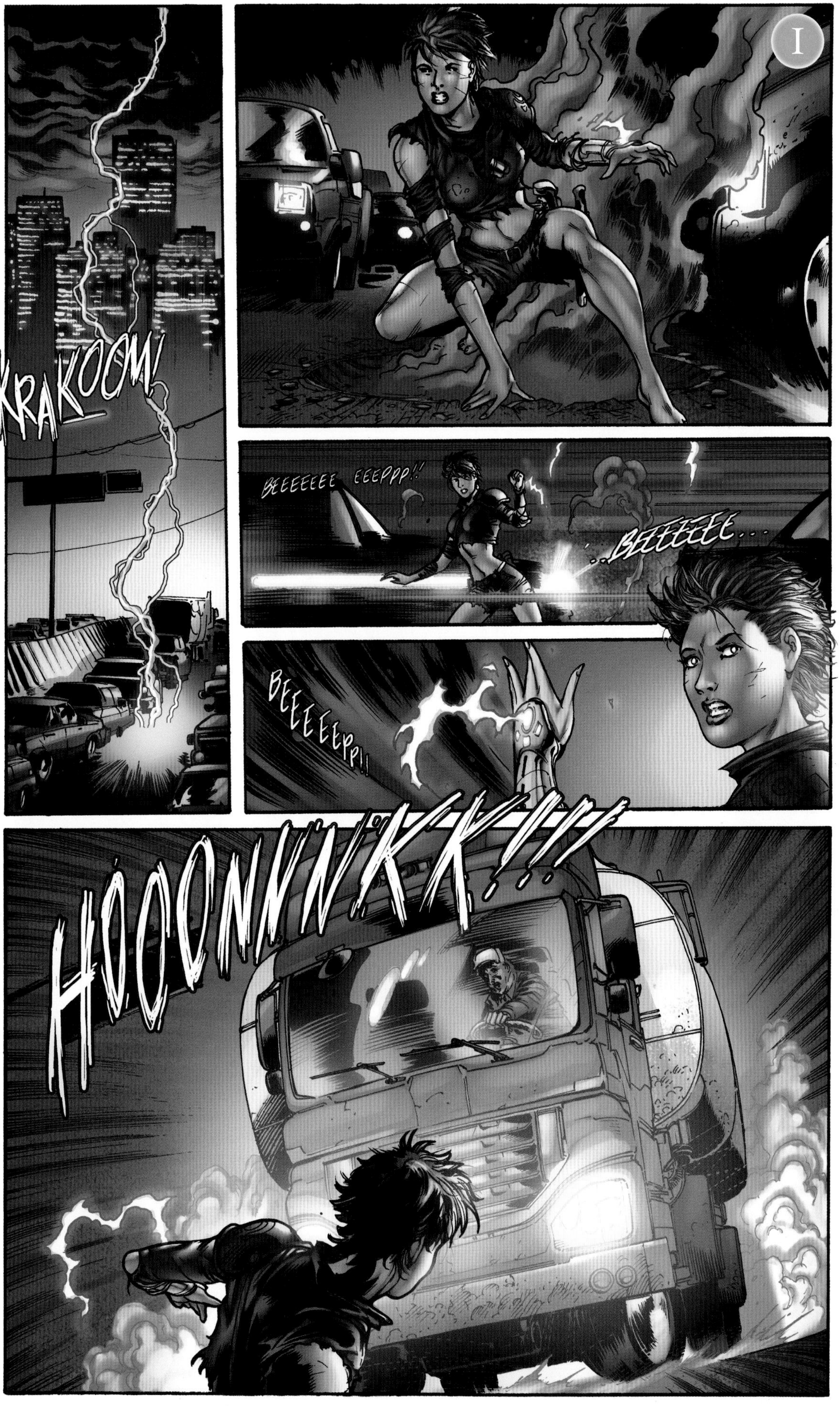
I
KRAKOOM!
BEEEEEEE EEEPPP!!
..BEEEEEE...
BEEEEEEPP!!
HOOONNNKK!!!

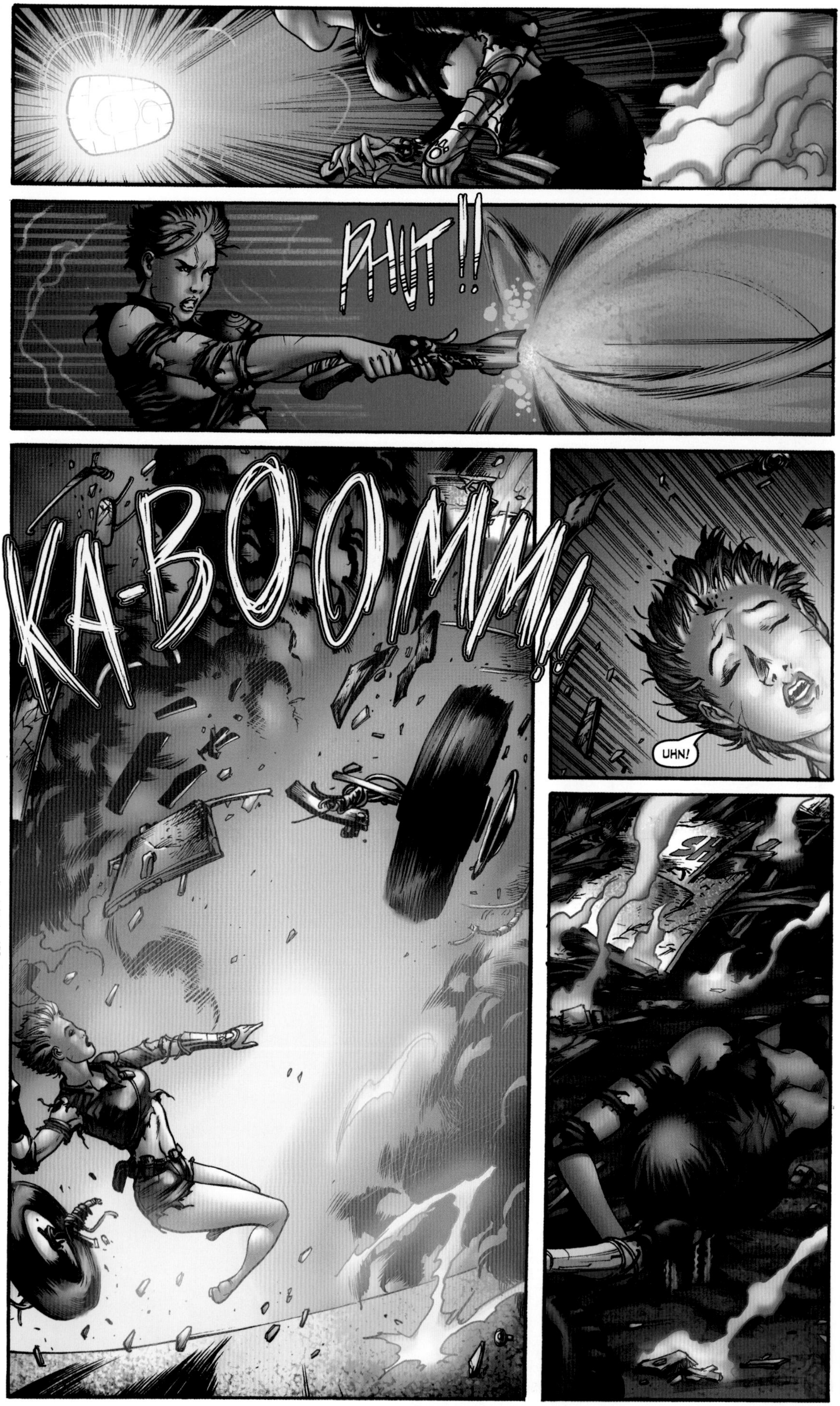
PHUT!!
KA-BOOMM!!
UHN!

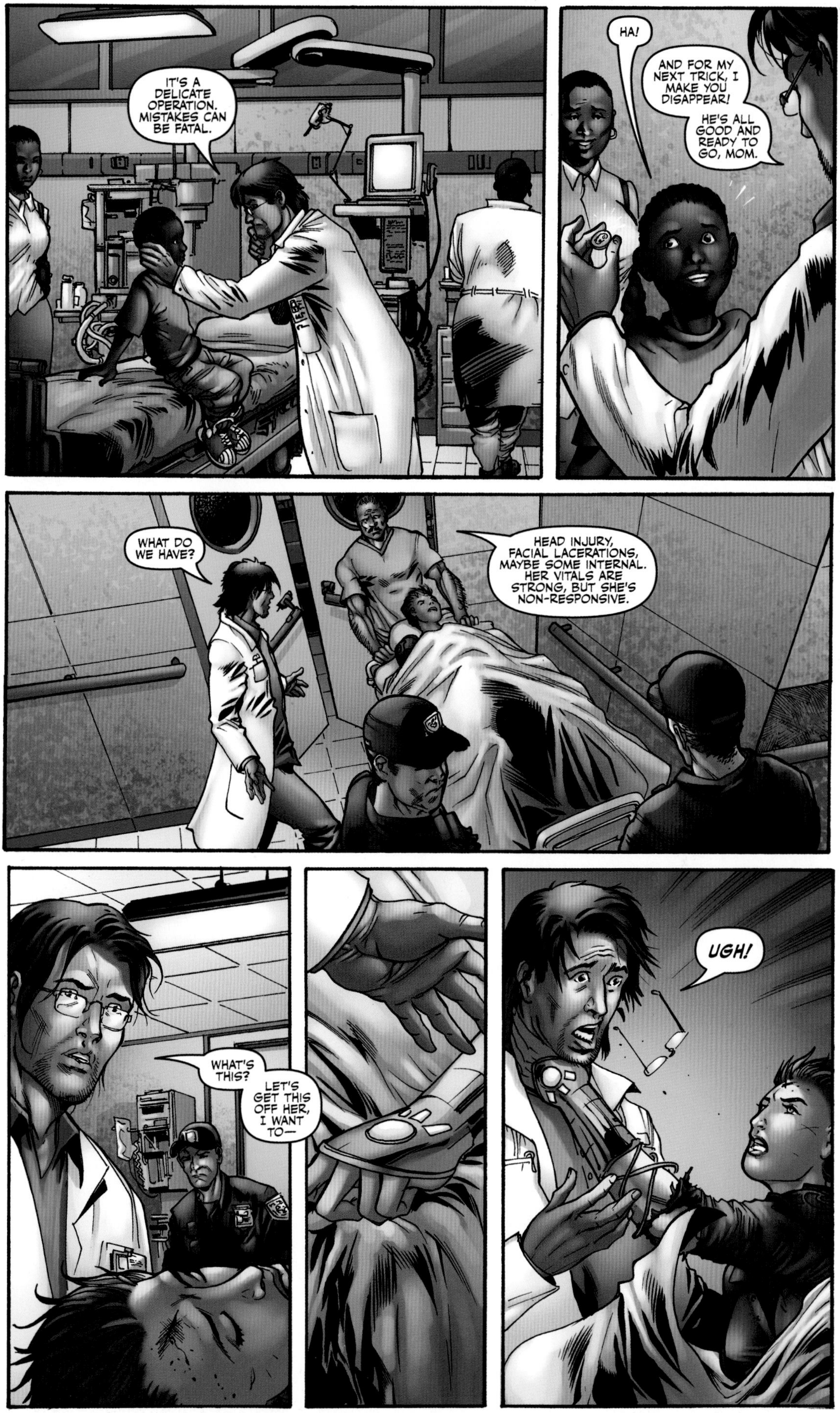
IT'S A DELICATE OPERATION. MISTAKES CAN BE FATAL.
HA!
AND FOR MY NEXT TRICK, I MAKE YOU DISAPPEAR!
HE'S ALL GOOD AND READY TO GO, MOM.
WHAT DO WE HAVE?
HEAD INJURY, FACIAL LACERATIONS, MAYBE SOME INTERNAL. HER VITALS ARE STRONG, BUT SHE'S NON-RESPONSIVE.
WHAT'S THIS?
LET'S GET THIS OFF HER, I WANT TO—
UGH!

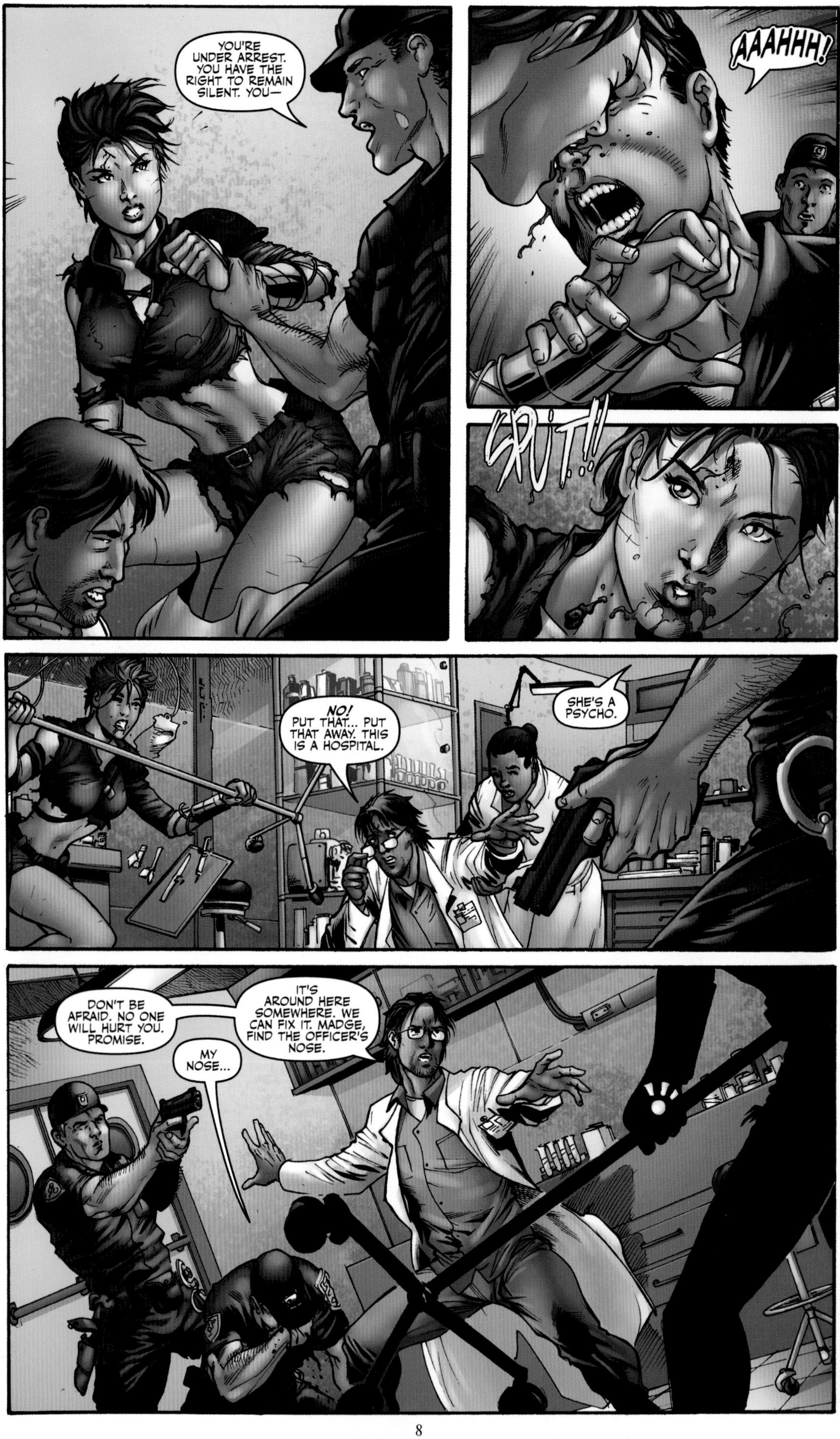
YOU'RE UNDER ARREST. YOU HAVE THE RIGHT TO REMAIN SILENT. YOU—
AAAHHH!
SPLUT!!
NO! PUT THAT... PUT THAT AWAY. THIS IS A HOSPITAL.
SHE'S A PSYCHO.
DON'T BE AFRAID. NO ONE WILL HURT YOU. PROMISE.
IT'S AROUND HERE SOMEWHERE. WE CAN FIX IT. MADGE, FIND THE OFFICER'S NOSE.
MY NOSE...

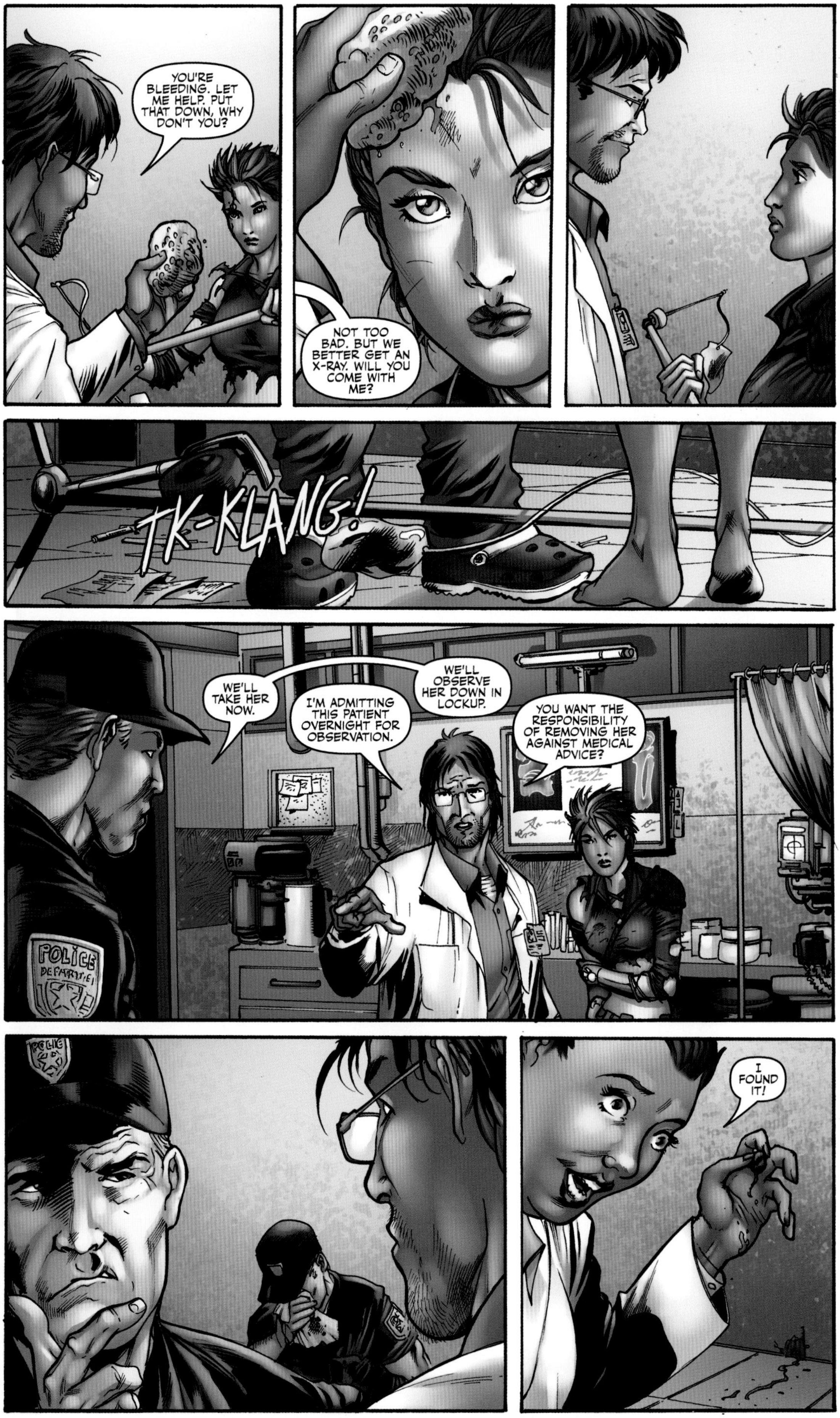
YOU'RE BLEEDING. LET ME HELP. PUT THAT DOWN, WHY DON'T YOU?
NOT TOO BAD. BUT WE BETTER GET AN X-RAY. WILL YOU COME WITH ME?
TK-KLANG!
WE'LL TAKE HER NOW.
I'M ADMITTING THIS PATIENT OVERNIGHT FOR OBSERVATION.
WE'LL OBSERVE HER DOWN IN LOCKUP.
YOU WANT THE RESPONSIBILITY OF REMOVING HER AGAINST MEDICAL ADVICE?
POLICE
I FOUND IT!

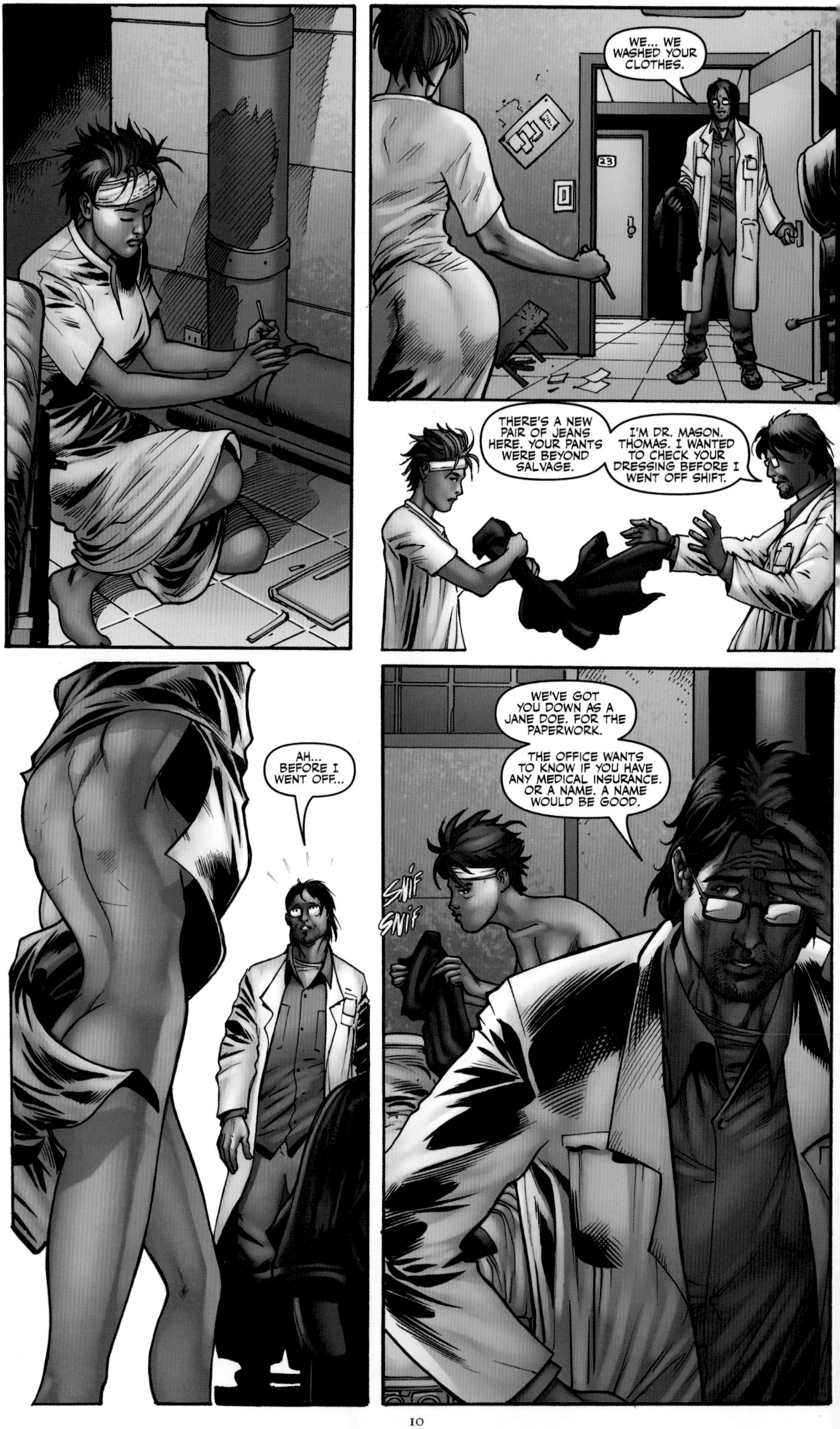
WE... WE WASHED YOUR CLOTHES.
THERE'S A NEW PAIR OF JEANS HERE. YOUR PANTS WERE BEYOND SALVAGE.
I'M DR. MASON. THOMAS. I WANTED TO CHECK YOUR DRESSING BEFORE I WENT OFF SHIFT.
AH... BEFORE I WENT OFF...
WE'VE GOT YOU DOWN AS A JANE DOE. FOR THE PAPERWORK.
THE OFFICE WANTS TO KNOW IF YOU HAVE ANY MEDICAL INSURANCE. OR A NAME. A NAME WOULD BE GOOD.
SNIF
SNIF

SORRY. THE POLICE DON'T WANT YOU GOING ANYWHERE RIGHT NOW.

BAM

STOP IT!

WHY ARE YOU SO ANGRY? WHAT ARE YOU AFRAID OF?

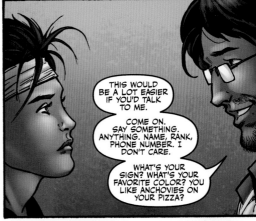

THIS WOULD BE A LOT EASIER IF YOU'D TALK TO ME.

COME ON. SAY SOMETHING. ANYTHING. NAME, RANK, PHONE NUMBER. I DON'T CARE.

WHAT'S YOUR SIGN? WHAT'S YOUR FAVORITE COLOR? YOU LIKE ANCHOVIES ON YOUR PIZZA?

CAT.

DID YOU SAY SOMETHING?

CAT. NAME. TOE MAS.

RIGHT. TOE MAS. TOE MAS MASON.

WHERE DO YOU LIVE, CAT? WHERE ARE YOU FROM?

EARTH.

THAT CLARIFIES THINGS.

NOT HERE. THERE. DOOR.

LEAVING NOW, TOE MAS. GOING NOW. GETTING OUT.

THAT DOOR ONLY OPENS FOR ME NOW. SORRY.

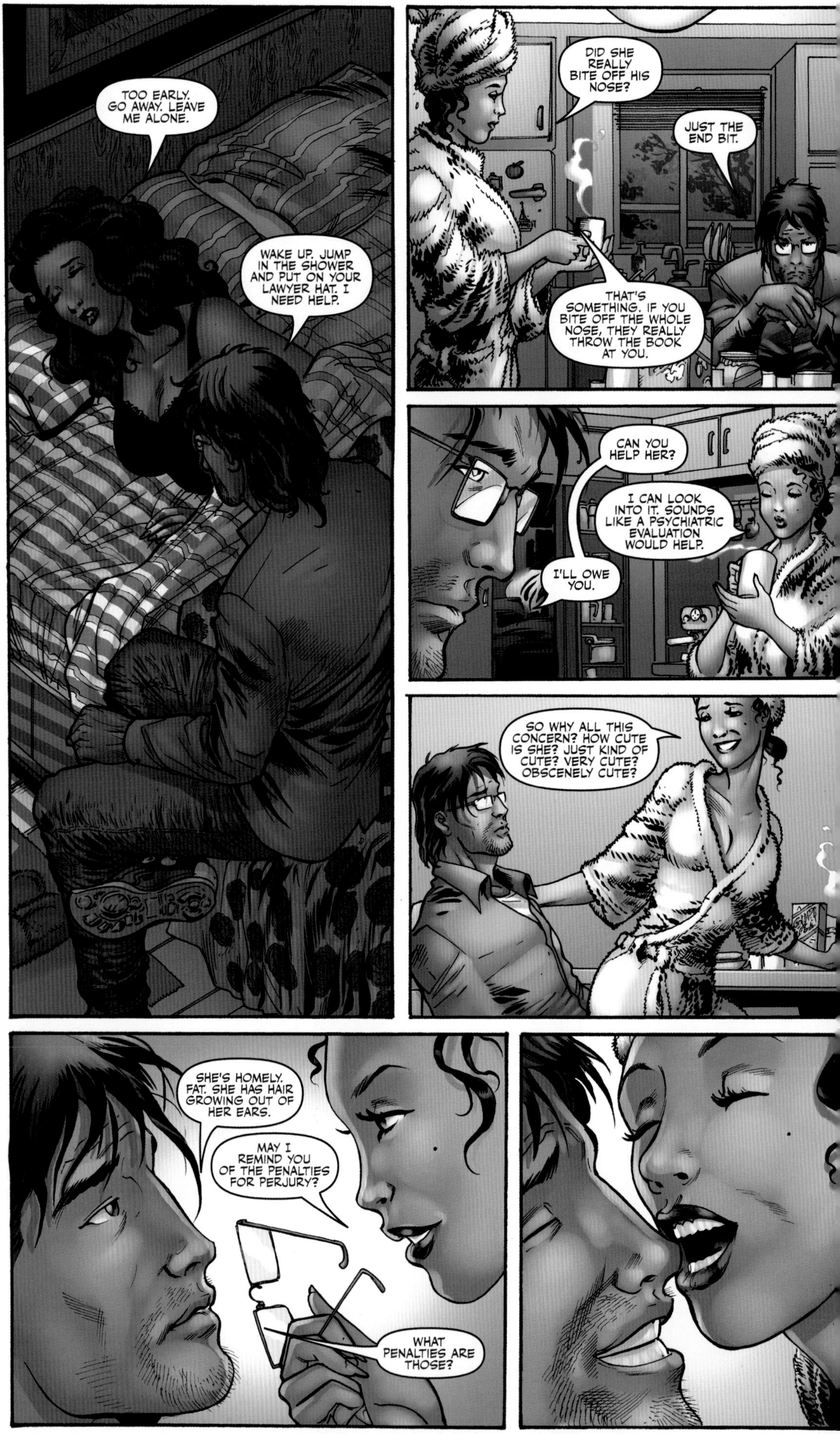
TOO EARLY. GO AWAY. LEAVE ME ALONE.
WAKE UP. JUMP IN THE SHOWER AND PUT ON YOUR LAWYER HAT. I NEED HELP.
DID SHE REALLY BITE OFF HIS NOSE?
JUST THE END BIT.
THAT'S SOMETHING. IF YOU BITE OFF THE WHOLE NOSE, THEY REALLY THROW THE BOOK AT YOU.
CAN YOU HELP HER?
I CAN LOOK INTO IT. SOUNDS LIKE A PSYCHIATRIC EVALUATION WOULD HELP.
I'LL OWE YOU.
SO WHY ALL THIS CONCERN? HOW CUTE IS SHE? JUST KIND OF CUTE? VERY CUTE? OBSCENELY CUTE?
SHE'S HOMELY. FAT. SHE HAS HAIR GROWING OUT OF HER EARS.
MAY I REMIND YOU OF THE PENALTIES FOR PERJURY?
WHAT PENALTIES ARE THOSE?

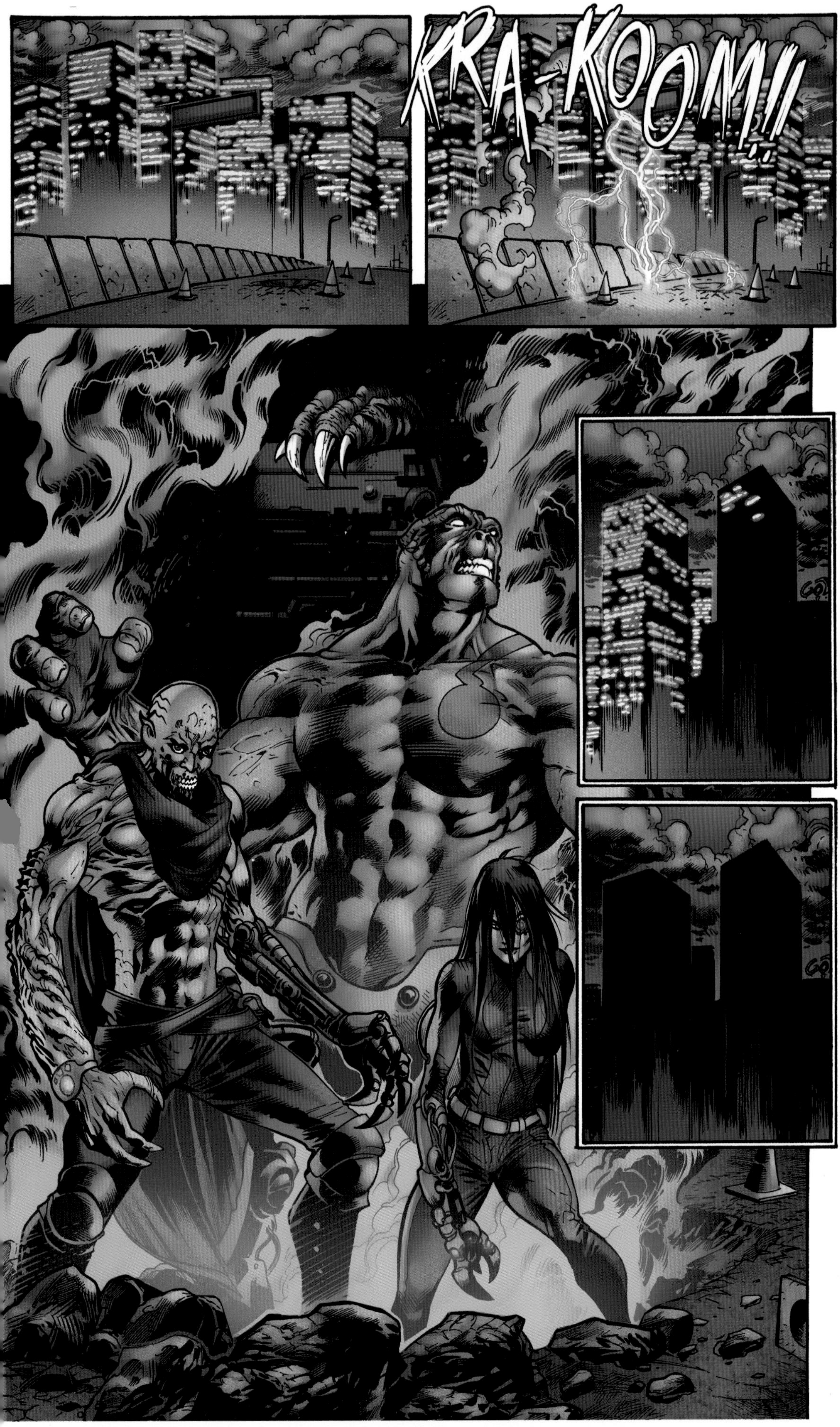
KRA-KOOM!!

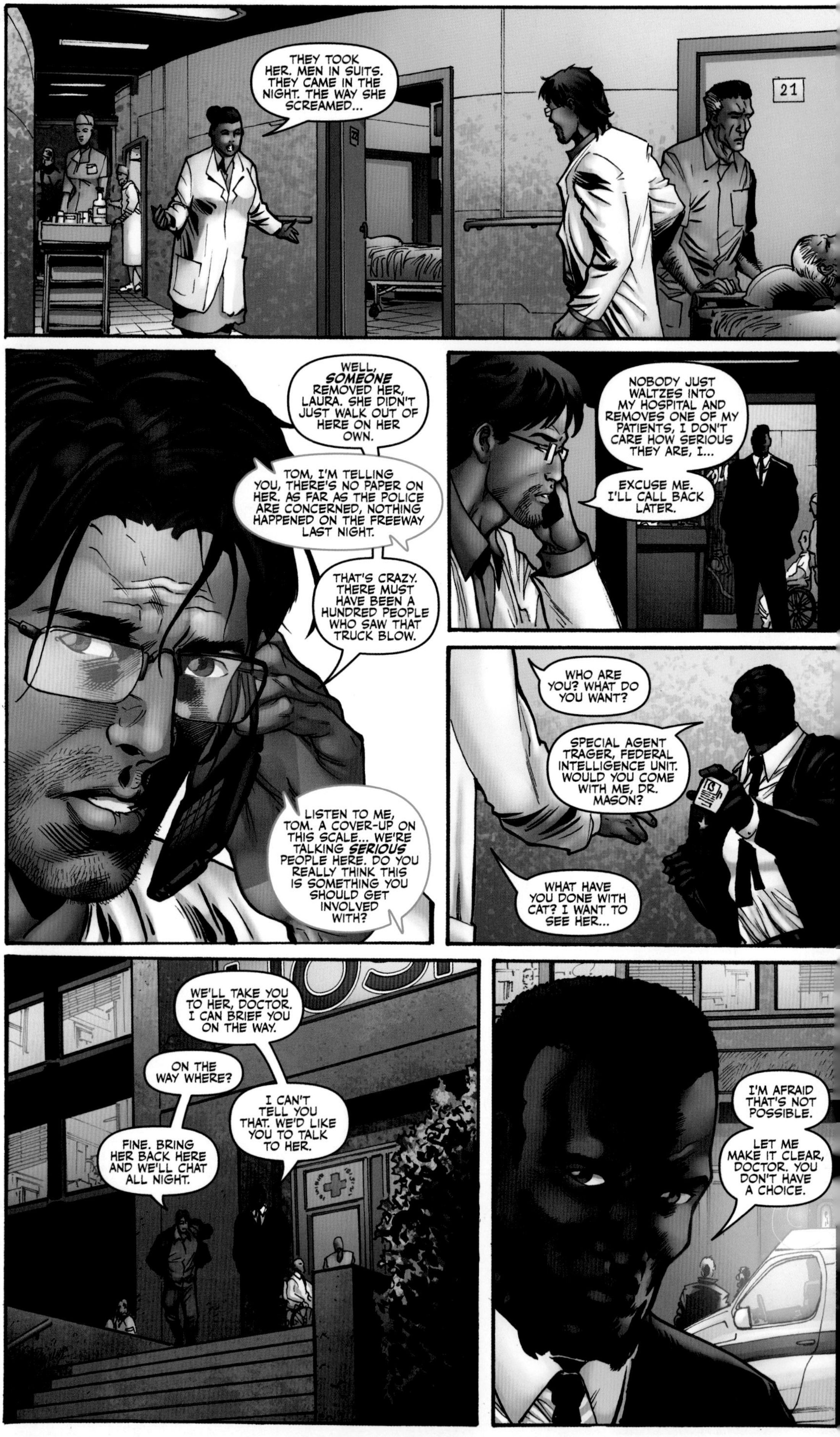
THEY TOOK HER. MEN IN SUITS. THEY CAME IN THE NIGHT. THE WAY SHE SCREAMED...
21
WELL, SOMEONE REMOVED HER, LAURA. SHE DIDN'T JUST WALK OUT OF HERE ON HER OWN.
TOM, I'M TELLING YOU, THERE'S NO PAPER ON HER. AS FAR AS THE POLICE ARE CONCERNED, NOTHING HAPPENED ON THE FREEWAY LAST NIGHT.
THAT'S CRAZY. THERE MUST HAVE BEEN A HUNDRED PEOPLE WHO SAW THAT TRUCK BLOW.
LISTEN TO ME, TOM. A COVER-UP ON THIS SCALE... WE'RE TALKING SERIOUS PEOPLE HERE. DO YOU REALLY THINK THIS IS SOMETHING YOU SHOULD GET INVOLVED WITH?
NOBODY JUST WALTZES INTO MY HOSPITAL AND REMOVES ONE OF MY PATIENTS, I DON'T CARE HOW SERIOUS THEY ARE, I...
EXCUSE ME. I'LL CALL BACK LATER.
WHO ARE YOU? WHAT DO YOU WANT?
SPECIAL AGENT TRAGER, FEDERAL INTELLIGENCE UNIT. WOULD YOU COME WITH ME, DR. MASON?
WHAT HAVE YOU DONE WITH CAT? I WANT TO SEE HER...
WE'LL TAKE YOU TO HER, DOCTOR. I CAN BRIEF YOU ON THE WAY.
ON THE WAY WHERE?
I CAN'T TELL YOU THAT. WE'D LIKE YOU TO TALK TO HER.
FINE. BRING HER BACK HERE AND WE'LL CHAT ALL NIGHT.
I'M AFRAID THAT'S NOT POSSIBLE.
LET ME MAKE IT CLEAR, DOCTOR. YOU DON'T HAVE A CHOICE.

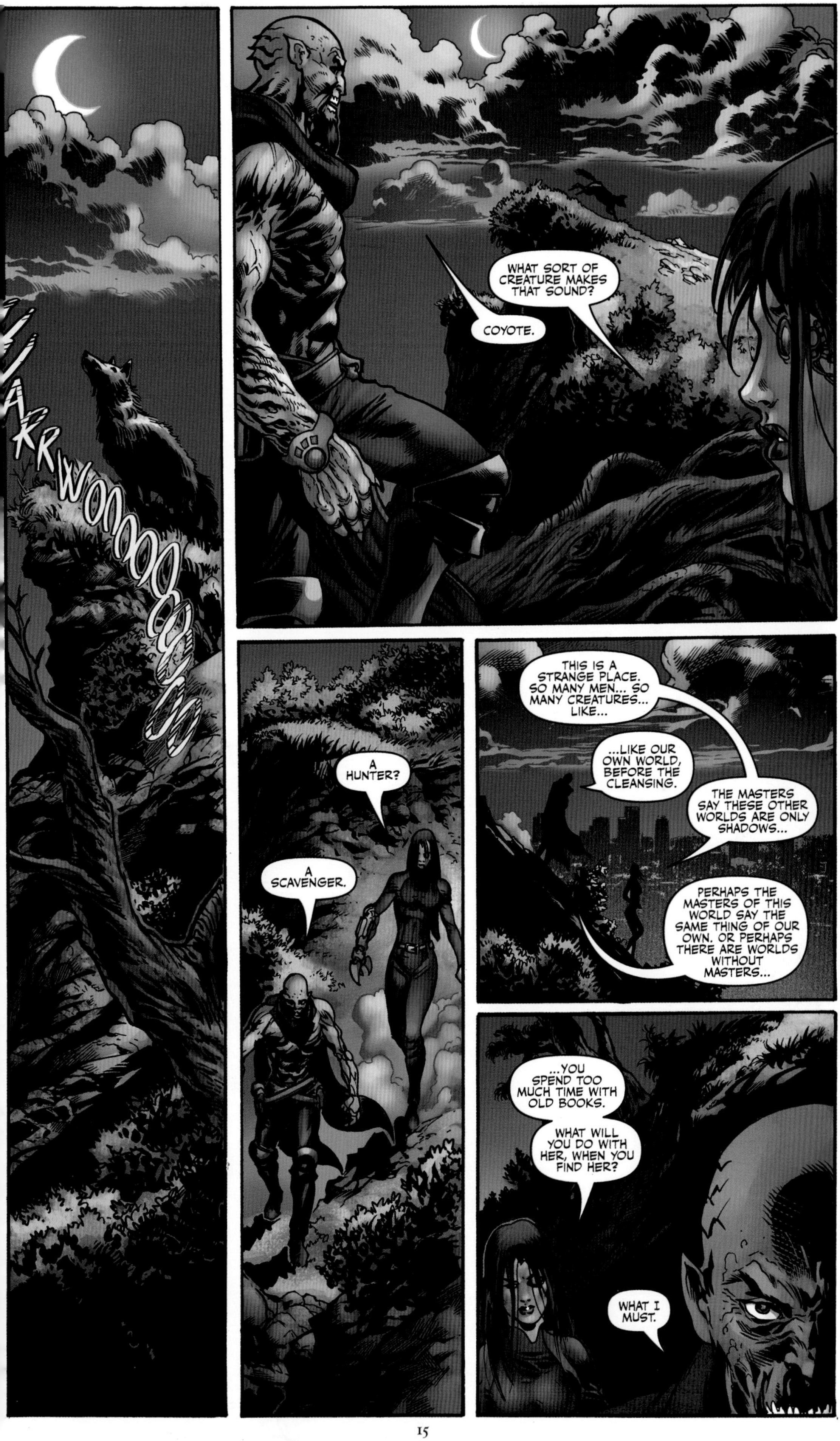
WHAT SORT OF CREATURE MAKES THAT SOUND?
COYOTE.
A HUNTER?
A SCAVENGER.
THIS IS A STRANGE PLACE. SO MANY MEN... SO MANY CREATURES... LIKE...
...LIKE OUR OWN WORLD, BEFORE THE CLEANSING.
THE MASTERS SAY THESE OTHER WORLDS ARE ONLY SHADOWS...
PERHAPS THE MASTERS OF THIS WORLD SAY THE SAME THING OF OUR OWN. OR PERHAPS THERE ARE WORLDS WITHOUT MASTERS...
...YOU SPEND TOO MUCH TIME WITH OLD BOOKS.
WHAT WILL YOU DO WITH HER, WHEN YOU FIND HER?
WHAT I MUST.

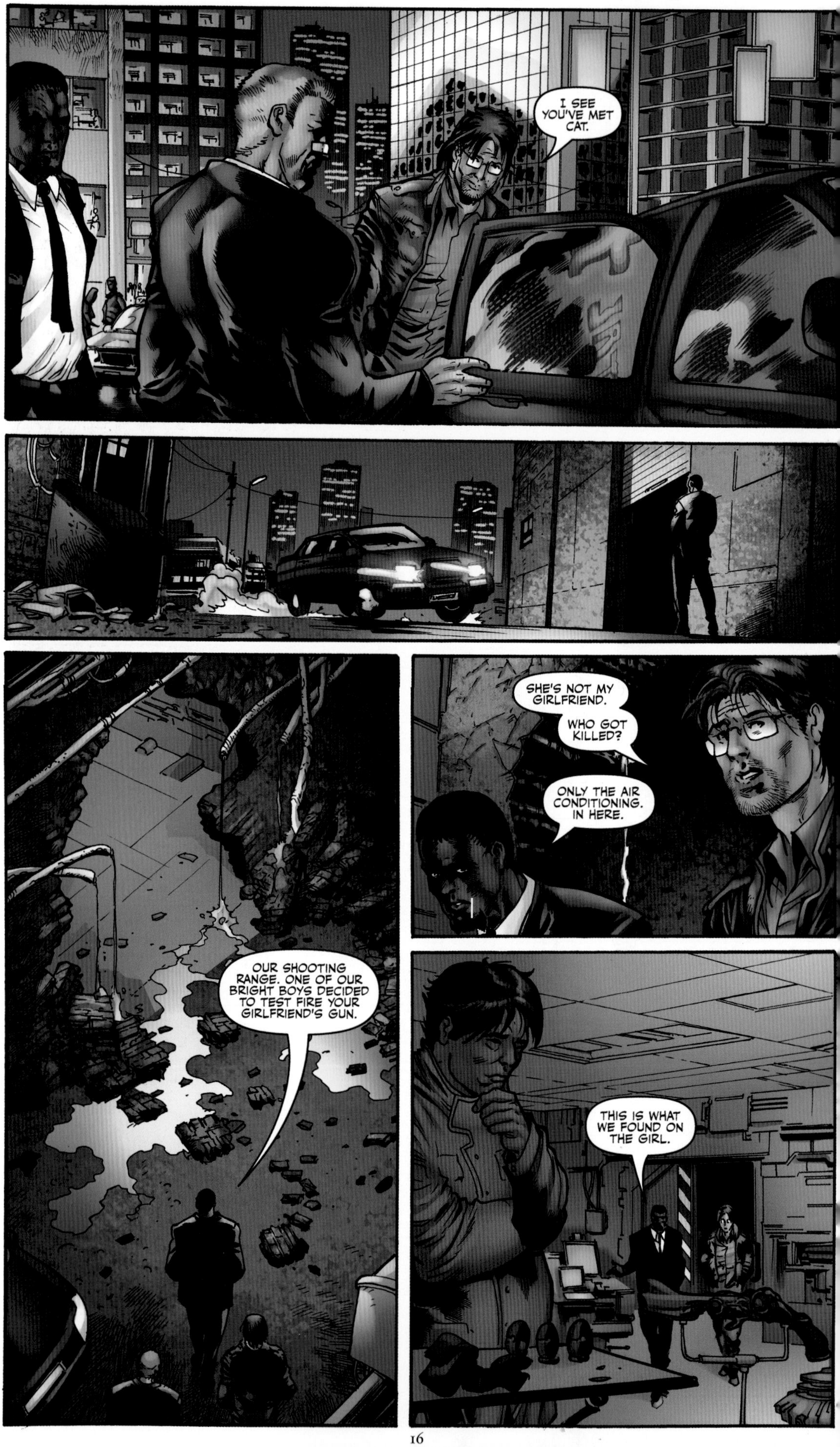
I SEE YOU'VE MET CAT.
OUR SHOOTING RANGE. ONE OF OUR BRIGHT BOYS DECIDED TO TEST FIRE YOUR GIRLFRIEND'S GUN.
SHE'S NOT MY GIRLFRIEND.
WHO GOT KILLED?
ONLY THE AIR CONDITIONING. IN HERE.
THIS IS WHAT WE FOUND ON THE GIRL.

I USED TO HAVE A WATER PISTOL THAT LOOKED LIKE THAT.

NOT WATER. AIR. QUITE SOPHISTICATED. IT USES A HIGH-VELOCITY JET OF PRESSURIZED AIR TO SPIT OUT NEEDLE-SIZED EXPLOSIVES THAT LOAD FROM EGG-SHAPED MAGAZINES.

NOTICE THE AWKWARD GRIP ON THE GUN? THE GIRL HAS TO USE BOTH HANDS TO FIRE.

WE BELIEVE THE WEAPON WAS ENGINEERED FOR SOMEONE WITH BIGGER HANDS.

YOU'D NEED FINGERS LIKE A SQUID.

THE POLICE FOUND THREE OF THESE MAGAZINES IN HER POCKETS. EACH ONE HOLDS ONE HUNDRED FORTY-FOUR NEEDLES. TAKE A LOOK AT THIS.

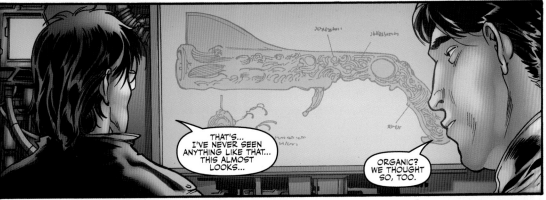

THAT'S... I'VE NEVER SEEN ANYTHING LIKE THAT... THIS ALMOST LOOKS...

ORGANIC? WE THOUGHT SO, TOO.

THE SHELL IS MORE LIKE HORN THAN METAL, BUT WITH A TENSILE STRENGTH GREATER THAN STEEL.

YOU COULD CALL IT MICROCIRCUITRY, BUT ONCE AGAIN IT HAS CERTAIN ORGANIC CHARACTERISTICS. AT FIVE-THIRTEEN THIS MORNING THESE INSETS EMITTED AN INTENSE YELLOW LIGHT FOR ABOUT NINE SECONDS. WE DON'T KNOW WHY.

WELL, I DIDN'T DO IT. LOOK, GUYS, THE SHOW-AND-TELL HAS BEEN FASCINATING, IF SLIGHTLY SURREAL, BUT I STILL DON'T KNOW WHAT YOU WANT FROM ME.

I'LL MAKE IT REAL SIMPLE FOR YOU. WE DIDN'T MAKE THESE. WE WANT TO KNOW WHO DID. YOU'RE GOING TO FIND OUT.

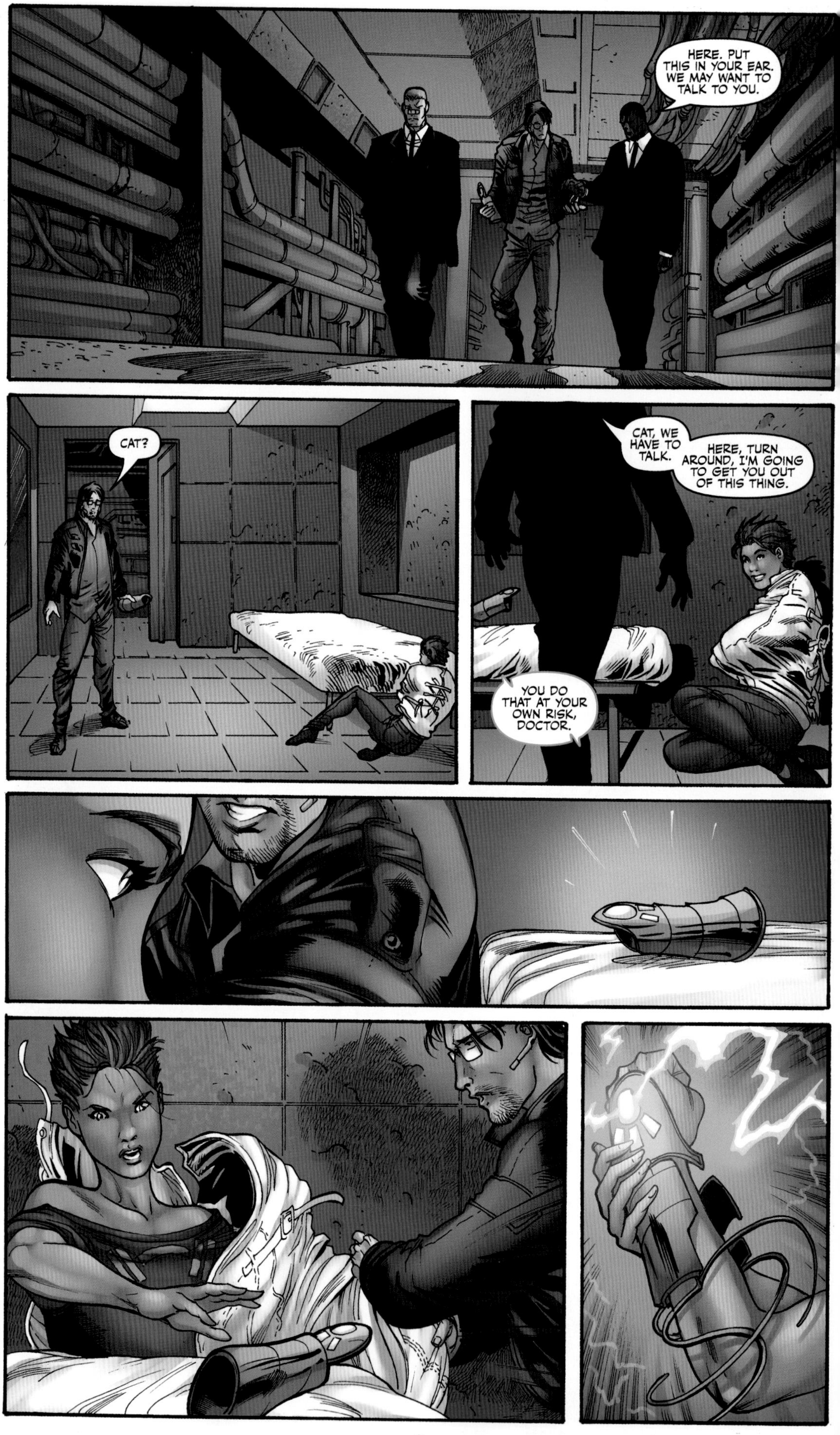
HERE. PUT THIS IN YOUR EAR. WE MAY WANT TO TALK TO YOU.
CAT?
CAT, WE HAVE TO TALK.
HERE, TURN AROUND, I'M GOING TO GET YOU OUT OF THIS THING.
YOU DO THAT AT YOUR OWN RISK, DOCTOR.

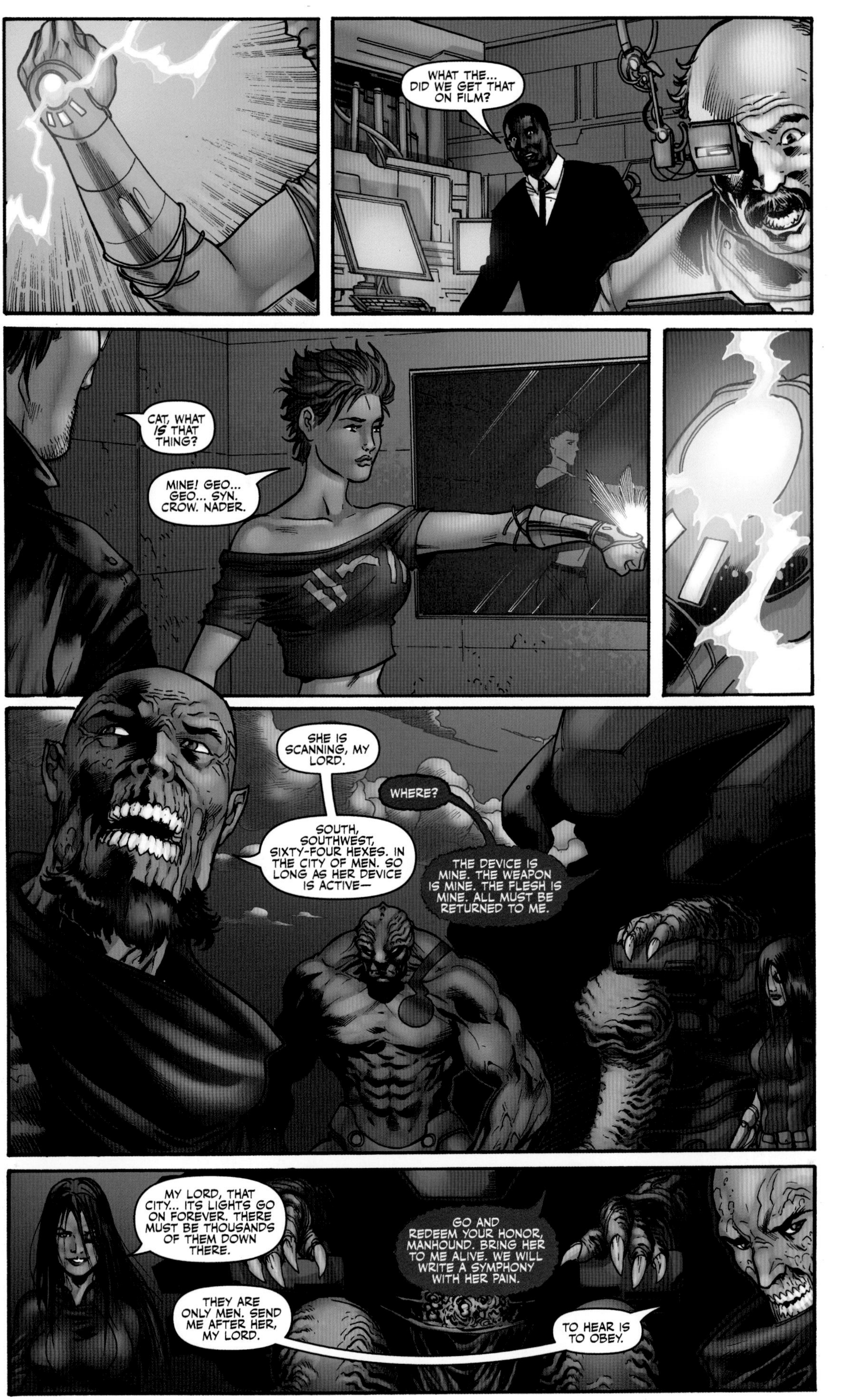
WHAT THE... DID WE GET THAT ON FILM?
CAT, WHAT IS THAT THING?
MINE! GEO... GEO... SYN. CROW. NADER.
SHE IS SCANNING, MY LORD.
WHERE?
SOUTH, SOUTHWEST, SIXTY-FOUR HEXES. IN THE CITY OF MEN. SO LONG AS HER DEVICE IS ACTIVE—
THE DEVICE IS MINE. THE WEAPON IS MINE. THE FLESH IS MINE. ALL MUST BE RETURNED TO ME.
MY LORD, THAT CITY... ITS LIGHTS GO ON FOREVER. THERE MUST BE THOUSANDS OF THEM DOWN THERE.
THEY ARE ONLY MEN. SEND ME AFTER HER, MY LORD.
GO AND REDEEM YOUR HONOR, MANHOUND. BRING HER TO ME ALIVE. WE WILL WRITE A SYMPHONY WITH HER PAIN.
TO HEAR IS TO OBEY.

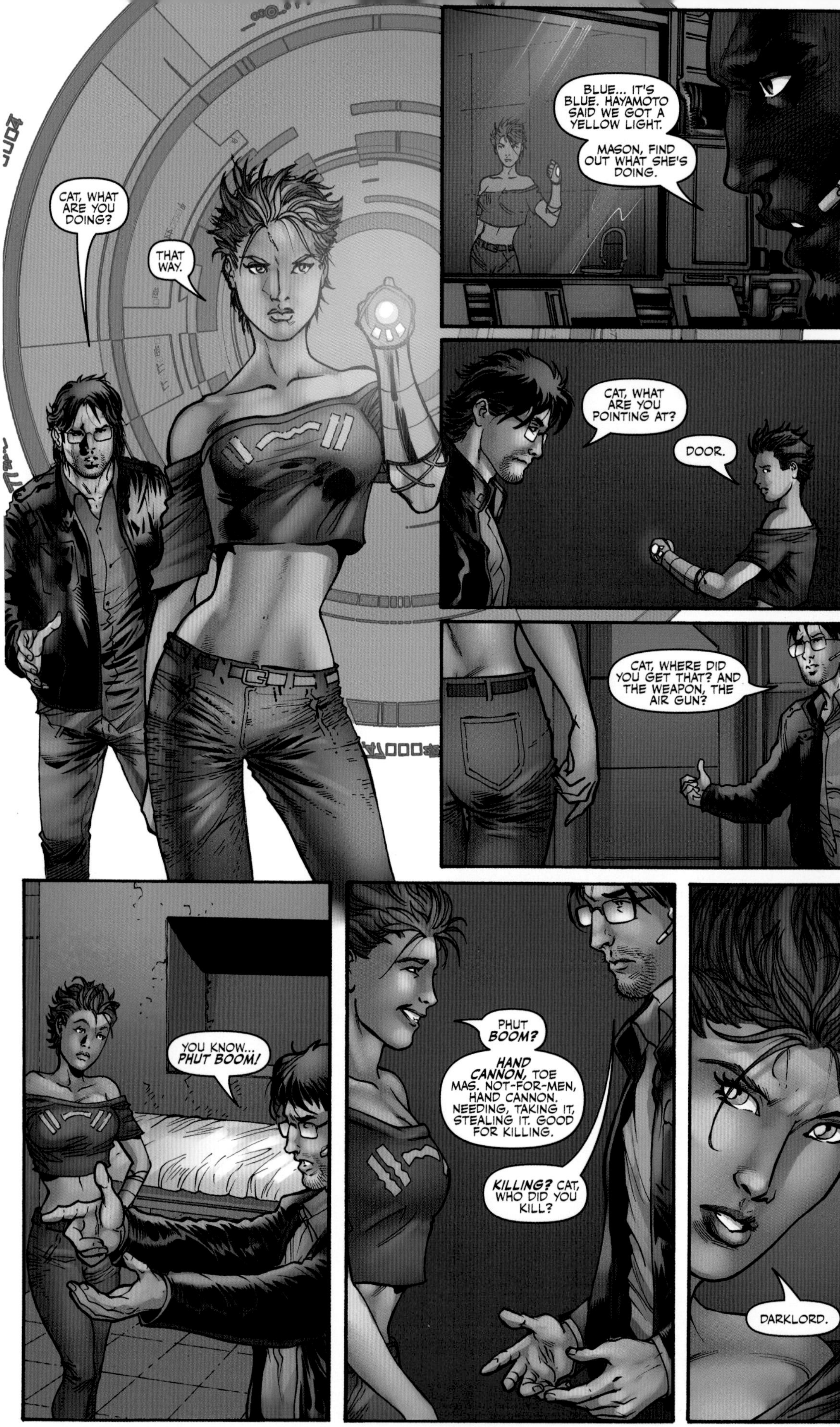
CAT, WHAT ARE YOU DOING?
THAT WAY.
BLUE... IT'S BLUE. HAYAMOTO SAID WE GOT A YELLOW LIGHT.
MASON, FIND OUT WHAT SHE'S DOING.
CAT, WHAT ARE YOU POINTING AT?
DOOR.
CAT, WHERE DID YOU GET THAT? AND THE WEAPON, THE AIR GUN?
YOU KNOW... *PHUT BOOM!*
PHUT *BOOM?*
HAND CANNON, TOE MAS. NOT-FOR-MEN, HAND CANNON. NEEDING, TAKING IT, STEALING IT. GOOD FOR KILLING.
KILLING? CAT, WHO DID YOU KILL?
DARKLORD.

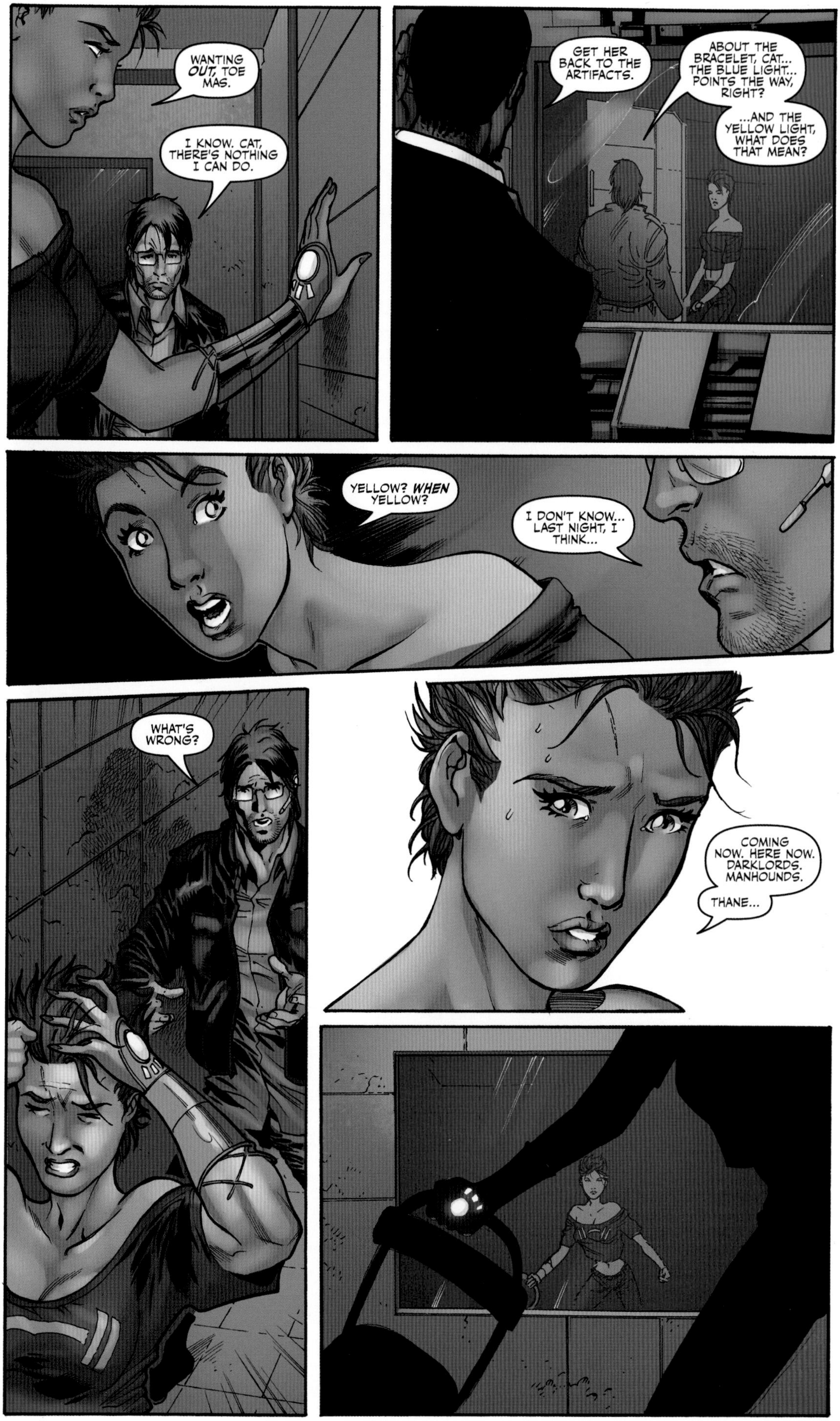
WANTING *OUT,* TOE MAS.
I KNOW. CAT, THERE'S NOTHING I CAN DO.
GET HER BACK TO THE ARTIFACTS.
ABOUT THE BRACELET, CAT... THE BLUE LIGHT... POINTS THE WAY, RIGHT?
...AND THE YELLOW LIGHT, WHAT DOES THAT MEAN?
YELLOW? *WHEN* YELLOW?
I DON'T KNOW... LAST NIGHT, I THINK...
WHAT'S WRONG?
COMING NOW. HERE NOW. DARKLORDS. MANHOUNDS.
THANE...

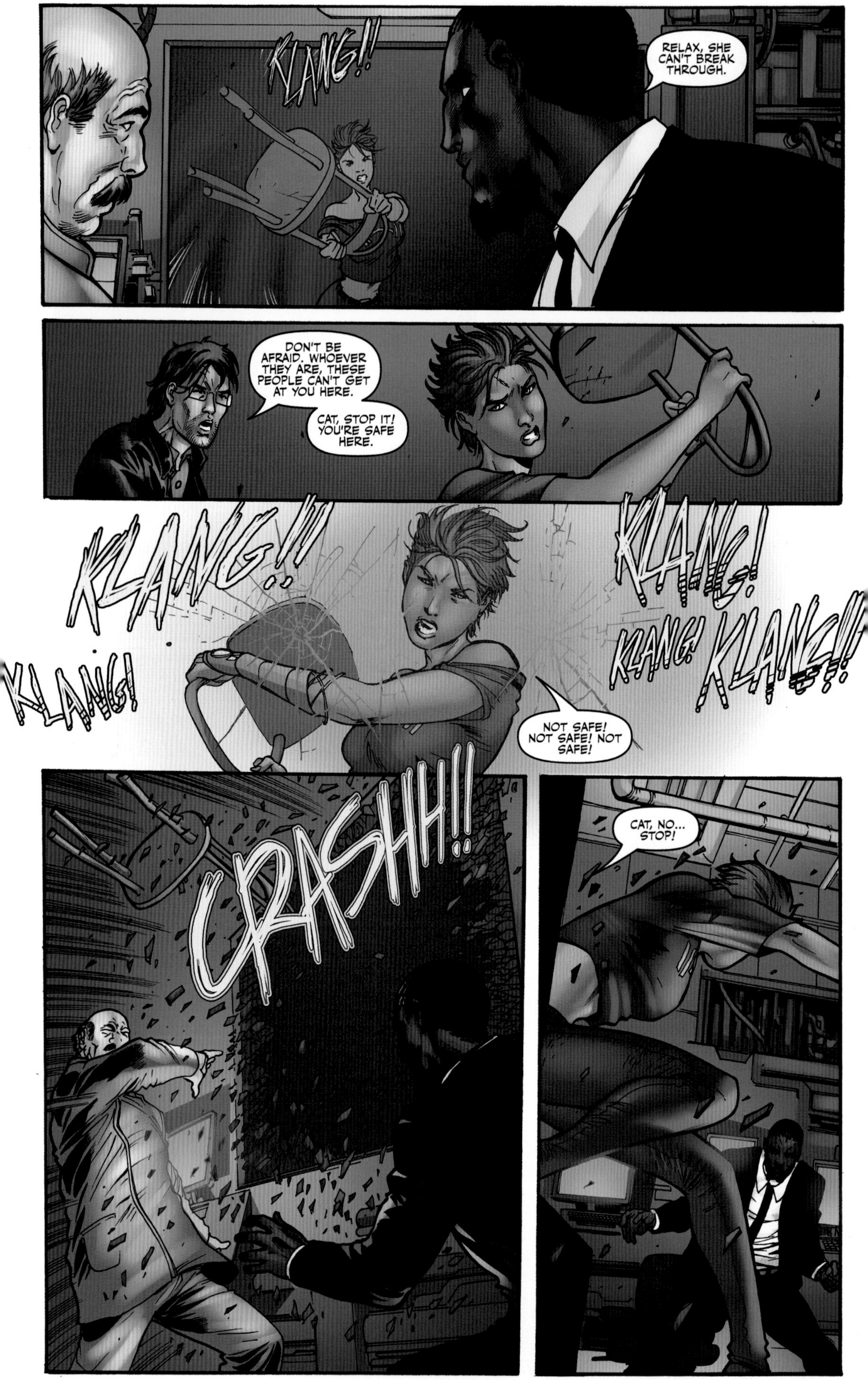
KLANG!!
RELAX, SHE CAN'T BREAK THROUGH.
DON'T BE AFRAID. WHOEVER THEY ARE, THESE PEOPLE CAN'T GET AT YOU HERE.
CAT, STOP IT! YOU'RE SAFE HERE.
KLANG!!
KLANG!
KLANG!
KLANG!
KLANG!!
NOT SAFE! NOT SAFE! NOT SAFE!
CRASHH!!
CAT, NO... STOP!

WHACK!!

UH!

KRAK!!

AAAAGGGGHH!

CAT!

MINE.

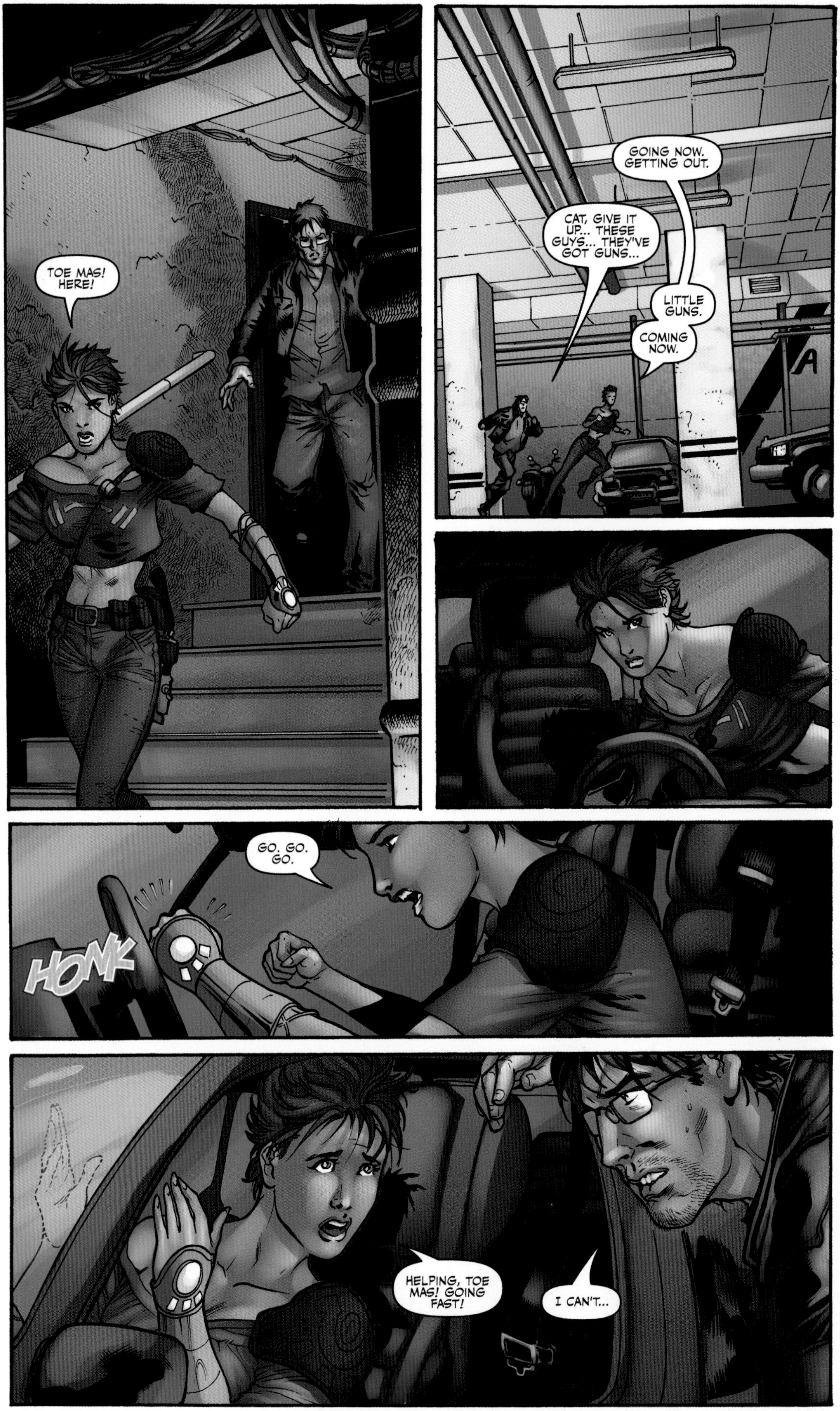
TOE MAS! HERE!
GOING NOW. GETTING OUT.
CAT, GIVE IT UP... THESE GUYS... THEY'VE GOT GUNS...
LITTLE GUNS.
COMING NOW.
GO. GO. GO.
HONK
HELPING, TOE MAS! GOING FAST!
I CAN'T...

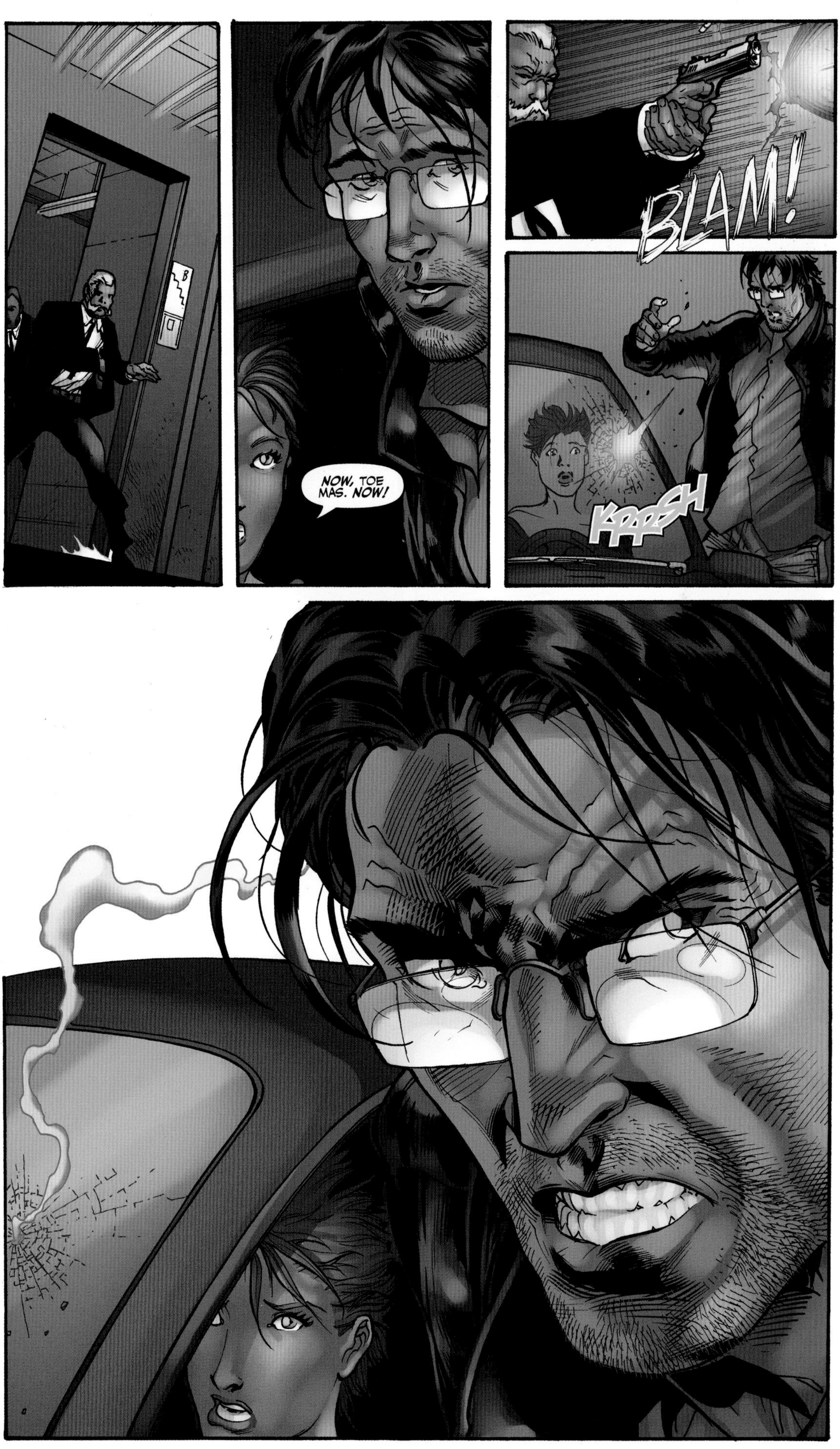
NOW, TOE MAS. NOW!
BLAM!
KRRSH

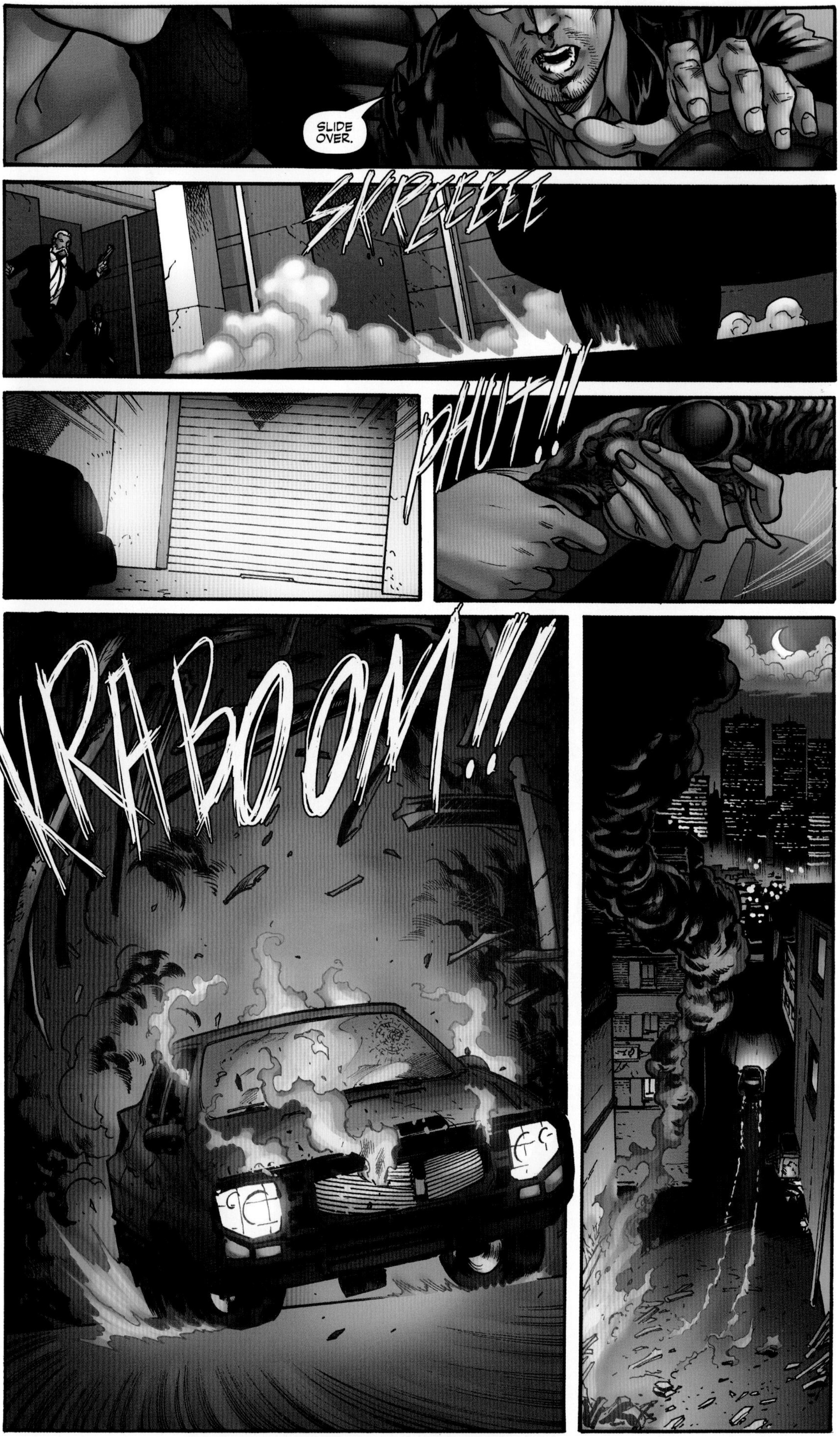
SLIDE OVER.
SKREEEEEE
PHUT!!
KRABOOM!!

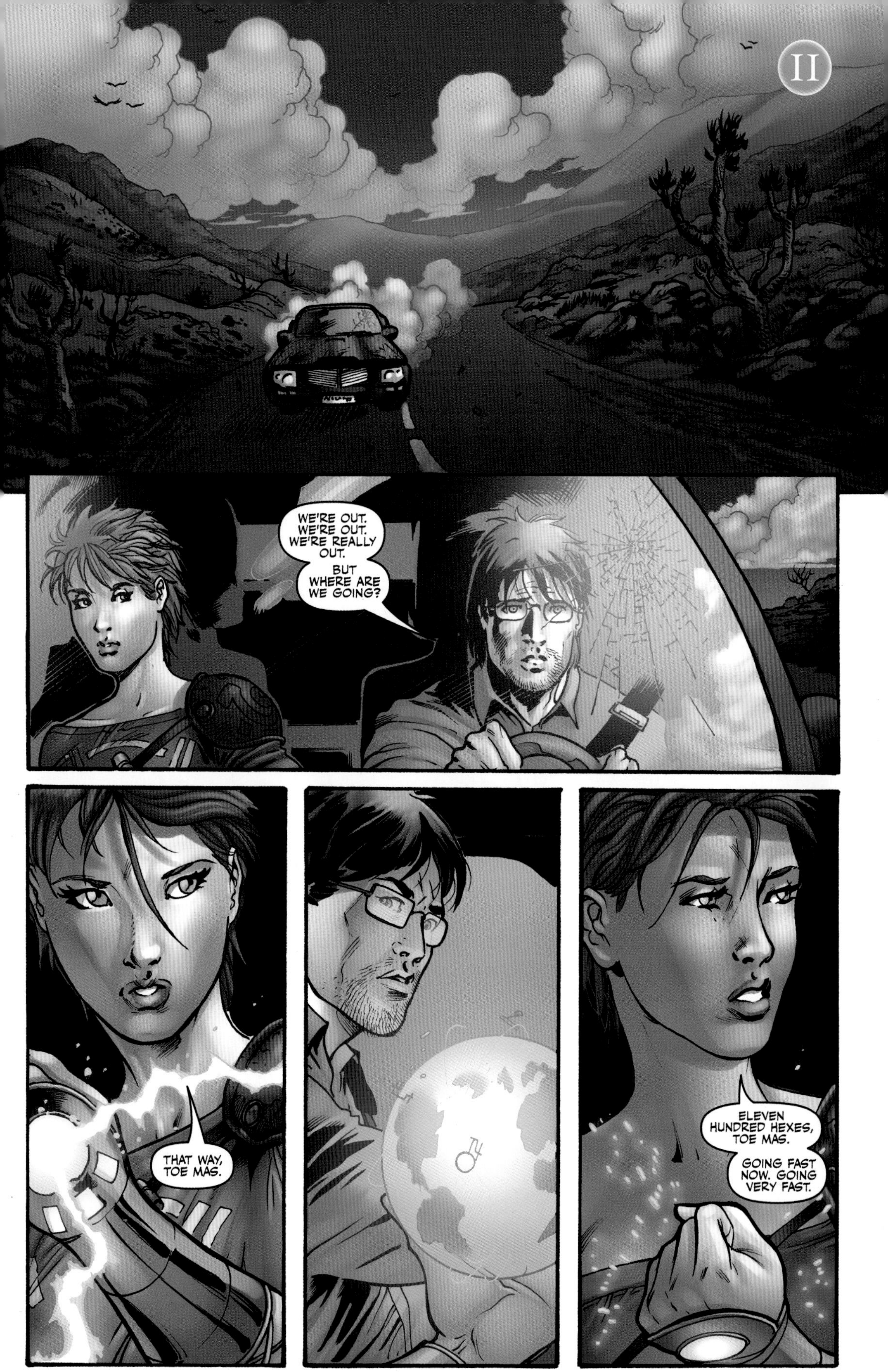
II
WE'RE OUT. WE'RE OUT. WE'RE REALLY OUT.
BUT WHERE ARE WE GOING?
THAT WAY, TOE MAS.
ELEVEN HUNDRED HEXES, TOE MAS.
GOING FAST NOW. GOING VERY FAST.

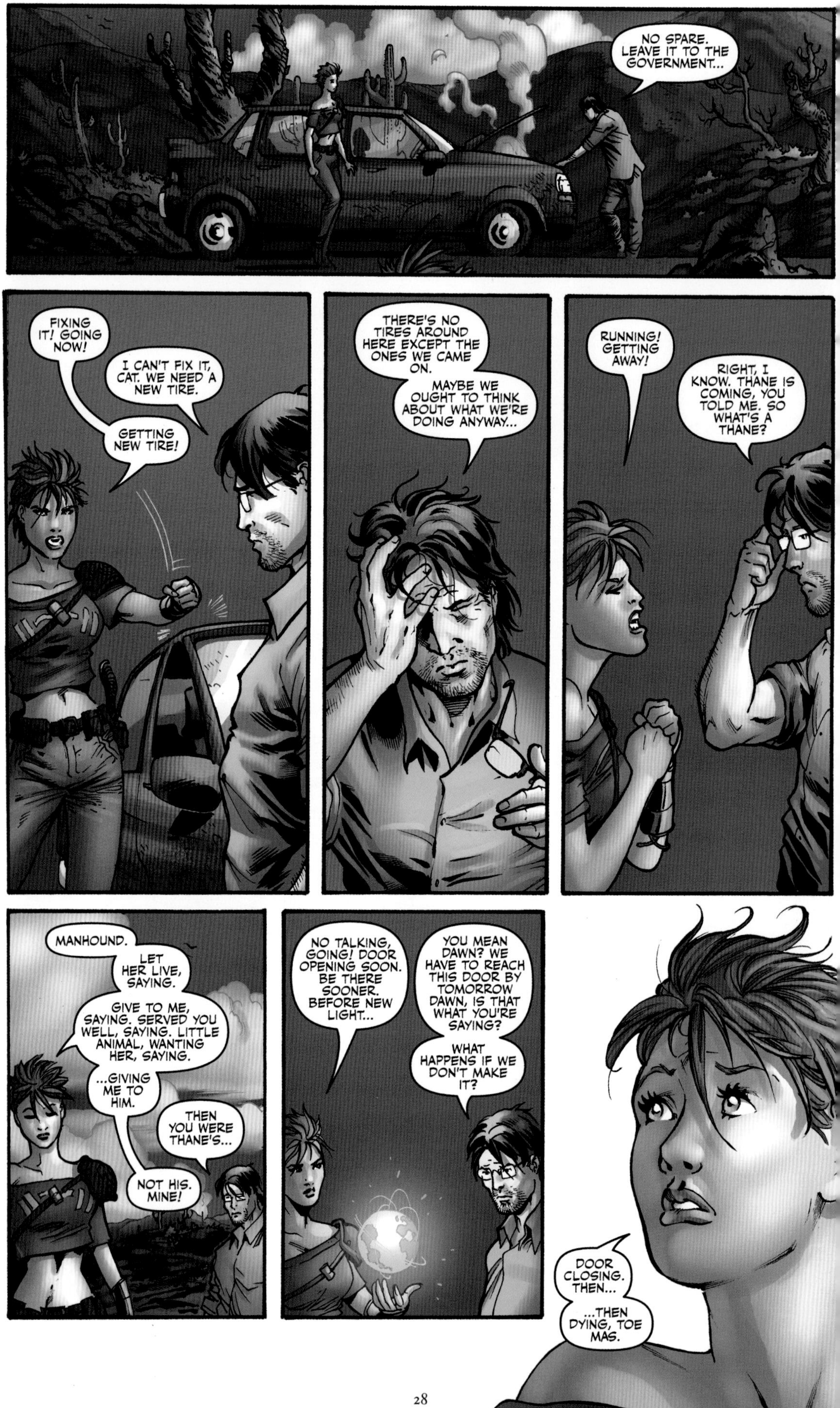
NO SPARE. LEAVE IT TO THE GOVERNMENT...
FIXING IT! GOING NOW!
I CAN'T FIX IT, CAT. WE NEED A NEW TIRE.
GETTING NEW TIRE!
THERE'S NO TIRES AROUND HERE EXCEPT THE ONES WE CAME ON.
MAYBE WE OUGHT TO THINK ABOUT WHAT WE'RE DOING ANYWAY...
RUNNING! GETTING AWAY!
RIGHT, I KNOW. THANE IS COMING, YOU TOLD ME. SO WHAT'S A THANE?
MANHOUND.
LET HER LIVE, SAYING.
GIVE TO ME, SAYING. SERVED YOU WELL, SAYING. LITTLE ANIMAL, WANTING HER, SAYING.
...GIVING ME TO HIM.
THEN YOU WERE THANE'S...
NOT HIS. MINE!
NO TALKING, GOING! DOOR OPENING SOON. BE THERE SOONER. BEFORE NEW LIGHT...
YOU MEAN DAWN? WE HAVE TO REACH THIS DOOR BY TOMORROW DAWN, IS THAT WHAT YOU'RE SAYING?
WHAT HAPPENS IF WE DON'T MAKE IT?
DOOR CLOSING. THEN...
...THEN DYING, TOE MAS.

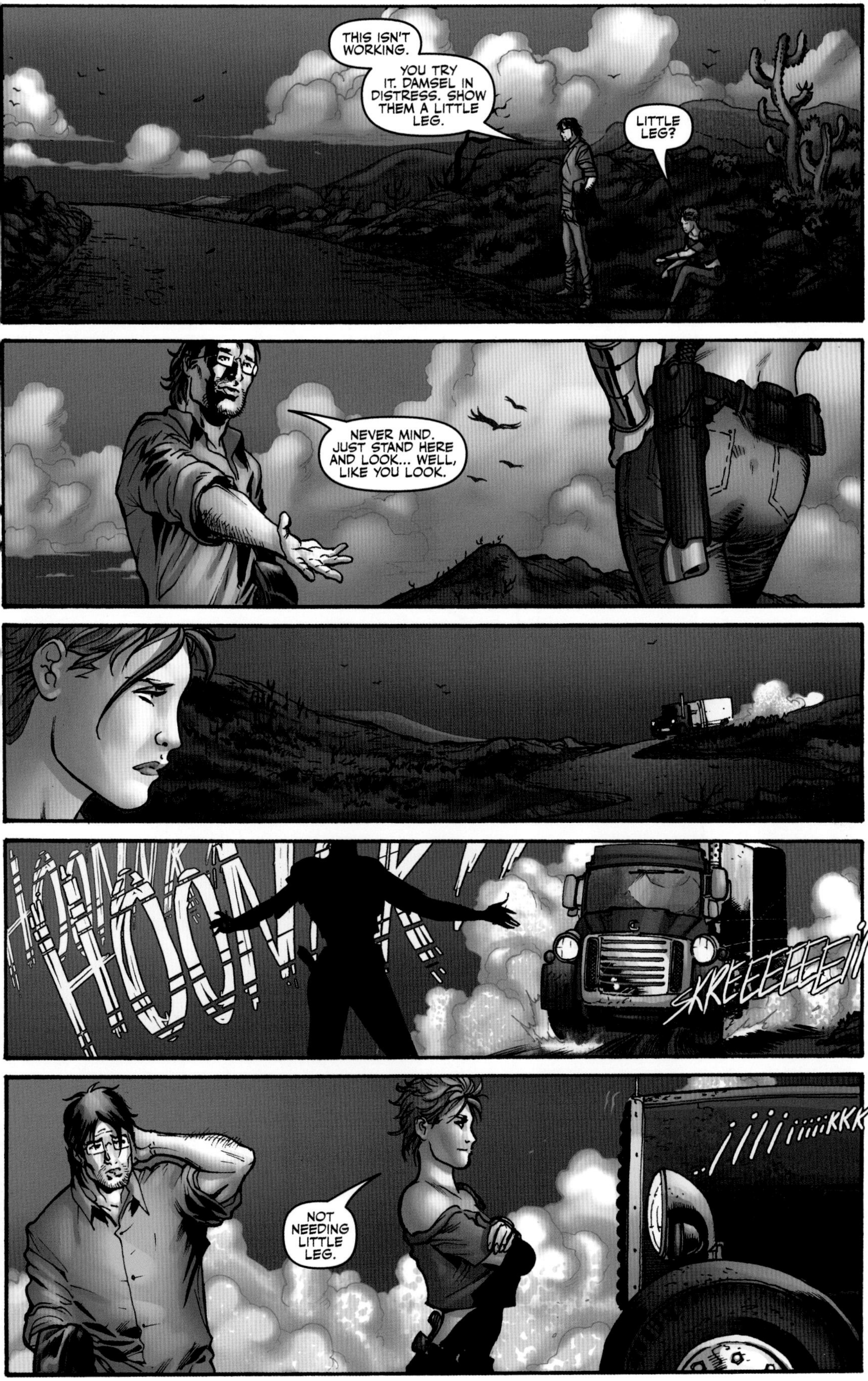
THIS ISN'T WORKING.
YOU TRY IT. DAMSEL IN DISTRESS. SHOW THEM A LITTLE LEG.
LITTLE LEG?
NEVER MIND. JUST STAND HERE AND LOOK... WELL, LIKE YOU LOOK.
NOT NEEDING LITTLE LEG.

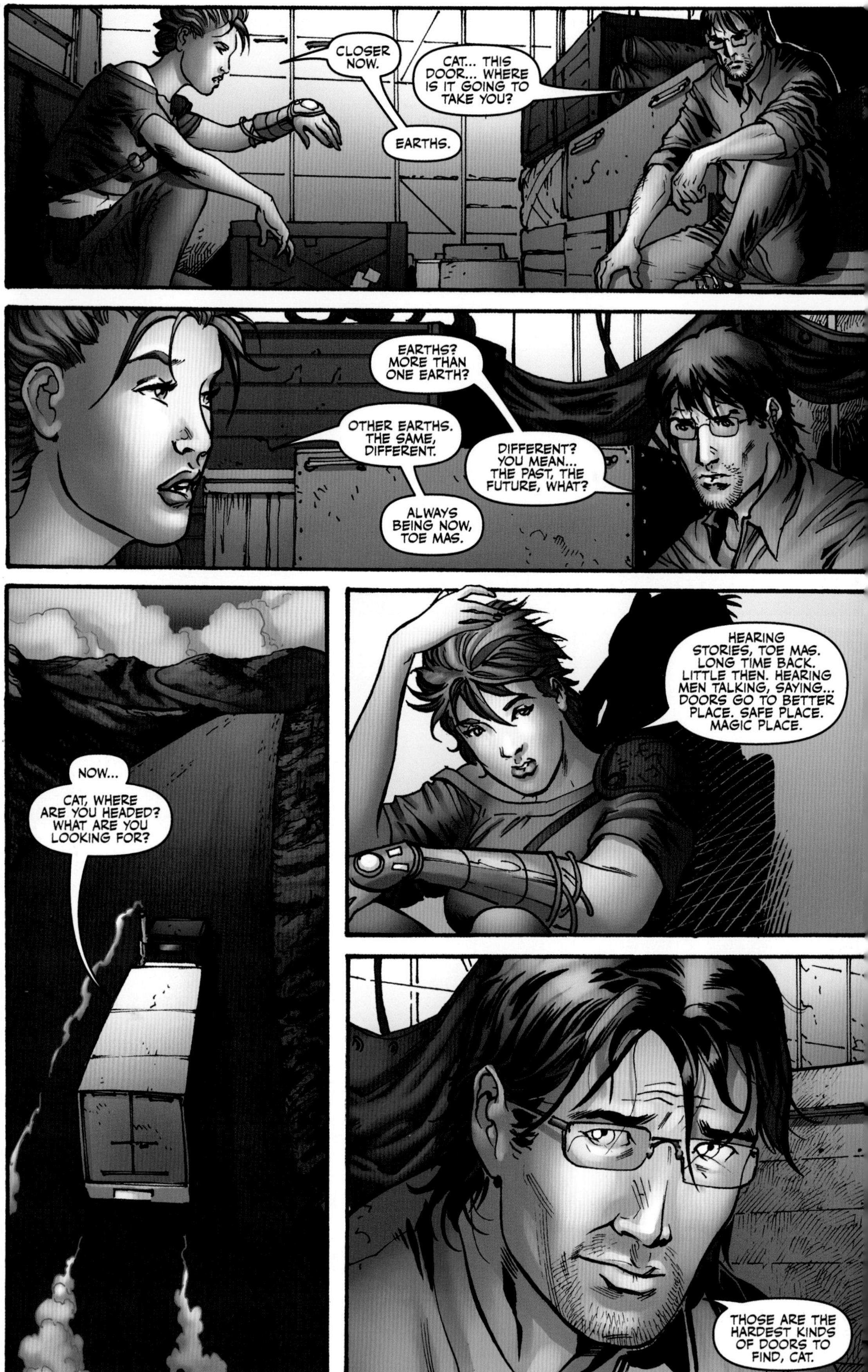
CLOSER NOW.
CAT... THIS DOOR... WHERE IS IT GOING TO TAKE YOU?
EARTHS.
EARTHS? MORE THAN ONE EARTH?
OTHER EARTHS. THE SAME, DIFFERENT.
DIFFERENT? YOU MEAN... THE PAST, THE FUTURE, WHAT?
ALWAYS BEING NOW, TOE MAS.
NOW...
CAT, WHERE ARE YOU HEADED? WHAT ARE YOU LOOKING FOR?
HEARING STORIES, TOE MAS. LONG TIME BACK. LITTLE THEN. HEARING MEN TALKING, SAYING... DOORS GO TO BETTER PLACE. SAFE PLACE. MAGIC PLACE.
THOSE ARE THE HARDEST KINDS OF DOORS TO FIND, CAT.

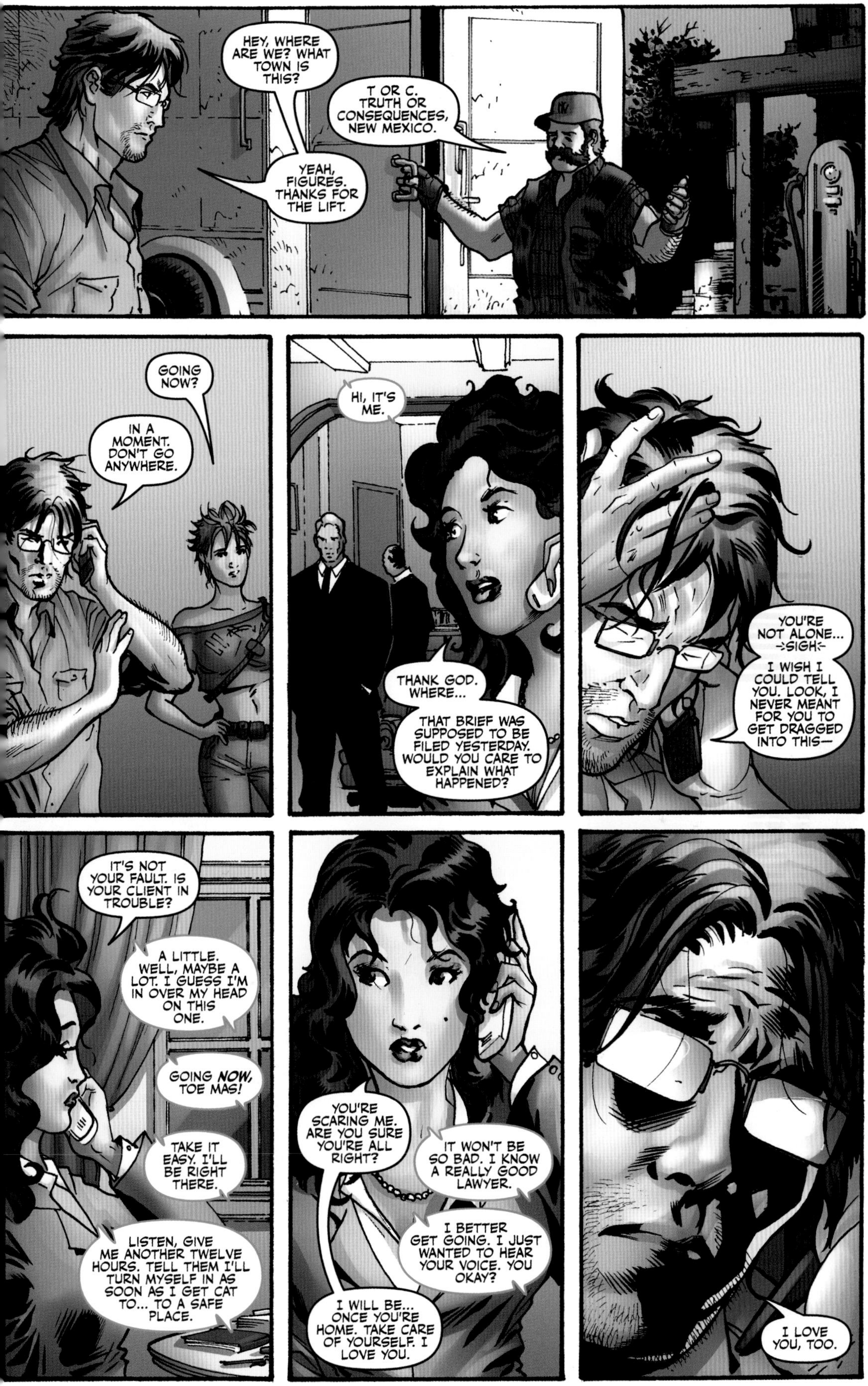
HEY, WHERE ARE WE? WHAT TOWN IS THIS?
T OR C. TRUTH OR CONSEQUENCES, NEW MEXICO.
YEAH, FIGURES. THANKS FOR THE LIFT.
GOING NOW?
IN A MOMENT. DON'T GO ANYWHERE.
HI, IT'S ME.
THANK GOD. WHERE...
THAT BRIEF WAS SUPPOSED TO BE FILED YESTERDAY. WOULD YOU CARE TO EXPLAIN WHAT HAPPENED?
YOU'RE NOT ALONE... -SIGH-
I WISH I COULD TELL YOU. LOOK, I NEVER MEANT FOR YOU TO GET DRAGGED INTO THIS—
IT'S NOT YOUR FAULT. IS YOUR CLIENT IN TROUBLE?
A LITTLE. WELL, MAYBE A LOT. I GUESS I'M IN OVER MY HEAD ON THIS ONE.
GOING *NOW,* TOE MAS!
TAKE IT EASY. I'LL BE RIGHT THERE.
LISTEN, GIVE ME ANOTHER TWELVE HOURS. TELL THEM I'LL TURN MYSELF IN AS SOON AS I GET CAT TO... TO A SAFE PLACE.
YOU'RE SCARING ME. ARE YOU SURE YOU'RE ALL RIGHT?
IT WON'T BE SO BAD. I KNOW A REALLY GOOD LAWYER.
I BETTER GET GOING. I JUST WANTED TO HEAR YOUR VOICE. YOU OKAY?
I WILL BE... ONCE YOU'RE HOME. TAKE CARE OF YOURSELF. I LOVE YOU.
I LOVE YOU, TOO.

THERE.

WE MUST BE CLOSE.

I HATE TO TELL YOU THIS, BUT IT'S A MEN'S ROOM.

TOO SOON. WAITING NOW.

TOE MAS... COMING?

I ALMOST WISH I COULD...

...MY FATHER WAS A MAGICIAN. CLOSE-UP STUFF MOSTLY, CARDS AND RINGS. HE COULD GET OUT OF HANDCUFFS AND PULL A COCKATOO FROM HIS HAT. WHEN I WAS LITTLE I THOUGHT HE WAS MERLIN. THEN ONE DAY I FOUND OUT IT WAS ALL JUST... TRICKS.

MAYBE THE REAL MAGIC IS RIGHT THROUGH THAT DOOR...

...BUT IT'S TOO LATE, CAT. I'M ALL GROWN UP NOW. I HAVE A GIRLFRIEND, A CAREER... I HAVE STUDENT LOANS TO REPAY, AND I DON'T BELIEVE IN FAIRIES ANYMORE. THIS IS AS FAR AS I GO.

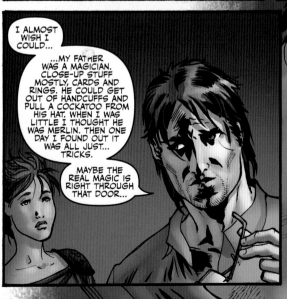

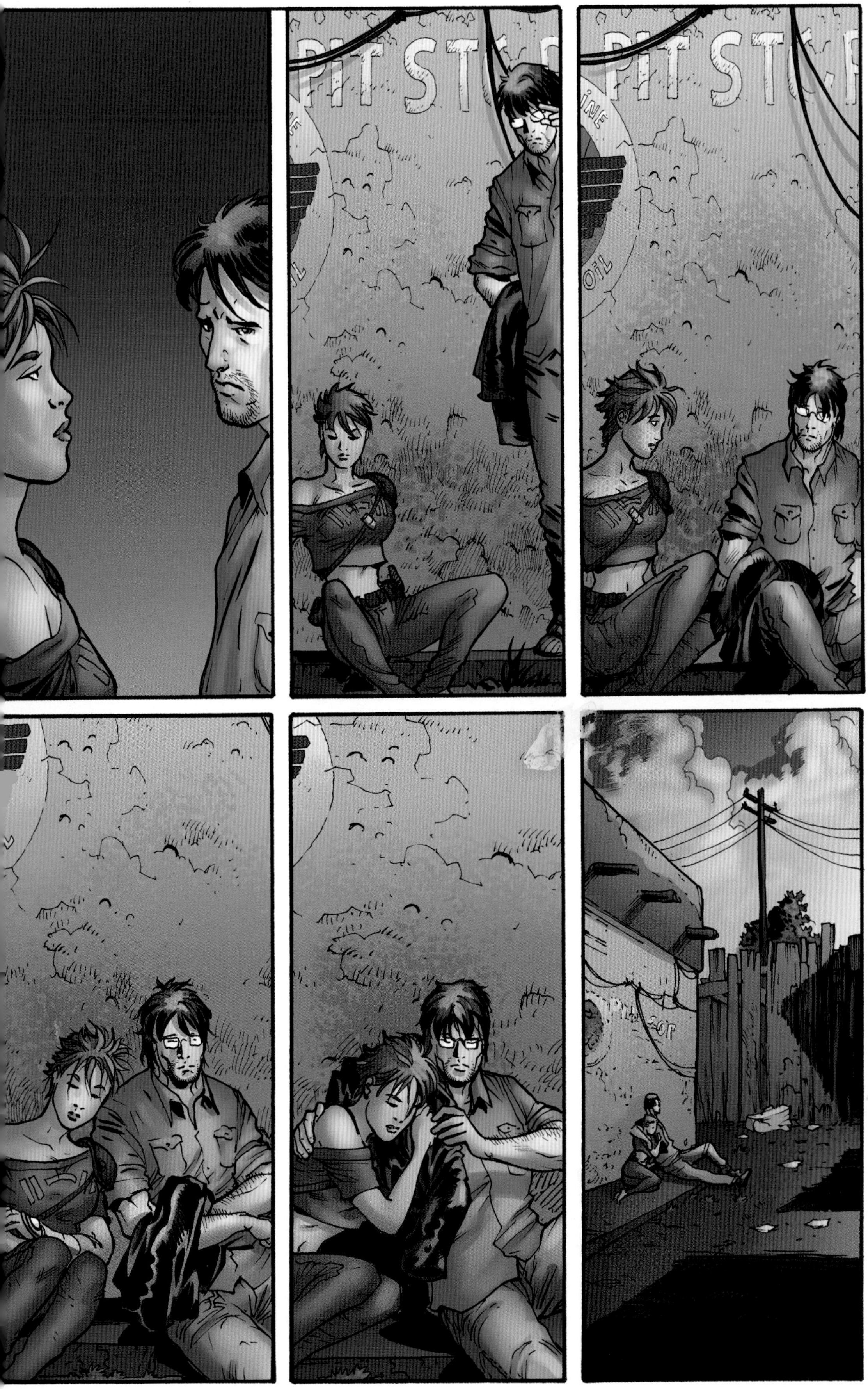

YOU'RE UNDER ARREST.

CAT, *DON'T.*

HOW DID YOU FIND US?

PLEASE, DOCTOR. WE NEVER LOST YOU. I JUST WANTED TO SEE WHERE SHE WOULD GO. I MUST ADMIT, I DIDN'T EXPECT... THIS.

$10.9 OIL

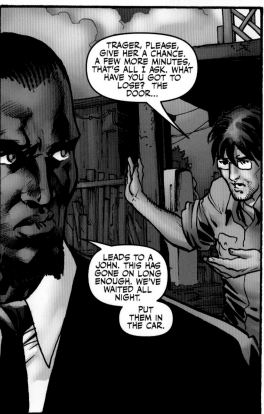

TRAGER, PLEASE, GIVE HER A CHANCE. A FEW MORE MINUTES, THAT'S ALL I ASK. WHAT HAVE YOU GOT TO LOSE? THE DOOR...

LEADS TO A JOHN. THIS HAS GONE ON LONG ENOUGH. WE'VE WAITED ALL NIGHT.

PUT THEM IN THE CAR.

GET HER UNDER CONTROL, DAMN IT.

TRAGER, WE'VE GOT COMPANY.

34

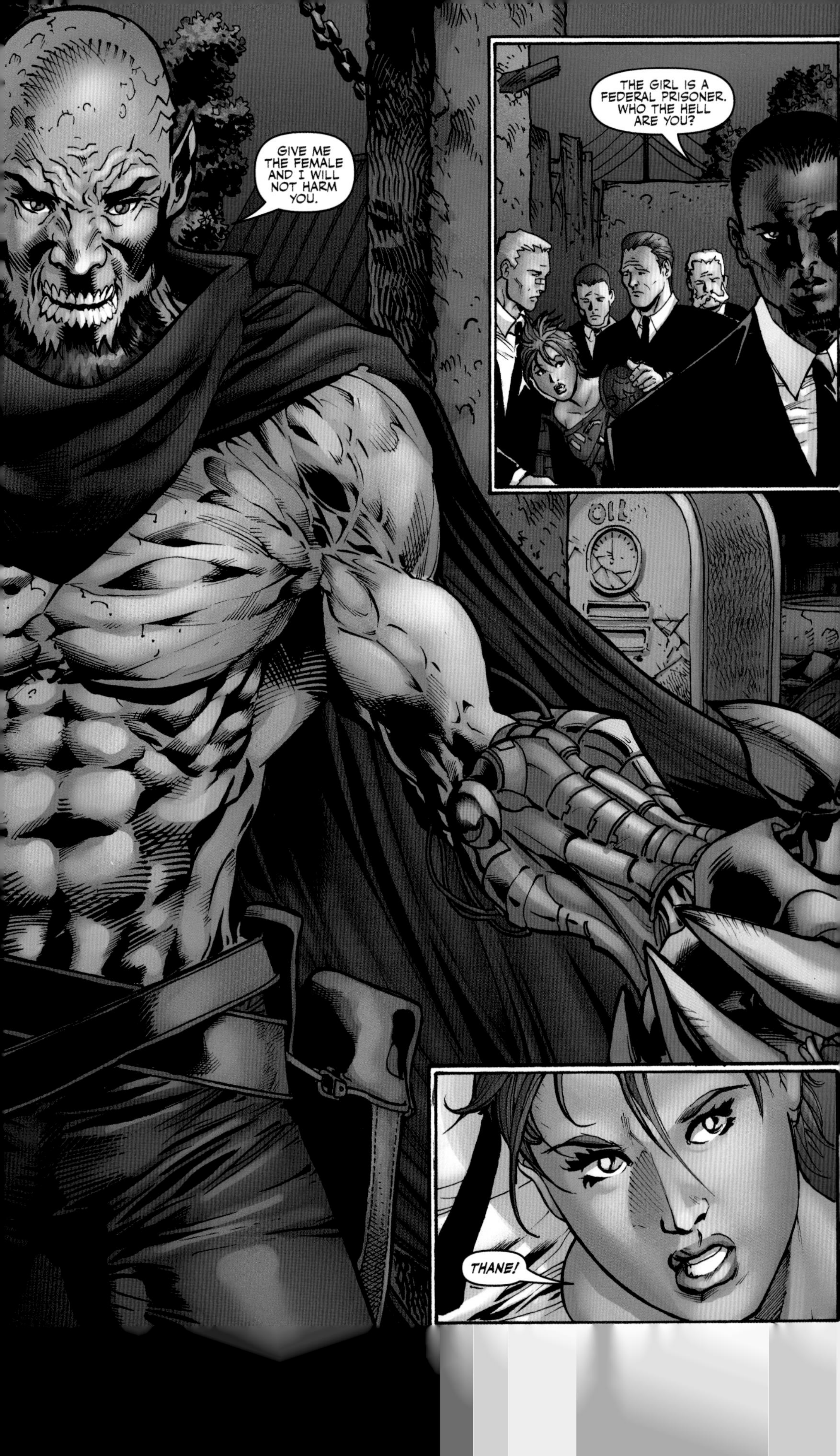
GIVE ME THE FEMALE AND I WILL NOT HARM YOU.
THE GIRL IS A FEDERAL PRISONER. WHO THE HELL ARE YOU?
THANE!

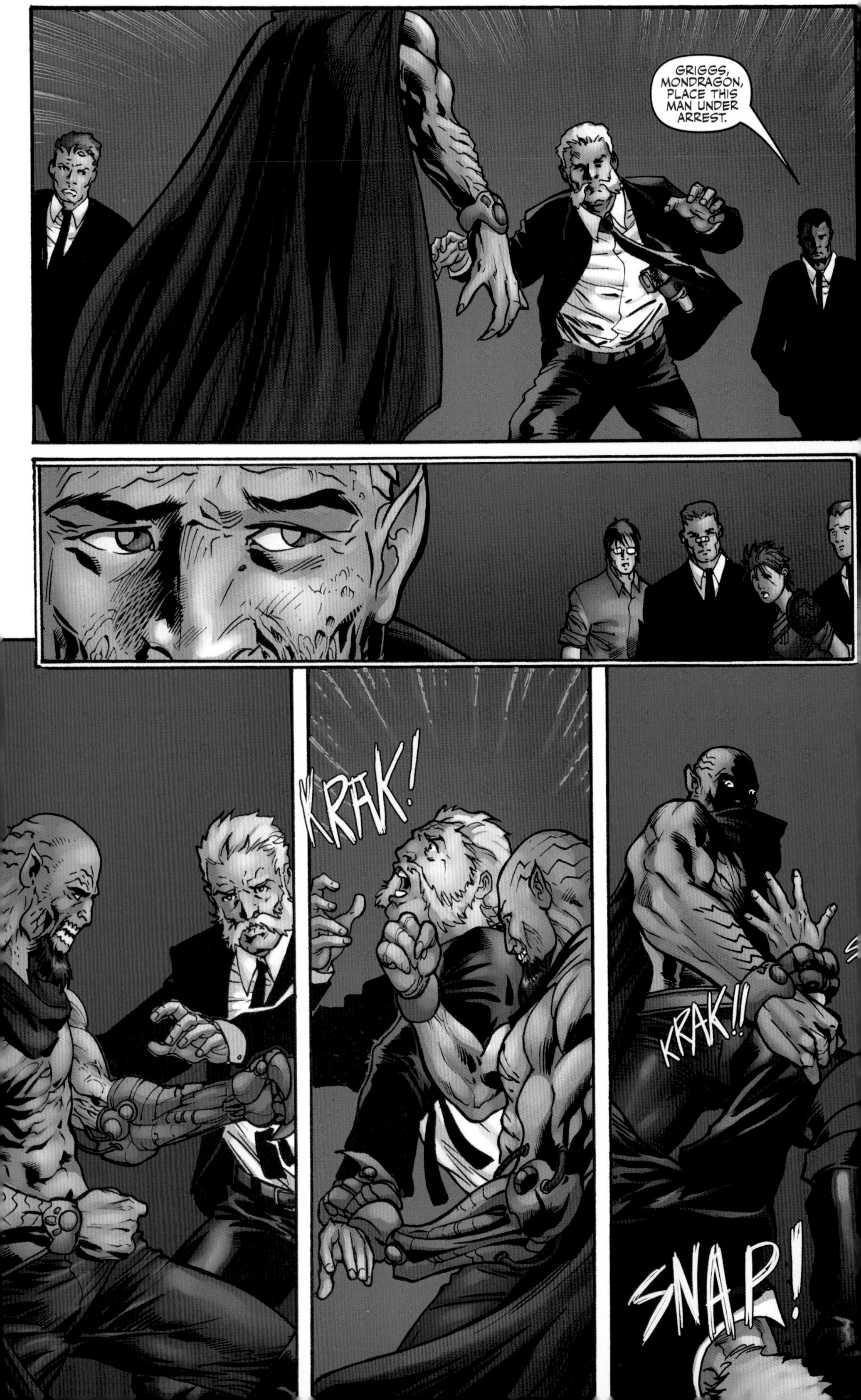
GRIGGS, MONDRAGON, PLACE THIS MAN UNDER ARREST.
KRAK!
KRAK!!
SNAP!

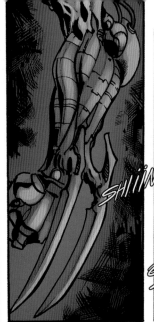

SHIING

SZLOCK!!

BLAM
BLAM!!

TUHP!!

TWIING

SLASH!!

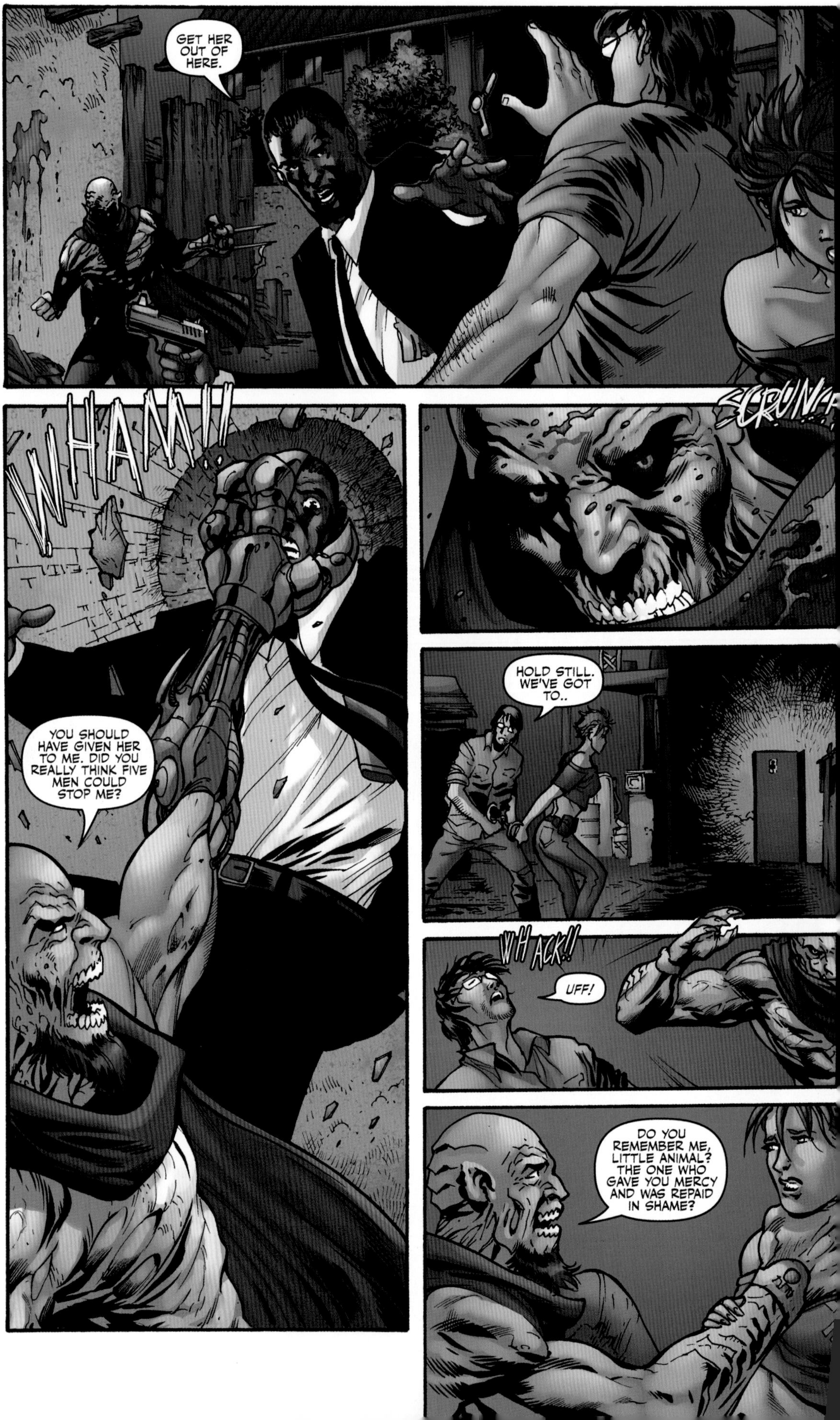
GET HER OUT OF HERE.
WHAM!!
YOU SHOULD HAVE GIVEN HER TO ME. DID YOU REALLY THINK FIVE MEN COULD STOP ME?
HOLD STILL. WE'VE GOT TO..
WHACK!!
UFF!
DO YOU REMEMBER ME, LITTLE ANIMAL? THE ONE WHO GAVE YOU MERCY AND WAS REPAID IN SHAME?

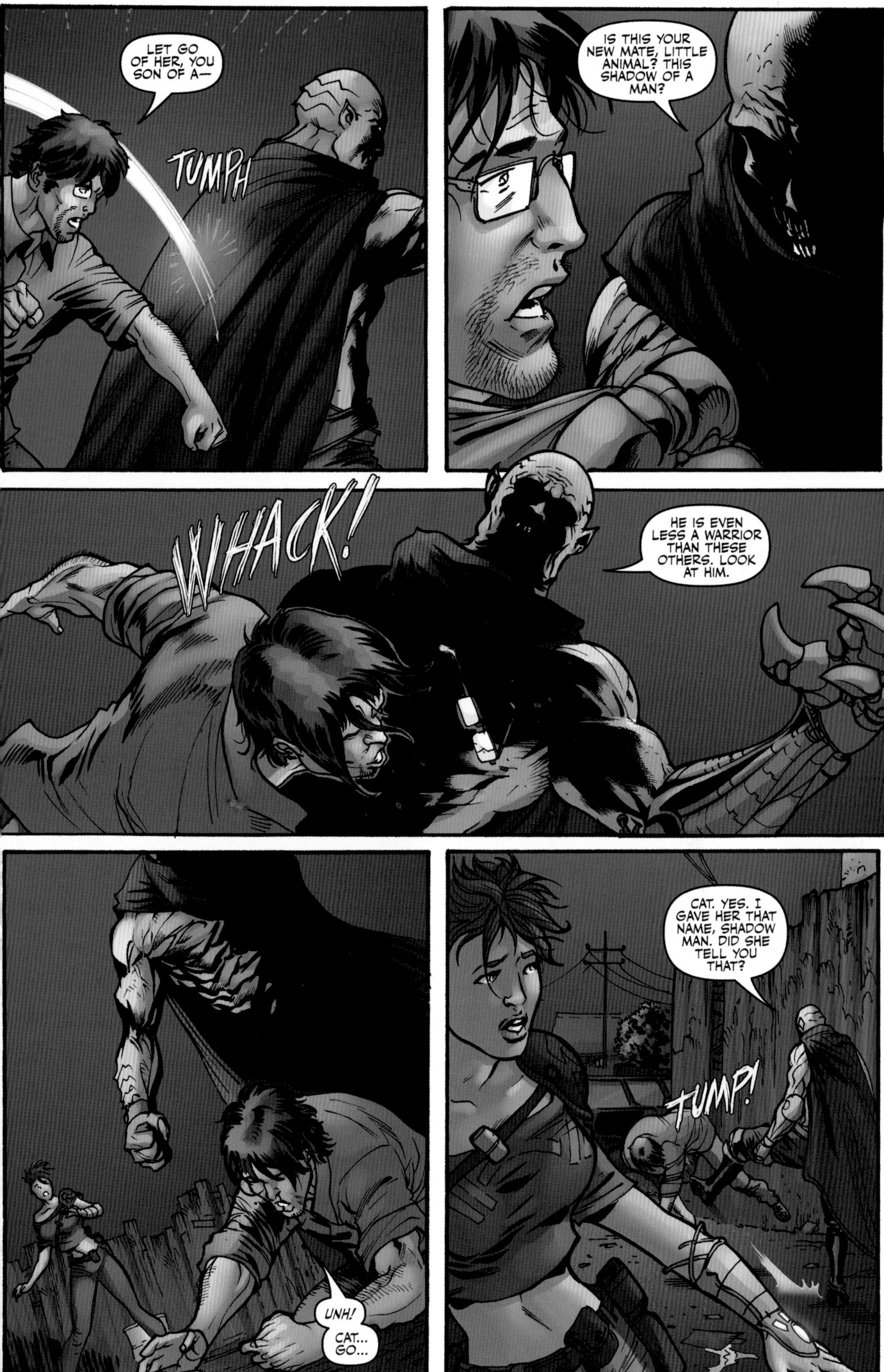
LET GO OF HER, YOU SON OF A—
TUMPH
IS THIS YOUR NEW MATE, LITTLE ANIMAL? THIS SHADOW OF A MAN?
WHACK!
HE IS EVEN LESS A WARRIOR THAN THESE OTHERS. LOOK AT HIM.
UNH!
CAT... GO...
CAT. YES. I GAVE HER THAT NAME, SHADOW MAN. DID SHE TELL YOU THAT?
TUMP!

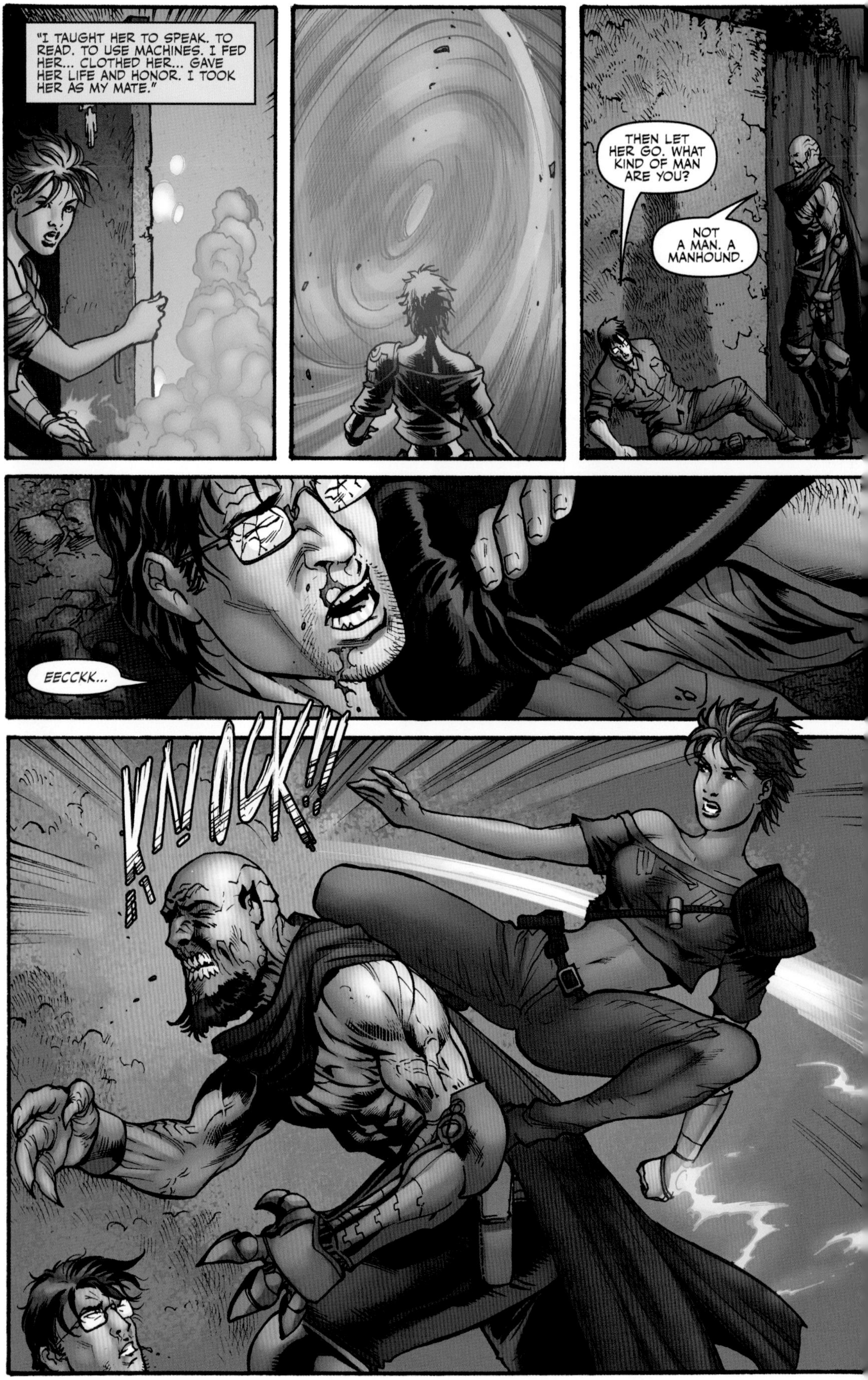
"I TAUGHT HER TO SPEAK. TO READ. TO USE MACHINES. I FED HER... CLOTHED HER... GAVE HER LIFE AND HONOR. I TOOK HER AS MY MATE."
THEN LET HER GO. WHAT KIND OF MAN ARE YOU?
NOT A MAN. A MANHOUND.
EECCKK...
KNOCK!!!

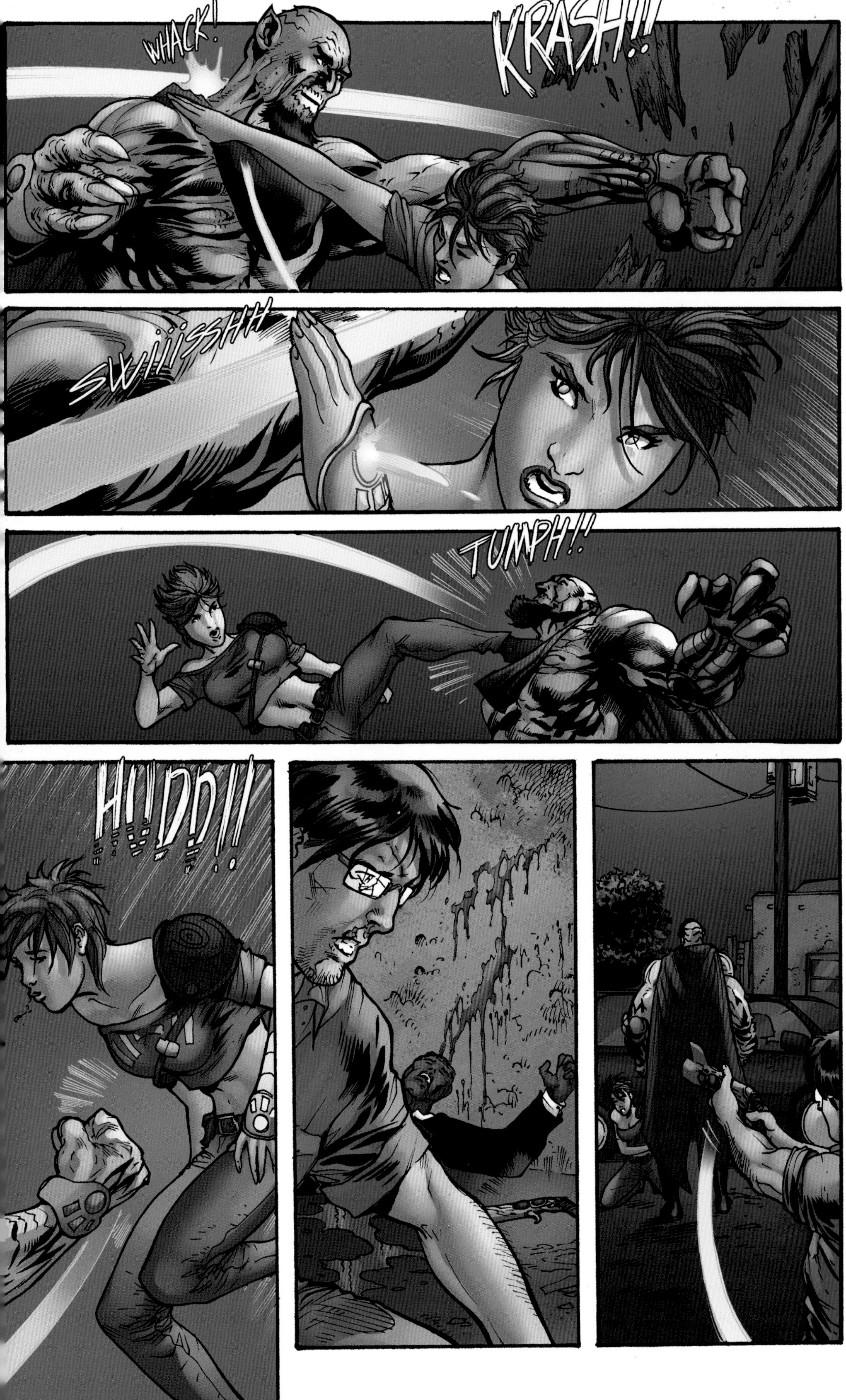
WHACK!
KRASH!!
SWIIIISSHH
TUMPH!!
H!!DD!!

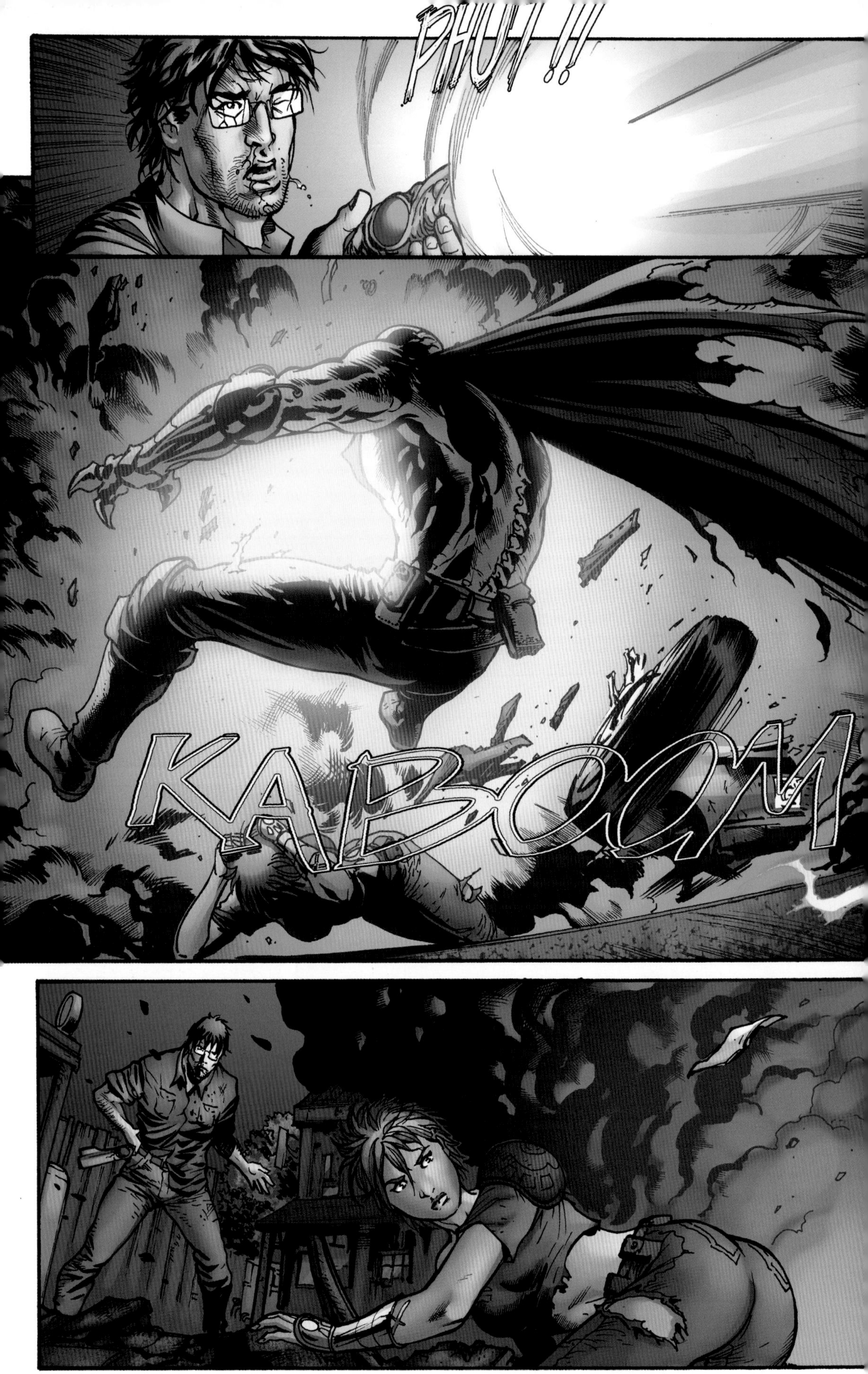
PHUT !!
KABOOM

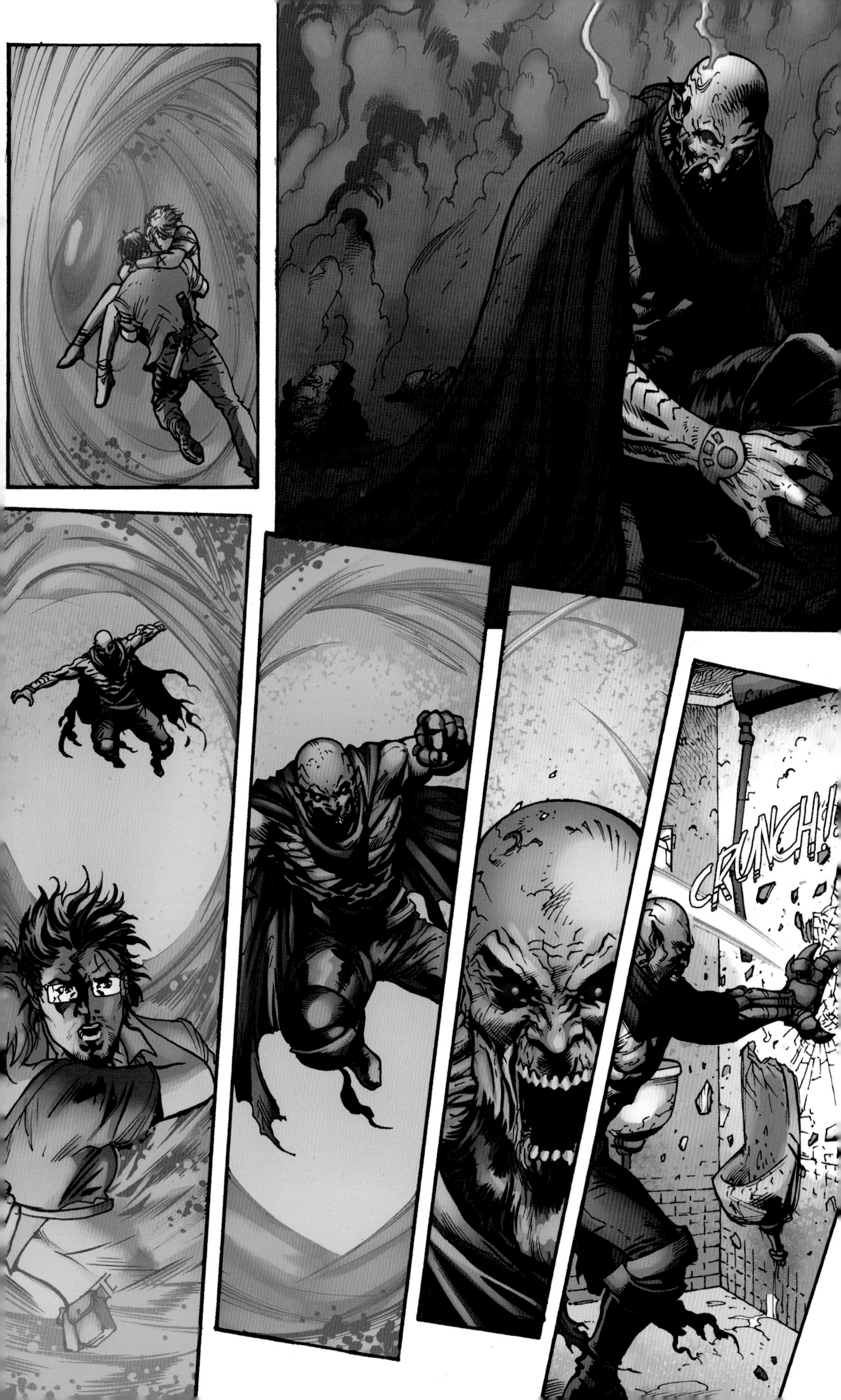
CRUNCH!!

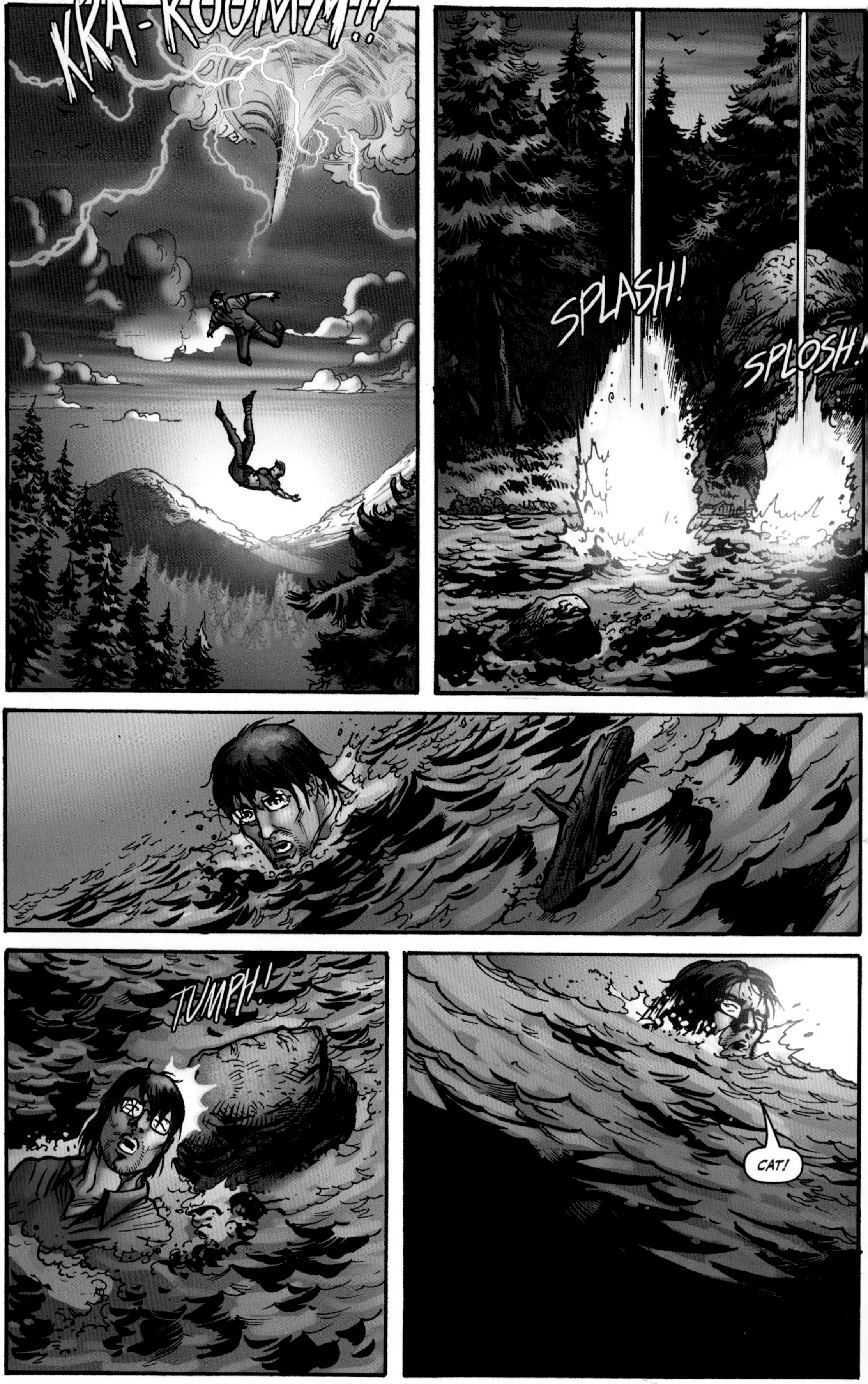
KRA-KOOMM!!
SPLASH!
SPLOSH!
TUMPH!
CAT!

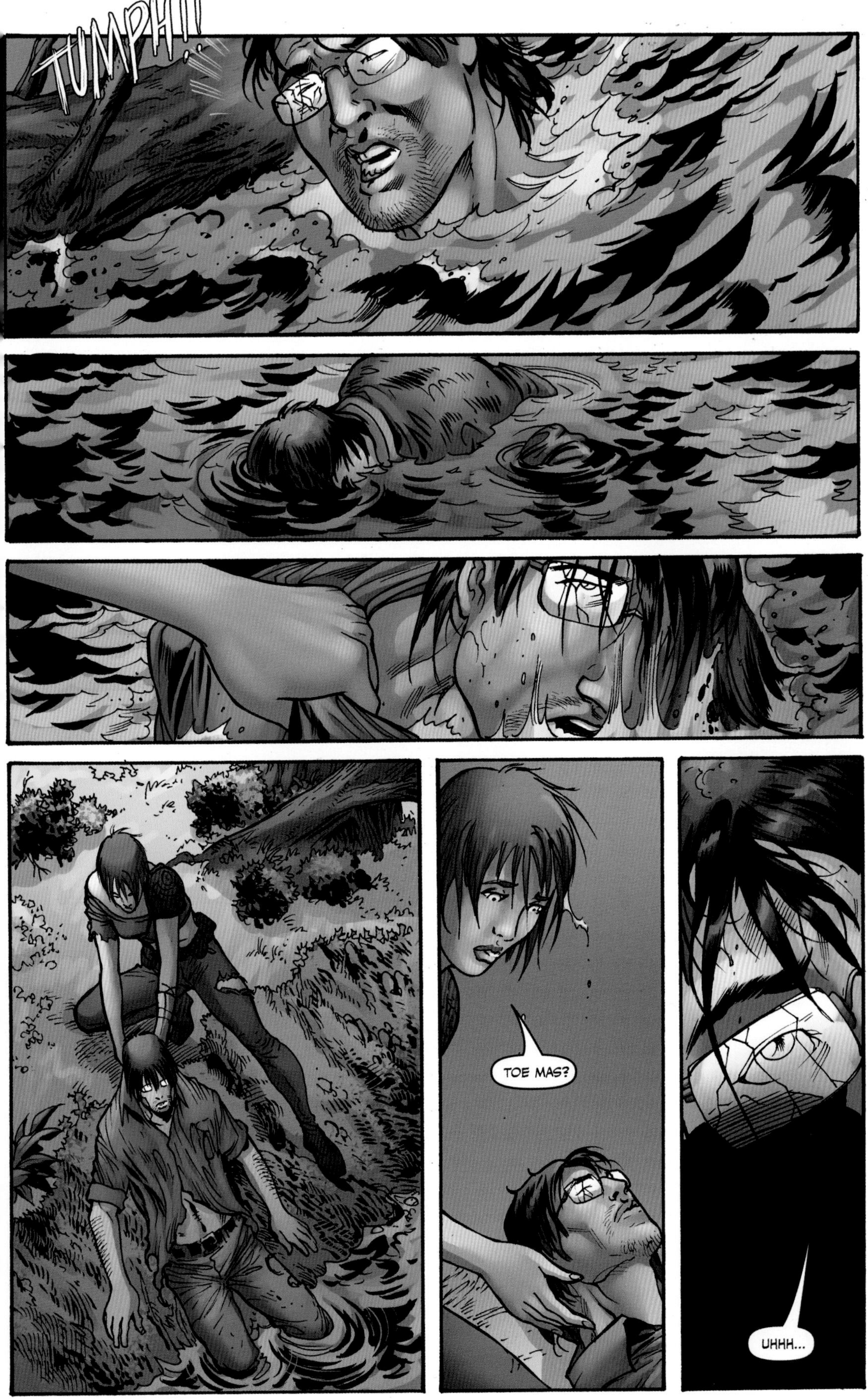
TUMPH!!
TOE MAS?
UHHH...

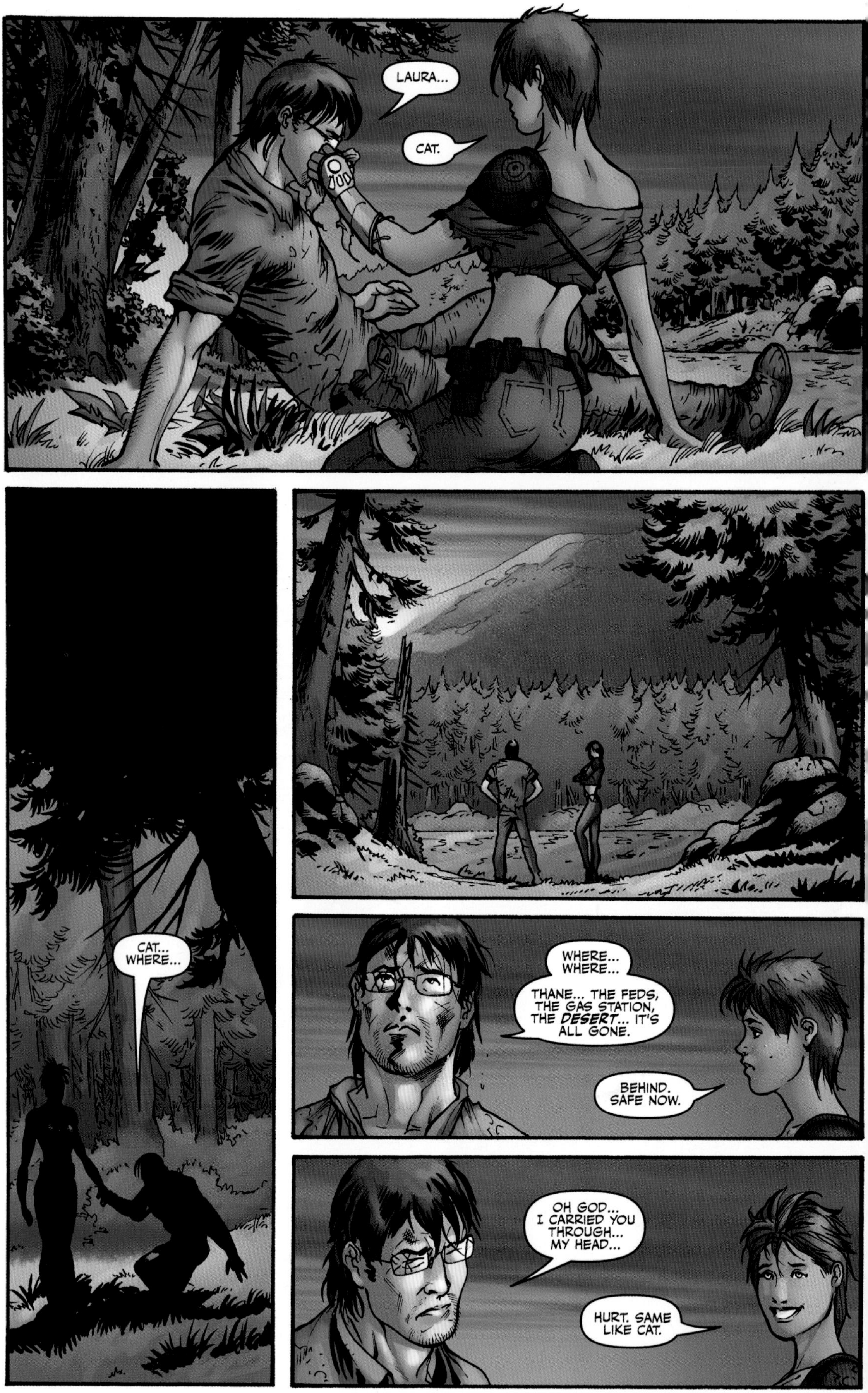

LAURA...
CAT.
CAT... WHERE...
WHERE... WHERE...
THANE... THE FEDS, THE GAS STATION, THE *DESERT*... IT'S ALL GONE.
BEHIND. SAFE NOW.
OH GOD... I CARRIED YOU THROUGH... MY HEAD...
HURT. SAME LIKE CAT.

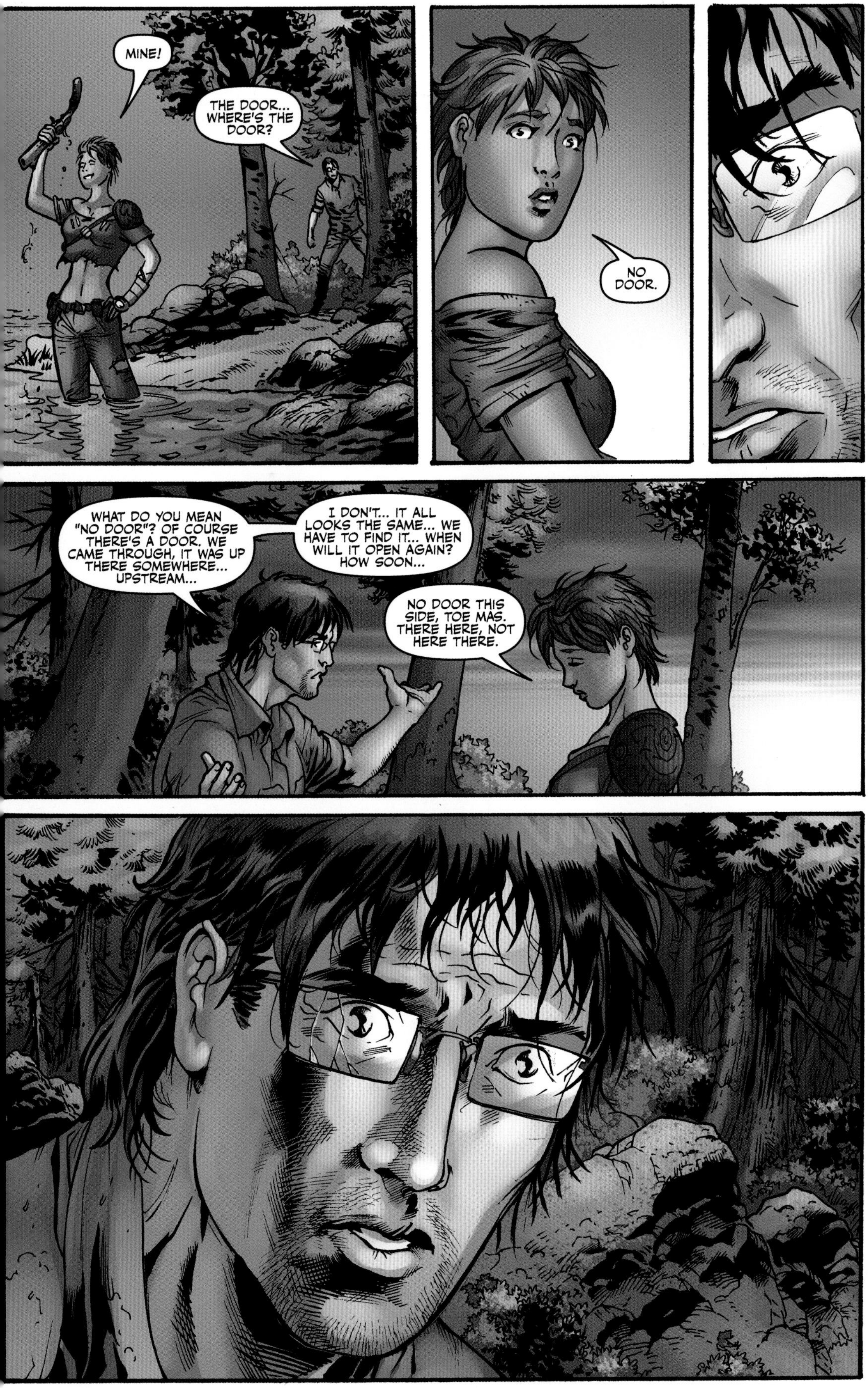
MINE!
THE DOOR... WHERE'S THE DOOR?
NO DOOR.
WHAT DO YOU MEAN "NO DOOR"? OF COURSE THERE'S A DOOR. WE CAME THROUGH, IT WAS UP THERE SOMEWHERE... UPSTREAM...
I DON'T... IT ALL LOOKS THE SAME... WE HAVE TO FIND IT... WHEN WILL IT OPEN AGAIN? HOW SOON...
NO DOOR THIS SIDE, TOE MAS. THERE HERE, NOT HERE THERE.

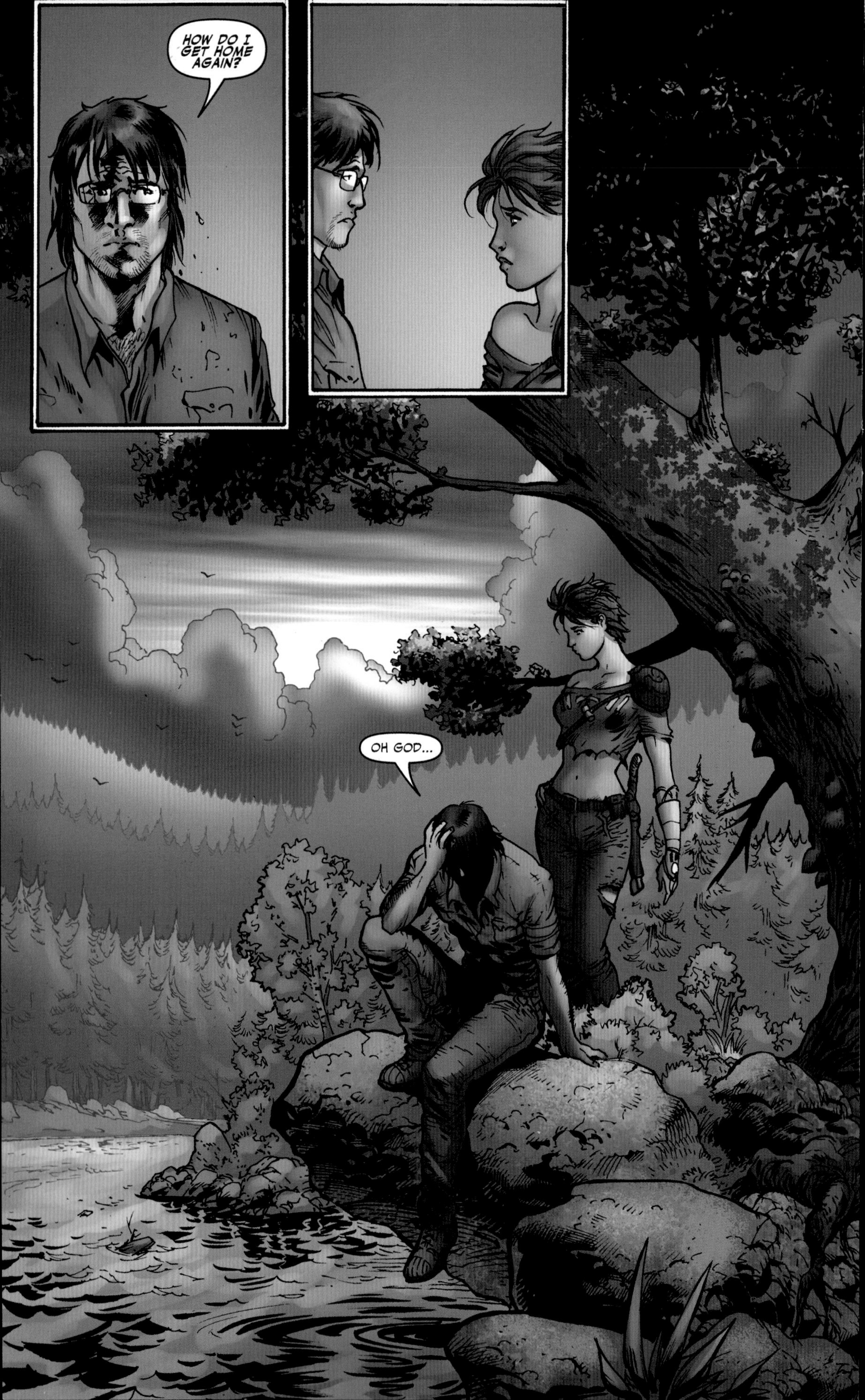
HOW DO I GET HOME AGAIN?
OH GOD...

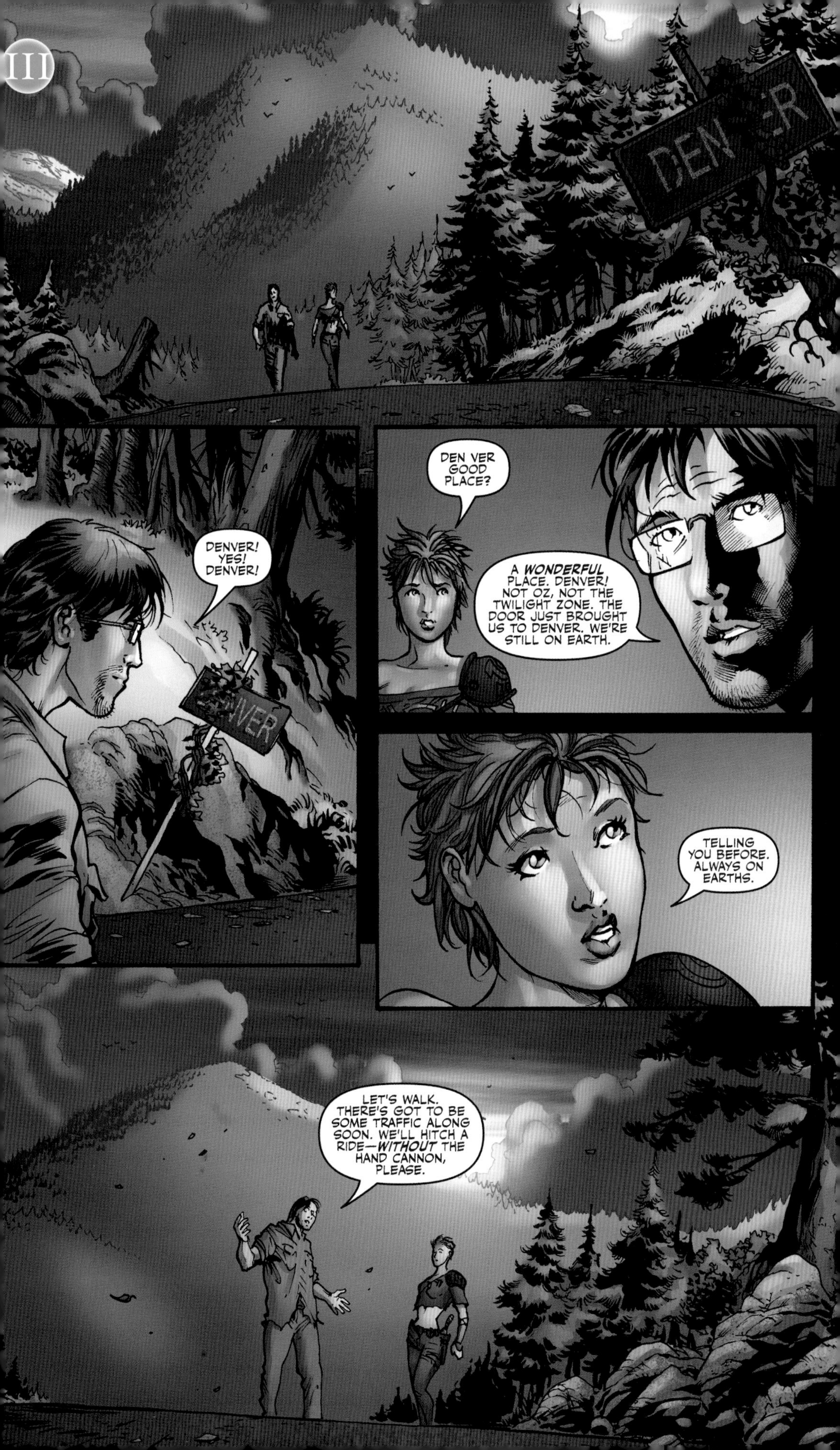
III
DEN ER
DENVER! YES! DENVER!
DENVER
DEN VER GOOD PLACE?
A WONDERFUL PLACE. DENVER! NOT OZ, NOT THE TWILIGHT ZONE. THE DOOR JUST BROUGHT US TO DENVER. WE'RE STILL ON EARTH.
TELLING YOU BEFORE. ALWAYS ON EARTHS.
LET'S WALK. THERE'S GOT TO BE SOME TRAFFIC ALONG SOON. WE'LL HITCH A RIDE—WITHOUT THE HAND CANNON, PLEASE.

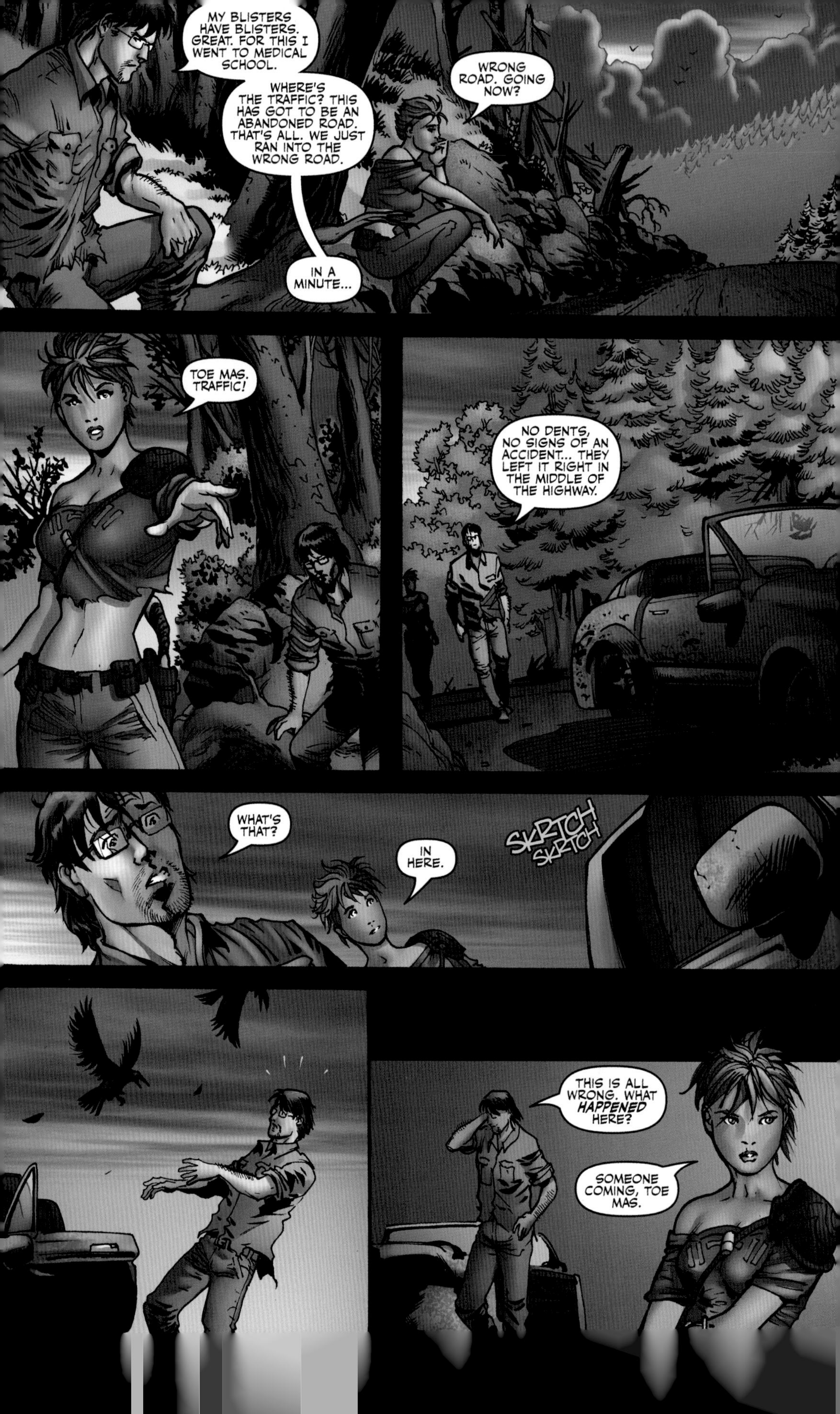
MY BLISTERS HAVE BLISTERS. GREAT. FOR THIS I WENT TO MEDICAL SCHOOL.
WRONG ROAD. GOING NOW?
WHERE'S THE TRAFFIC? THIS HAS GOT TO BE AN ABANDONED ROAD. THAT'S ALL. WE JUST RAN INTO THE WRONG ROAD.
IN A MINUTE...
TOE MAS. TRAFFIC!
NO DENTS, NO SIGNS OF AN ACCIDENT... THEY LEFT IT RIGHT IN THE MIDDLE OF THE HIGHWAY.
WHAT'S THAT?
IN HERE.
SKRTCH SKRTCH
THIS IS ALL WRONG. WHAT *HAPPENED* HERE?
SOMEONE COMING, TOE MAS.

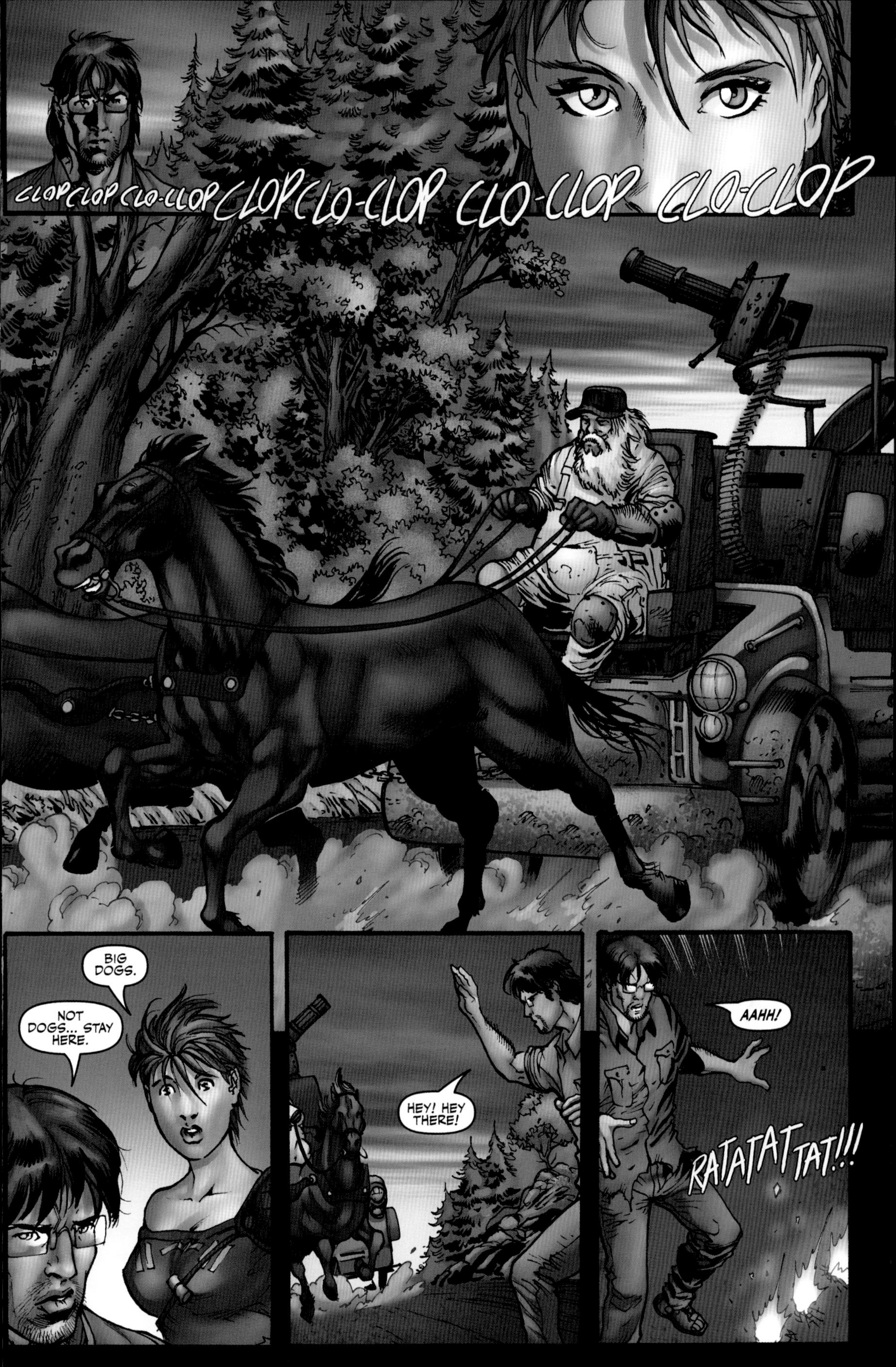
CLOP CLOP CLO-CLOP CLOP CLO-CLOP CLO-CLOP CLO-CLOP
BIG DOGS.
NOT DOGS... STAY HERE.
HEY! HEY THERE!
AAHH!
RATATAT TAT!!!

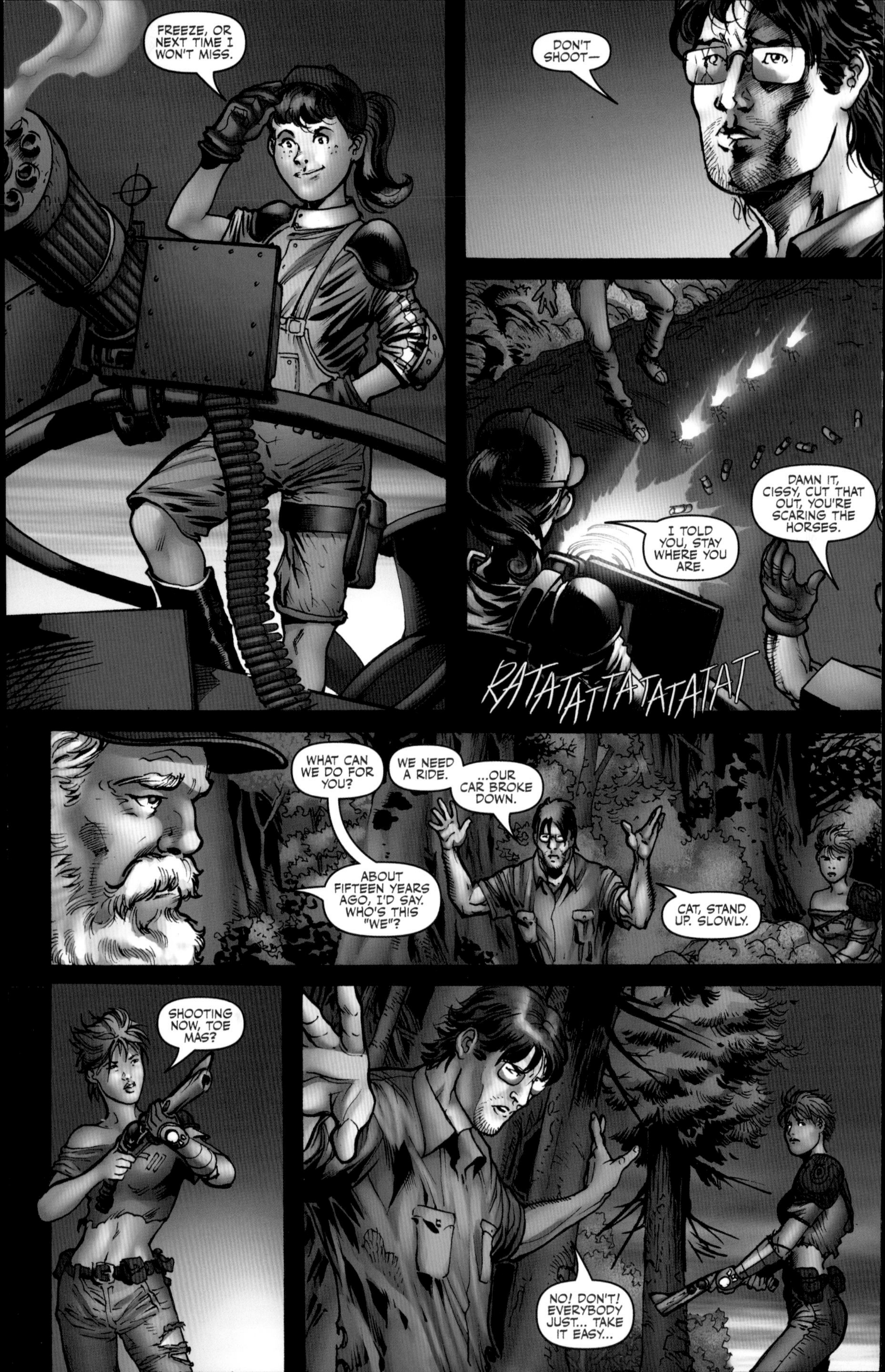
FREEZE, OR NEXT TIME I WON'T MISS.
DON'T SHOOT—
I TOLD YOU, STAY WHERE YOU ARE.
DAMN IT, CISSY, CUT THAT OUT, YOU'RE SCARING THE HORSES.
RATATATTATATATAT
WHAT CAN WE DO FOR YOU?
WE NEED A RIDE.
...OUR CAR BROKE DOWN.
ABOUT FIFTEEN YEARS AGO, I'D SAY. WHO'S THIS "WE"?
CAT, STAND UP. SLOWLY.
SHOOTING NOW, TOE MÁS?
NO! DON'T! EVERYBODY JUST... TAKE IT EASY...

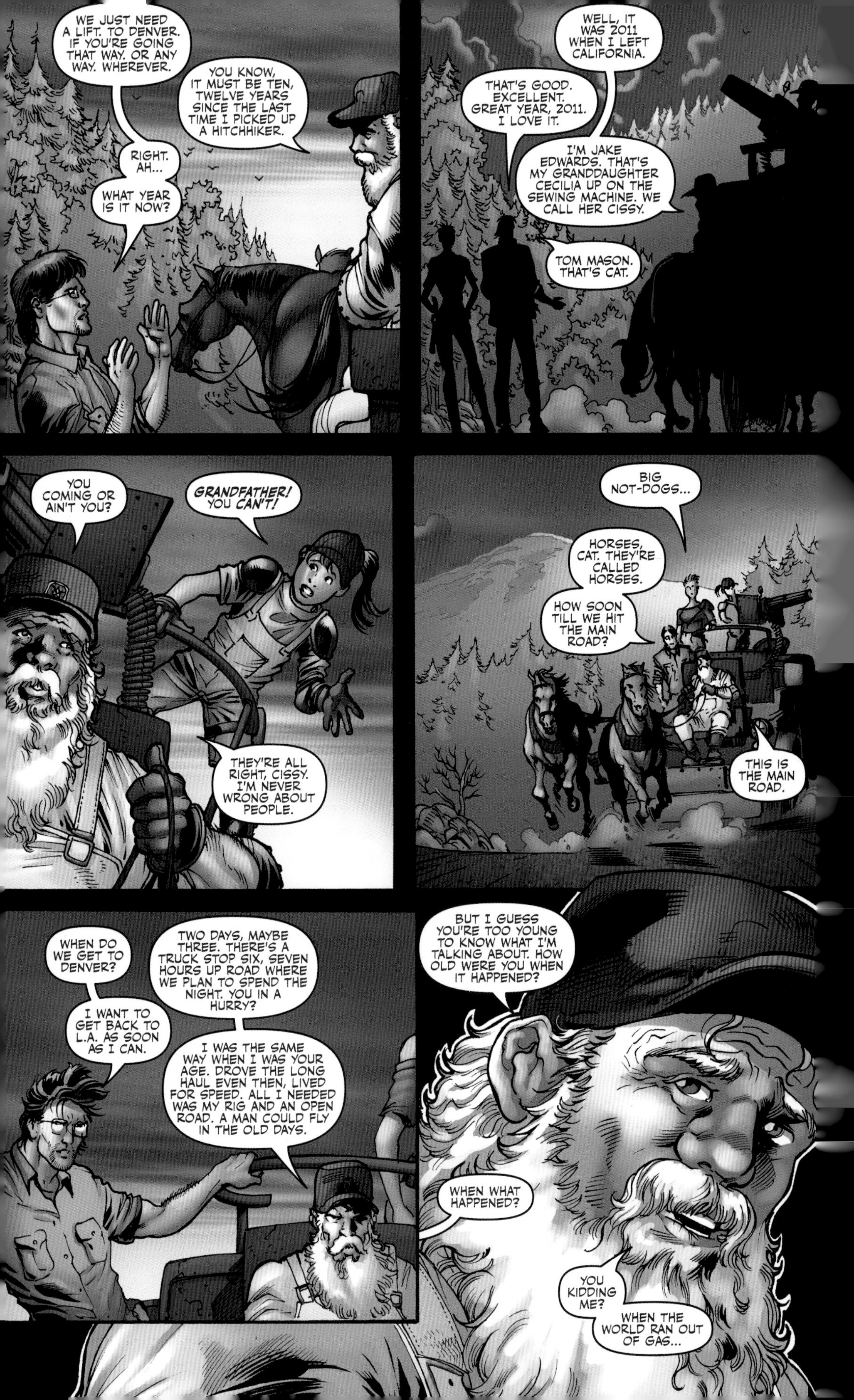
WE JUST NEED A LIFT. TO DENVER. IF YOU'RE GOING THAT WAY. OR ANY WAY. WHEREVER.
YOU KNOW, IT MUST BE TEN, TWELVE YEARS SINCE THE LAST TIME I PICKED UP A HITCHHIKER.
RIGHT. AH...
WHAT YEAR IS IT NOW?
WELL, IT WAS 2011 WHEN I LEFT CALIFORNIA.
THAT'S GOOD. EXCELLENT. GREAT YEAR, 2011. I LOVE IT.
I'M JAKE EDWARDS. THAT'S MY GRANDDAUGHTER CECILIA UP ON THE SEWING MACHINE. WE CALL HER CISSY.
TOM MASON. THAT'S CAT.
YOU COMING OR AIN'T YOU?
GRANDFATHER! YOU CAN'T!
THEY'RE ALL RIGHT, CISSY. I'M NEVER WRONG ABOUT PEOPLE.
BIG NOT-DOGS...
HORSES, CAT. THEY'RE CALLED HORSES.
HOW SOON TILL WE HIT THE MAIN ROAD?
THIS IS THE MAIN ROAD.
WHEN DO WE GET TO DENVER?
TWO DAYS, MAYBE THREE. THERE'S A TRUCK STOP SIX, SEVEN HOURS UP ROAD WHERE WE PLAN TO SPEND THE NIGHT. YOU IN A HURRY?
I WANT TO GET BACK TO L.A. AS SOON AS I CAN.
I WAS THE SAME WAY WHEN I WAS YOUR AGE. DROVE THE LONG HAUL EVEN THEN, LIVED FOR SPEED. ALL I NEEDED WAS MY RIG AND AN OPEN ROAD. A MAN COULD FLY IN THE OLD DAYS.
BUT I GUESS YOU'RE TOO YOUNG TO KNOW WHAT I'M TALKING ABOUT. HOW OLD WERE YOU WHEN IT HAPPENED?
WHEN WHAT HAPPENED?
YOU KIDDING ME?
WHEN THE WORLD RAN OUT OF GAS...

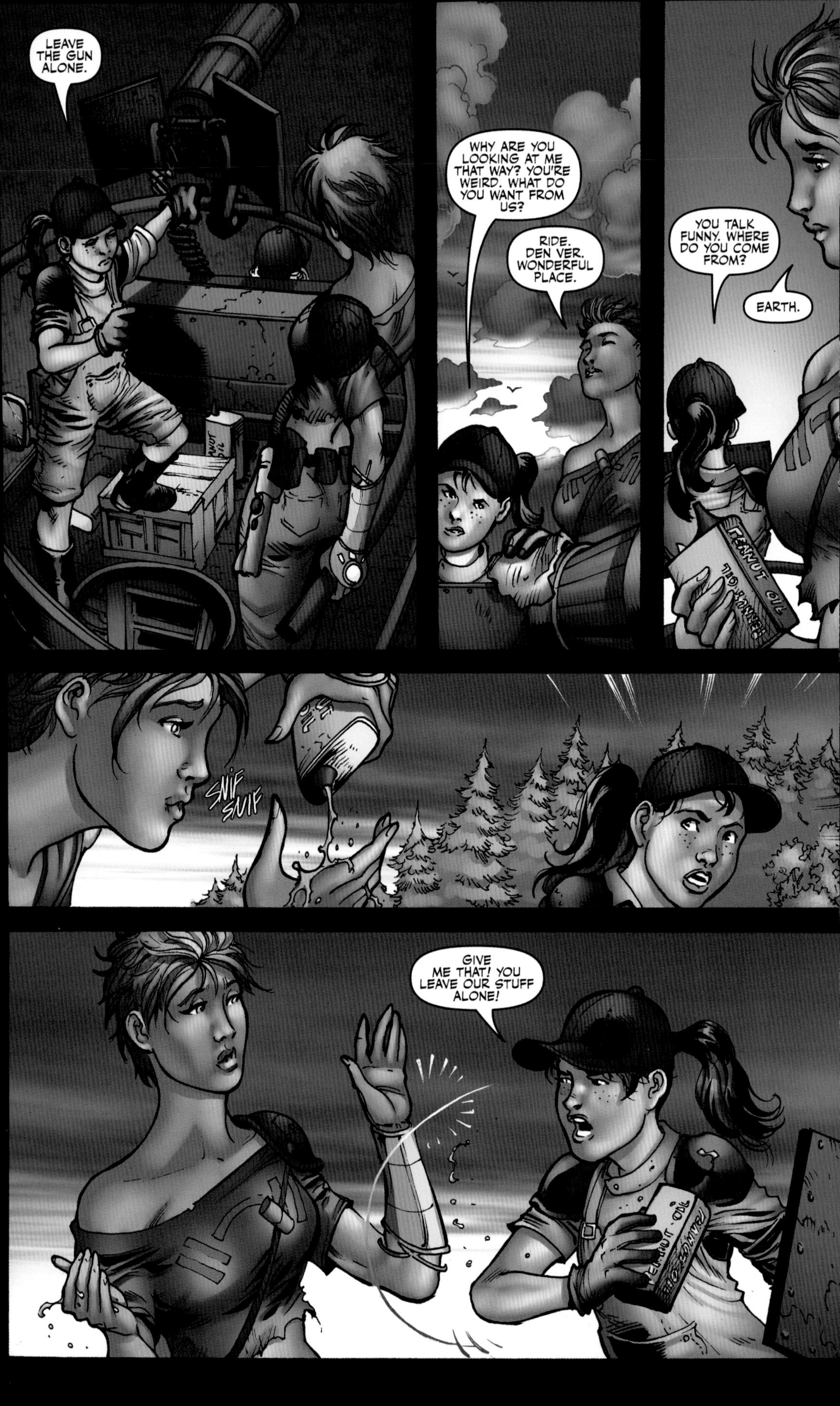
LEAVE THE GUN ALONE.
WHY ARE YOU LOOKING AT ME THAT WAY? YOU'RE WEIRD. WHAT DO YOU WANT FROM US?
RIDE. DEN VER. WONDERFUL PLACE.
YOU TALK FUNNY. WHERE DO YOU COME FROM?
EARTH.
PEANUT OIL
SNIF SNIF
GIVE ME THAT! YOU LEAVE OUR STUFF ALONE!

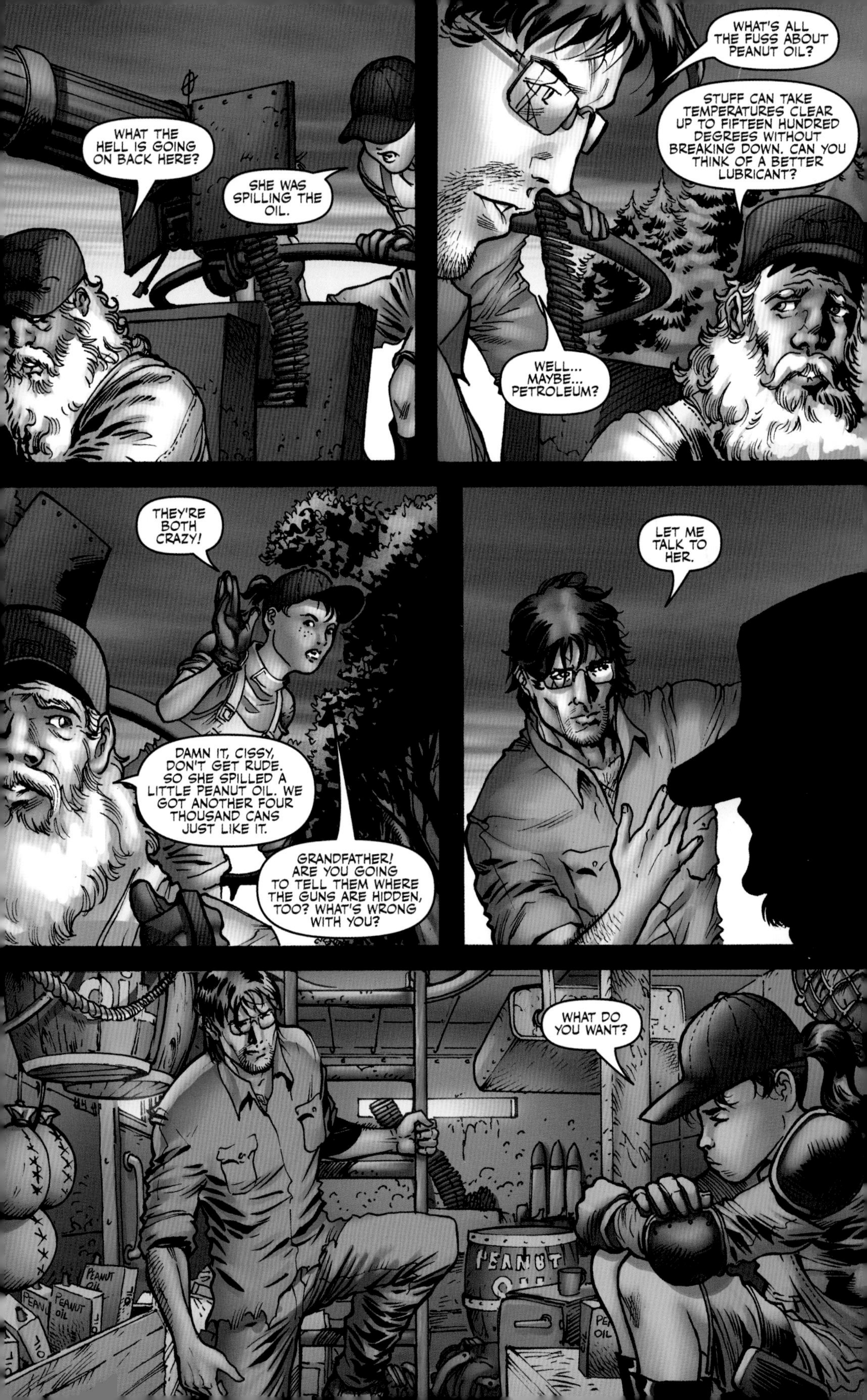
WHAT THE HELL IS GOING ON BACK HERE?
SHE WAS SPILLING THE OIL.
WHAT'S ALL THE FUSS ABOUT PEANUT OIL?
STUFF CAN TAKE TEMPERATURES CLEAR UP TO FIFTEEN HUNDRED DEGREES WITHOUT BREAKING DOWN. CAN YOU THINK OF A BETTER LUBRICANT?
WELL... MAYBE... PETROLEUM?
THEY'RE BOTH CRAZY!
DAMN IT, CISSY, DON'T GET RUDE. SO SHE SPILLED A LITTLE PEANUT OIL. WE GOT ANOTHER FOUR THOUSAND CANS JUST LIKE IT.
GRANDFATHER! ARE YOU GOING TO TELL THEM WHERE THE GUNS ARE HIDDEN, TOO? WHAT'S WRONG WITH YOU?
LET ME TALK TO HER.
WHAT DO YOU WANT?
PEANUT OIL
PEANUT OIL

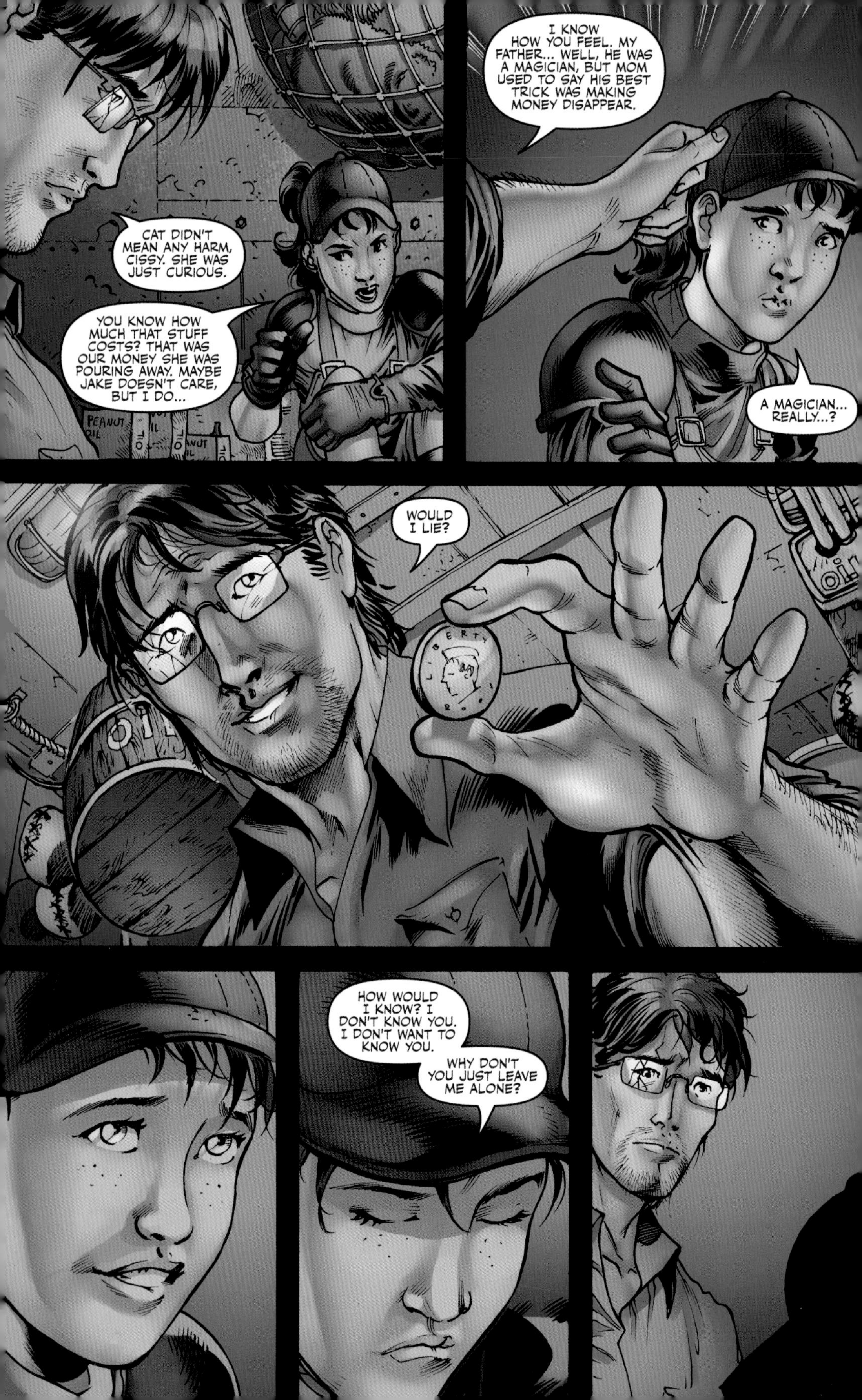

CAT DIDN'T MEAN ANY HARM, CISSY. SHE WAS JUST CURIOUS.
YOU KNOW HOW MUCH THAT STUFF COSTS? THAT WAS OUR MONEY SHE WAS POURING AWAY. MAYBE JAKE DOESN'T CARE, BUT I DO...
PEANUT OIL
I KNOW HOW YOU FEEL. MY FATHER... WELL, HE WAS A MAGICIAN, BUT MOM USED TO SAY HIS BEST TRICK WAS MAKING MONEY DISAPPEAR.
A MAGICIAN... REALLY...?
WOULD I LIE?
LIBERTY
HOW WOULD I KNOW? I DON'T KNOW YOU. I DON'T WANT TO KNOW YOU.
WHY DON'T YOU JUST LEAVE ME ALONE?

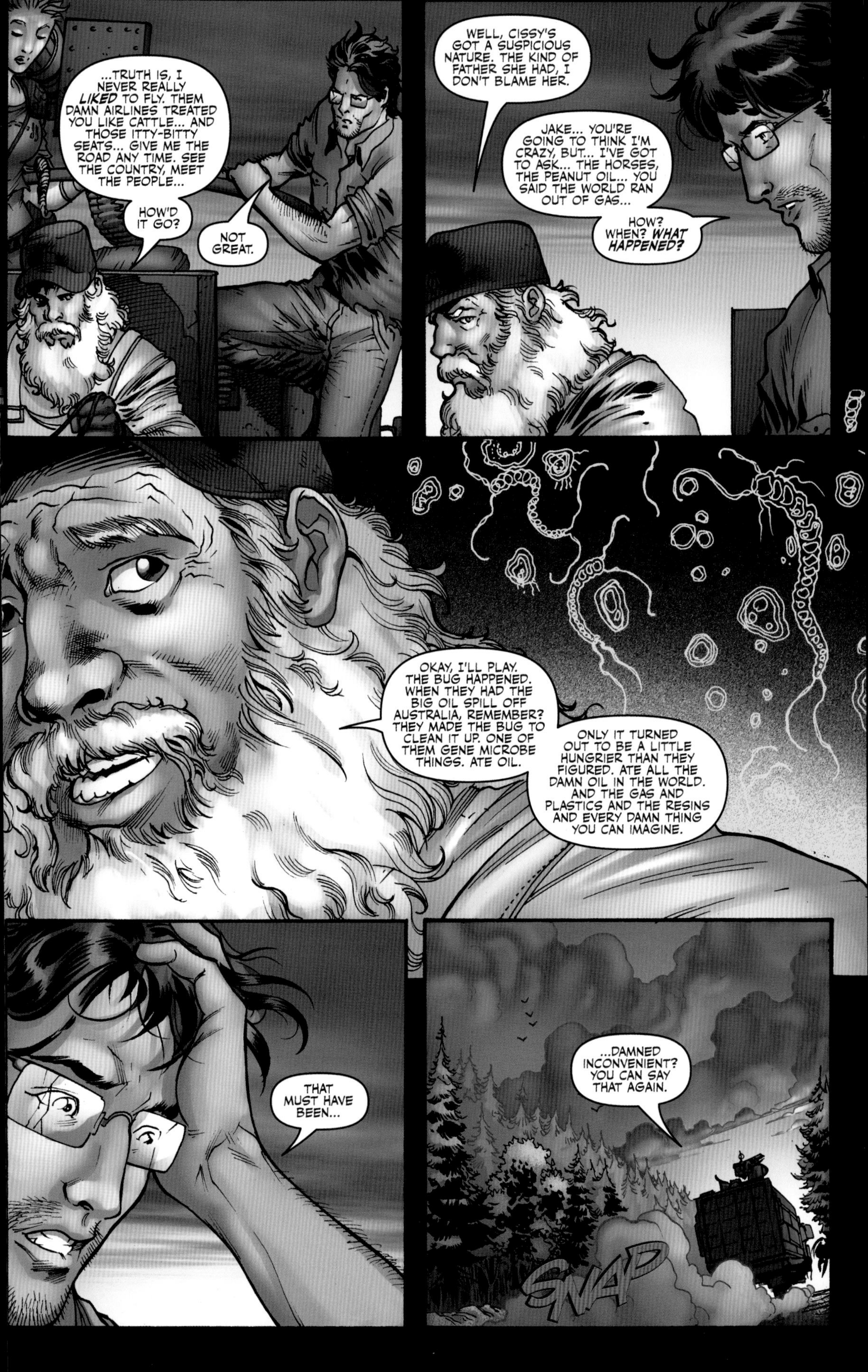
...TRUTH IS, I NEVER REALLY *LIKED* TO FLY. THEM DAMN AIRLINES TREATED YOU LIKE CATTLE... AND THOSE ITTY-BITTY SEATS... GIVE ME THE ROAD ANY TIME. SEE THE COUNTRY, MEET THE PEOPLE...
HOW'D IT GO?
NOT GREAT.
WELL, CISSY'S GOT A SUSPICIOUS NATURE. THE KIND OF FATHER SHE HAD, I DON'T BLAME HER.
JAKE... YOU'RE GOING TO THINK I'M CRAZY, BUT... I'VE GOT TO ASK... THE HORSES, THE PEANUT OIL... YOU SAID THE WORLD RAN OUT OF GAS...
HOW? WHEN? ***WHAT HAPPENED?***
OKAY, I'LL PLAY. THE BUG HAPPENED. WHEN THEY HAD THE BIG OIL SPILL OFF AUSTRALIA, REMEMBER? THEY MADE THE BUG TO CLEAN IT UP. ONE OF THEM GENE MICROBE THINGS. ATE OIL.
ONLY IT TURNED OUT TO BE A LITTLE HUNGRIER THAN THEY FIGURED. ATE ALL THE DAMN OIL IN THE WORLD. AND THE GAS AND PLASTICS AND THE RESINS AND EVERY DAMN THING YOU CAN IMAGINE.
THAT MUST HAVE BEEN...
...DAMNED INCONVENIENT? YOU CAN SAY THAT AGAIN.
SNAP

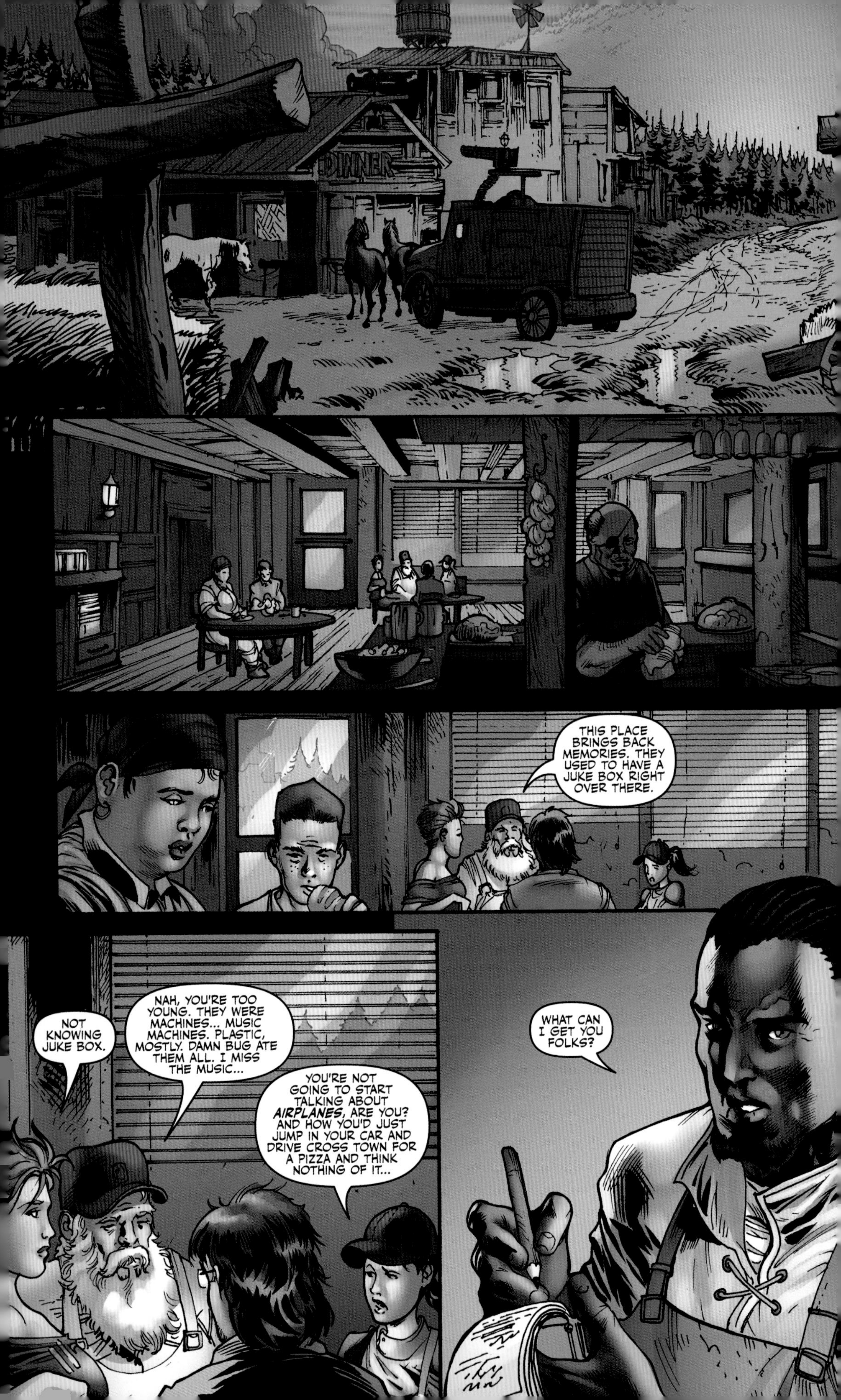
DINNER
THIS PLACE BRINGS BACK MEMORIES. THEY USED TO HAVE A JUKE BOX RIGHT OVER THERE.
NOT KNOWING JUKE BOX.
NAH, YOU'RE TOO YOUNG. THEY WERE MACHINES... MUSIC MACHINES. PLASTIC, MOSTLY. DAMN BUG ATE THEM ALL. I MISS THE MUSIC...
YOU'RE NOT GOING TO START TALKING ABOUT *AIRPLANES*, ARE YOU? AND HOW YOU'D JUST JUMP IN YOUR CAR AND DRIVE CROSS TOWN FOR A PIZZA AND THINK NOTHING OF IT...
WHAT CAN I GET YOU FOLKS?

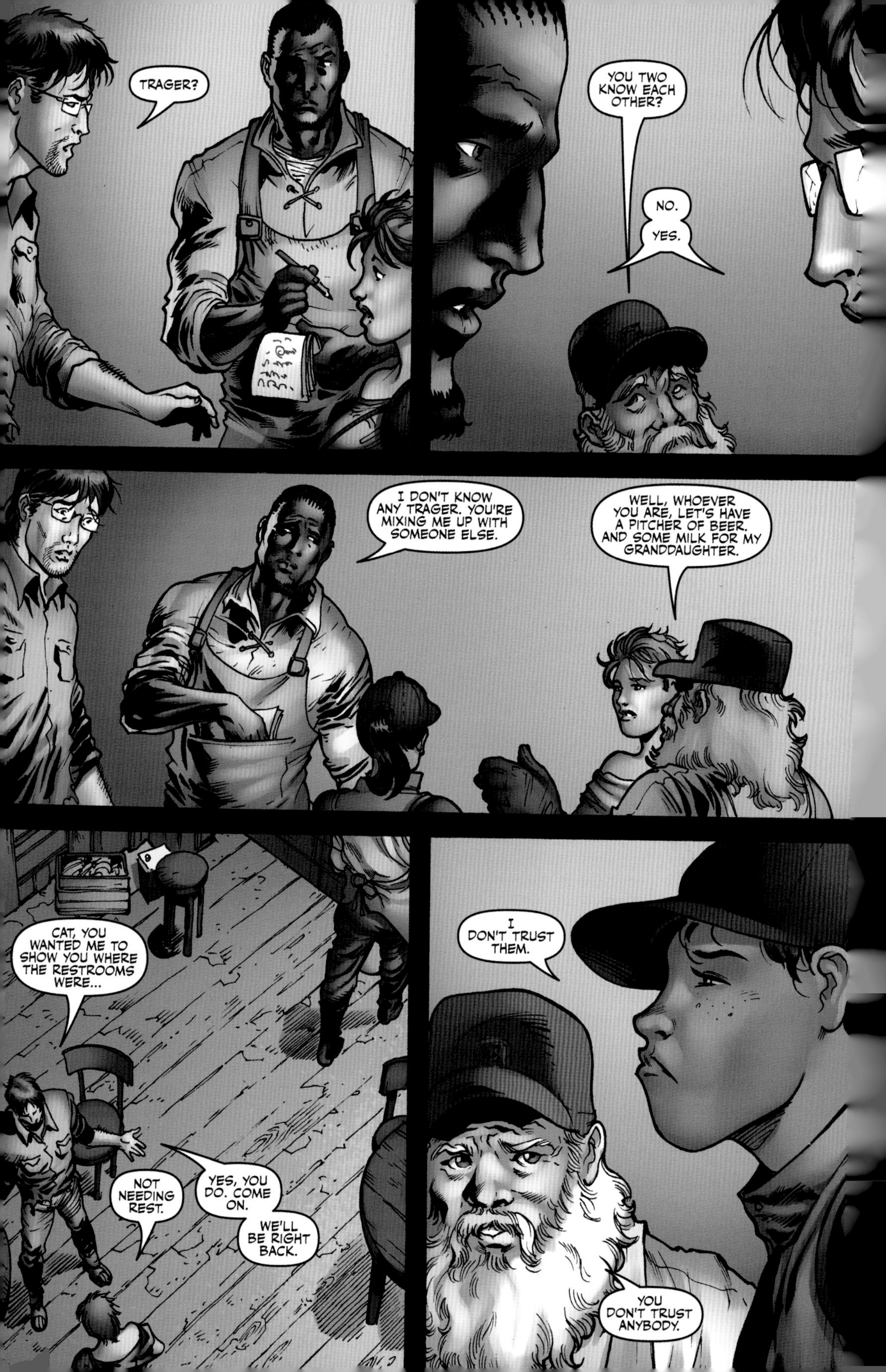
TRAGER?
YOU TWO KNOW EACH OTHER?
NO.
YES.
I DON'T KNOW ANY TRAGER. YOU'RE MIXING ME UP WITH SOMEONE ELSE.
WELL, WHOEVER YOU ARE, LET'S HAVE A PITCHER OF BEER. AND SOME MILK FOR MY GRANDDAUGHTER.
CAT, YOU WANTED ME TO SHOW YOU WHERE THE RESTROOMS WERE...
NOT NEEDING REST.
YES, YOU DO. COME ON.
WE'LL BE RIGHT BACK.
I DON'T TRUST THEM.
YOU DON'T TRUST ANYBODY.

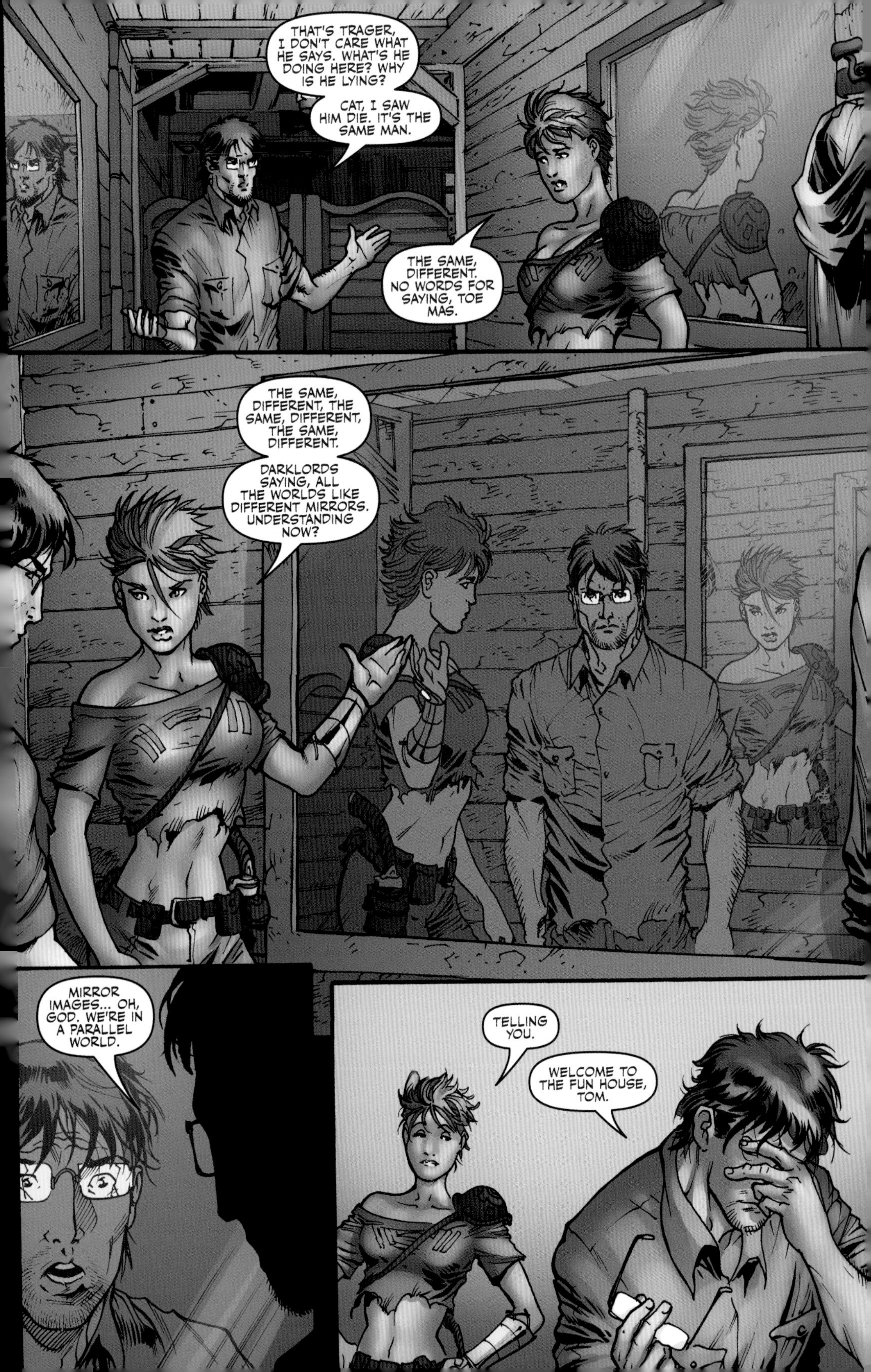
THAT'S TRAGER, I DON'T CARE WHAT HE SAYS. WHAT'S HE DOING HERE? WHY IS HE LYING?
CAT, I SAW HIM DIE. IT'S THE SAME MAN.
THE SAME, DIFFERENT. NO WORDS FOR SAYING, TOE MAS.
THE SAME, DIFFERENT, THE SAME, DIFFERENT, THE SAME, DIFFERENT.
DARKLORDS SAYING, ALL THE WORLDS LIKE DIFFERENT MIRRORS. UNDERSTANDING NOW?
MIRROR IMAGES... OH, GOD. WE'RE IN A PARALLEL WORLD.
TELLING YOU.
WELCOME TO THE FUN HOUSE, TOM.

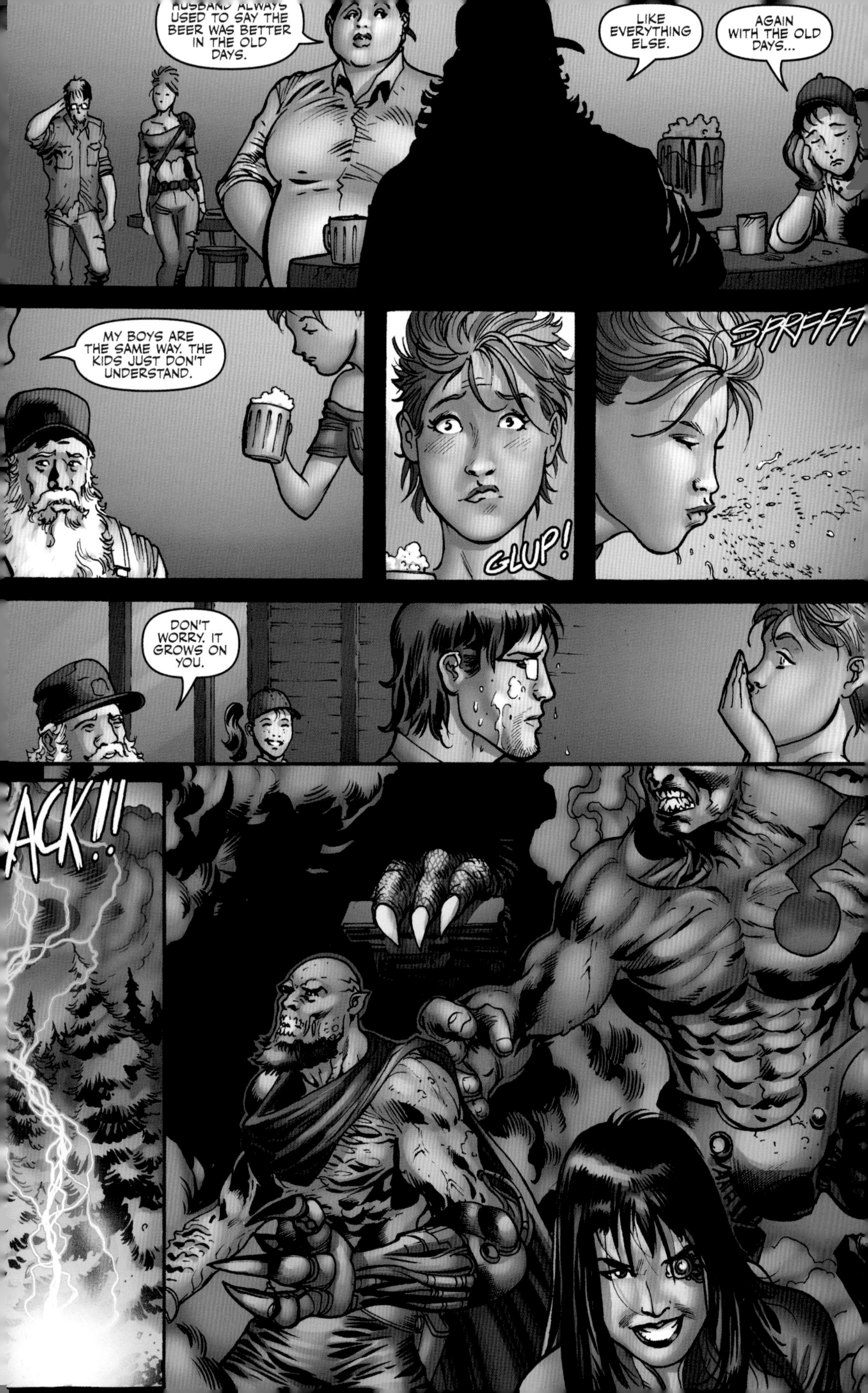
HUSBAND ALWAYS USED TO SAY THE BEER WAS BETTER IN THE OLD DAYS.
LIKE EVERYTHING ELSE.
AGAIN WITH THE OLD DAYS...
MY BOYS ARE THE SAME WAY. THE KIDS JUST DON'T UNDERSTAND.
GLUP!
SPRFFFT
DON'T WORRY. IT GROWS ON YOU.
ACK!!

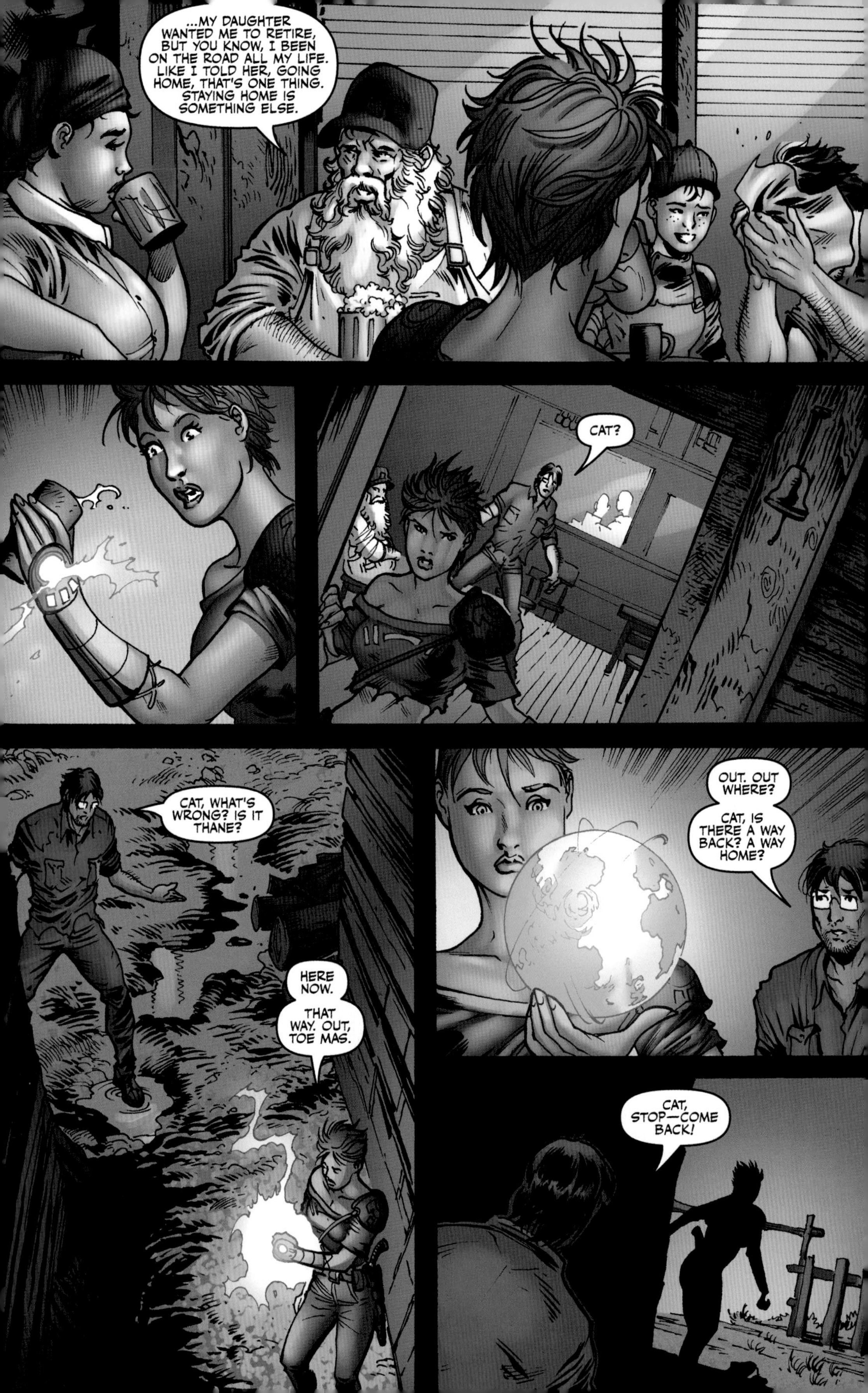
...MY DAUGHTER WANTED ME TO RETIRE, BUT YOU KNOW, I BEEN ON THE ROAD ALL MY LIFE. LIKE I TOLD HER, GOING HOME, THAT'S ONE THING. STAYING HOME IS SOMETHING ELSE.
CAT?
CAT, WHAT'S WRONG? IS IT THANE?
HERE NOW.
THAT WAY. OUT, TOE MAS.
OUT. OUT WHERE?
CAT, IS THERE A WAY BACK? A WAY HOME?
CAT, STOP—COME BACK!

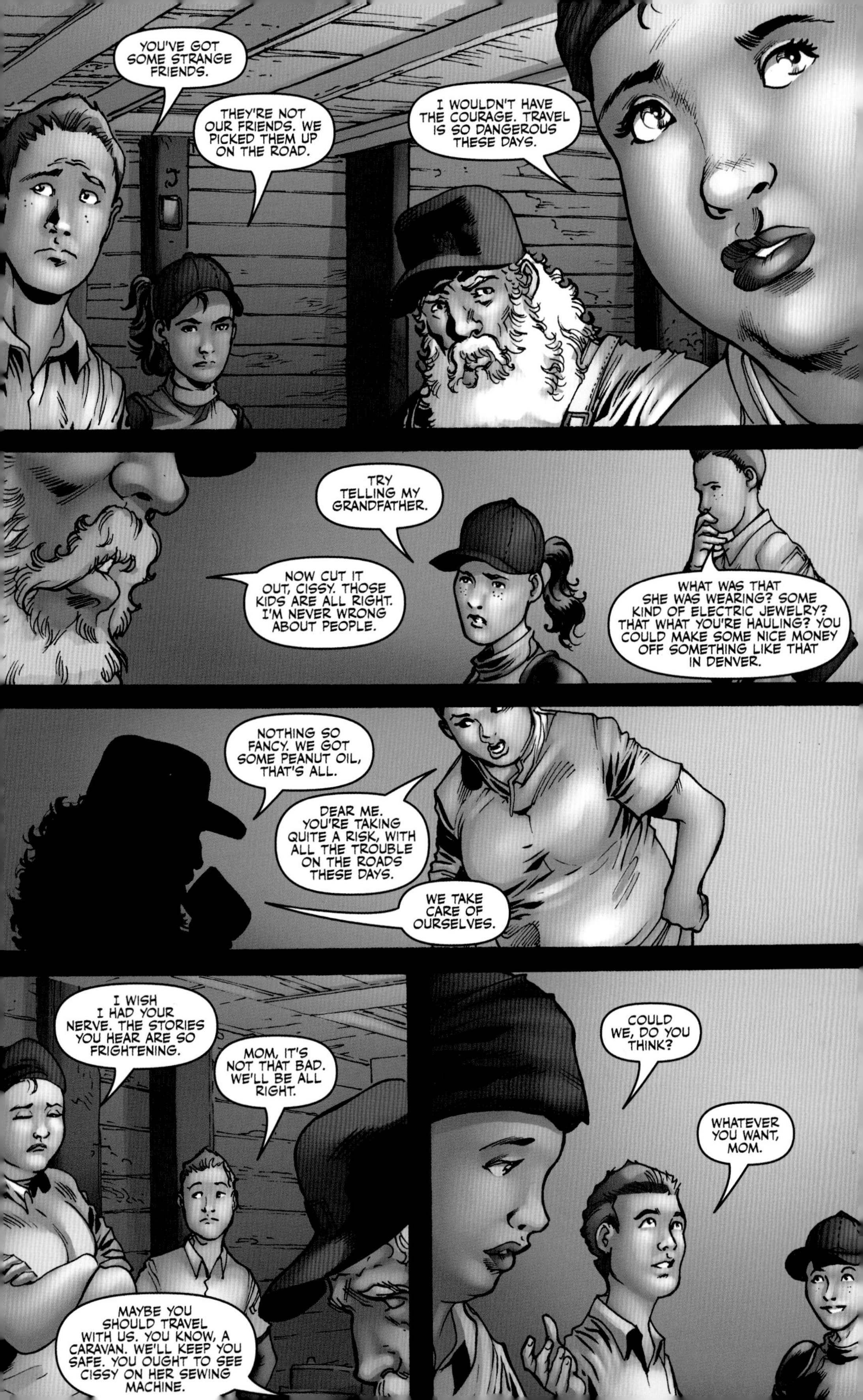
YOU'VE GOT SOME STRANGE FRIENDS.
THEY'RE NOT OUR FRIENDS. WE PICKED THEM UP ON THE ROAD.
I WOULDN'T HAVE THE COURAGE. TRAVEL IS SO DANGEROUS THESE DAYS.
TRY TELLING MY GRANDFATHER.
NOW CUT IT OUT, CISSY. THOSE KIDS ARE ALL RIGHT. I'M NEVER WRONG ABOUT PEOPLE.
WHAT WAS THAT SHE WAS WEARING? SOME KIND OF ELECTRIC JEWELRY? THAT WHAT YOU'RE HAULING? YOU COULD MAKE SOME NICE MONEY OFF SOMETHING LIKE THAT IN DENVER.
NOTHING SO FANCY. WE GOT SOME PEANUT OIL, THAT'S ALL.
DEAR ME. YOU'RE TAKING QUITE A RISK, WITH ALL THE TROUBLE ON THE ROADS THESE DAYS.
WE TAKE CARE OF OURSELVES.
I WISH I HAD YOUR NERVE. THE STORIES YOU HEAR ARE SO FRIGHTENING.
MOM, IT'S NOT THAT BAD. WE'LL BE ALL RIGHT.
MAYBE YOU SHOULD TRAVEL WITH US. YOU KNOW, A CARAVAN. WE'LL KEEP YOU SAFE. YOU OUGHT TO SEE CISSY ON HER SEWING MACHINE.
COULD WE, DO YOU THINK?
WHATEVER YOU WANT, MOM.

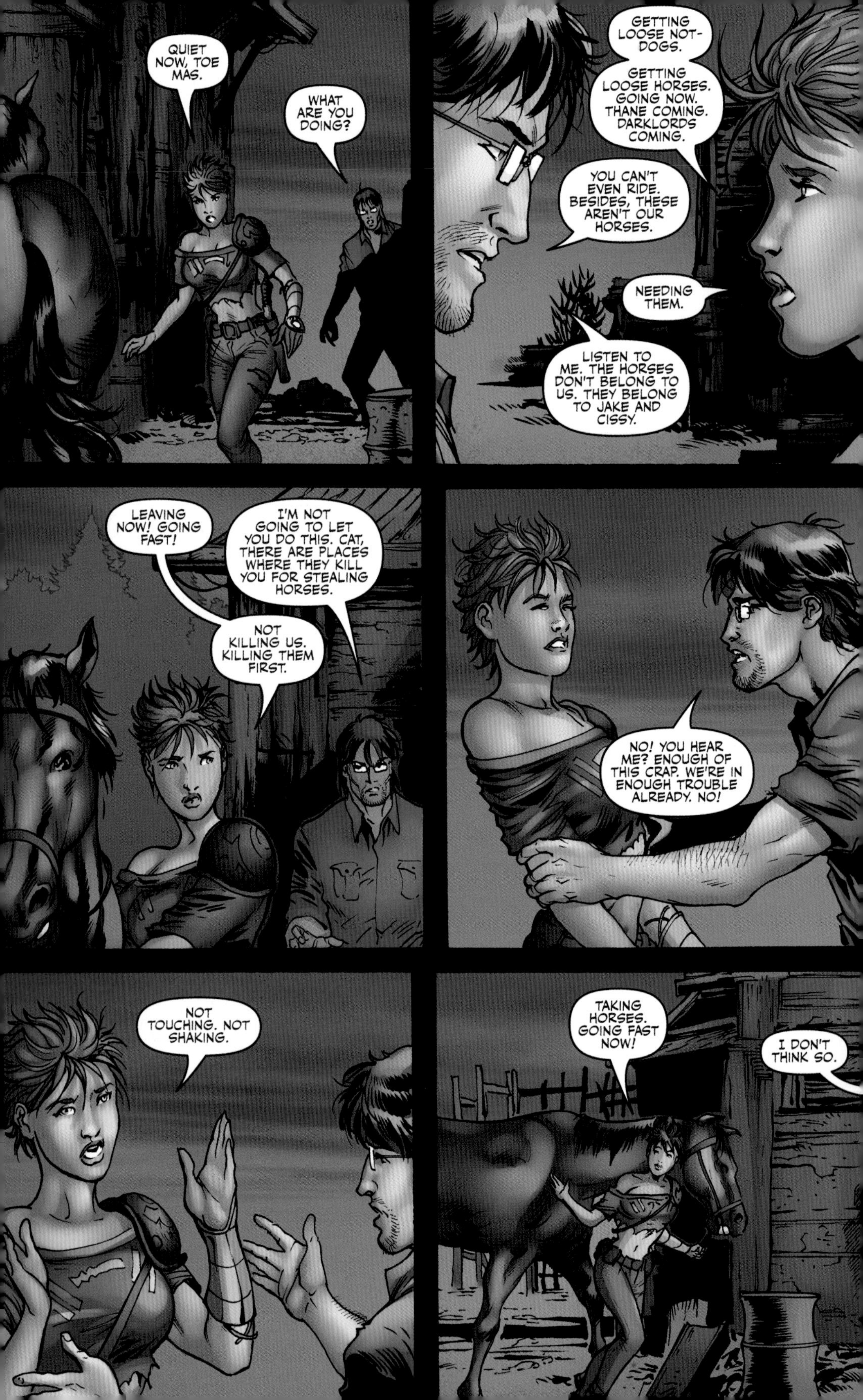
QUIET NOW, TOE MAS.
WHAT ARE YOU DOING?
GETTING LOOSE NOT-DOGS.
GETTING LOOSE HORSES. GOING NOW. THANE COMING. DARKLORDS COMING.
YOU CAN'T EVEN RIDE. BESIDES, THESE AREN'T OUR HORSES.
NEEDING THEM.
LISTEN TO ME. THE HORSES DON'T BELONG TO US. THEY BELONG TO JAKE AND CISSY.
LEAVING NOW! GOING FAST!
I'M NOT GOING TO LET YOU DO THIS. CAT, THERE ARE PLACES WHERE THEY KILL YOU FOR STEALING HORSES.
NOT KILLING US. KILLING THEM FIRST.
NO! YOU HEAR ME? ENOUGH OF THIS CRAP. WE'RE IN ENOUGH TROUBLE ALREADY. NO!
NOT TOUCHING. NOT SHAKING.
TAKING HORSES. GOING FAST NOW!
I DON'T THINK SO.

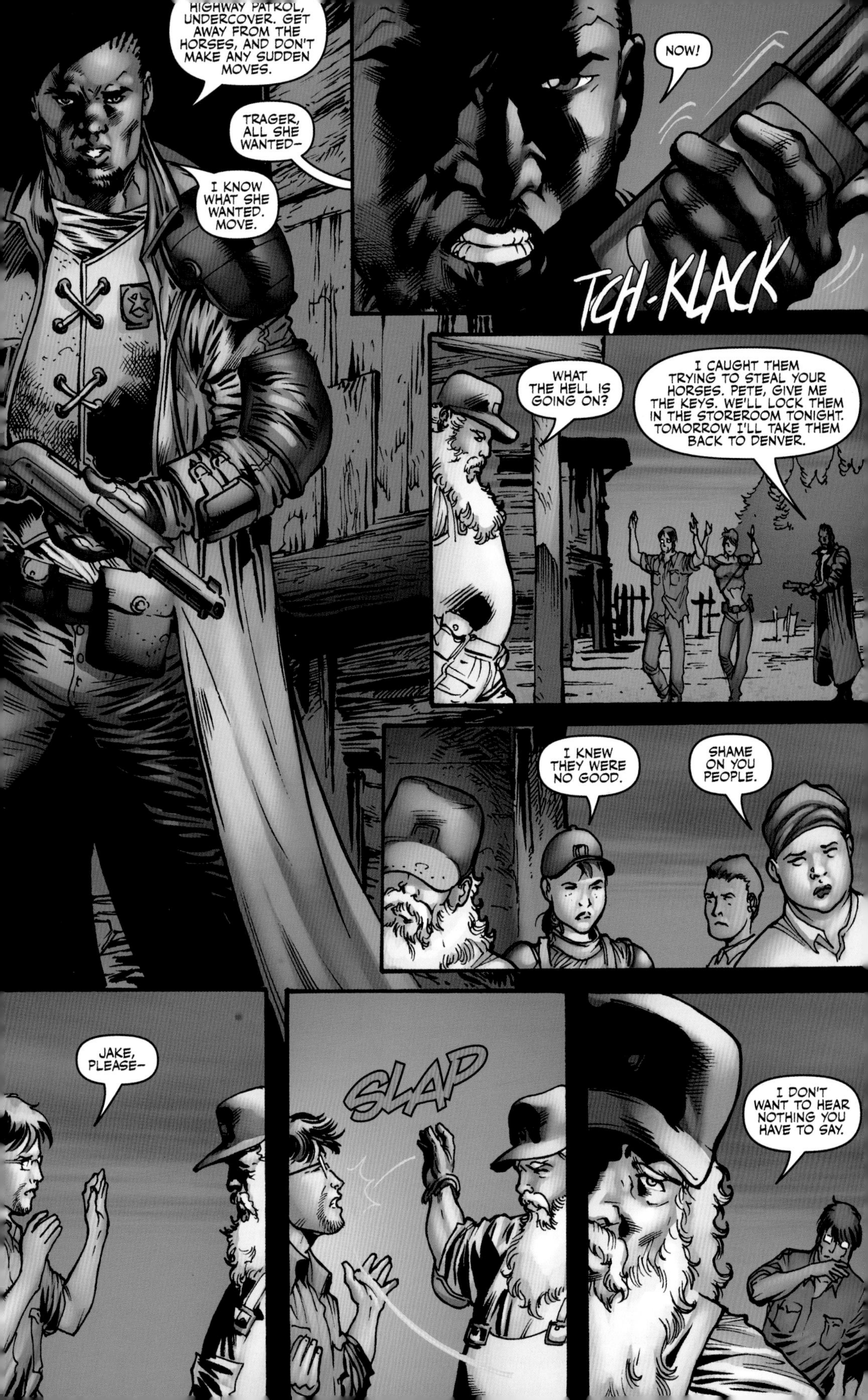
HIGHWAY PATROL, UNDERCOVER. GET AWAY FROM THE HORSES, AND DON'T MAKE ANY SUDDEN MOVES.
TRAGER, ALL SHE WANTED–
I KNOW WHAT SHE WANTED. MOVE.
NOW!
TCH-KLACK
WHAT THE HELL IS GOING ON?
I CAUGHT THEM TRYING TO STEAL YOUR HORSES. PETE, GIVE ME THE KEYS. WE'LL LOCK THEM IN THE STOREROOM TONIGHT. TOMORROW I'LL TAKE THEM BACK TO DENVER.
I KNEW THEY WERE NO GOOD.
SHAME ON YOU PEOPLE.
JAKE, PLEASE–
SLAP
I DON'T WANT TO HEAR NOTHING YOU HAVE TO SAY.

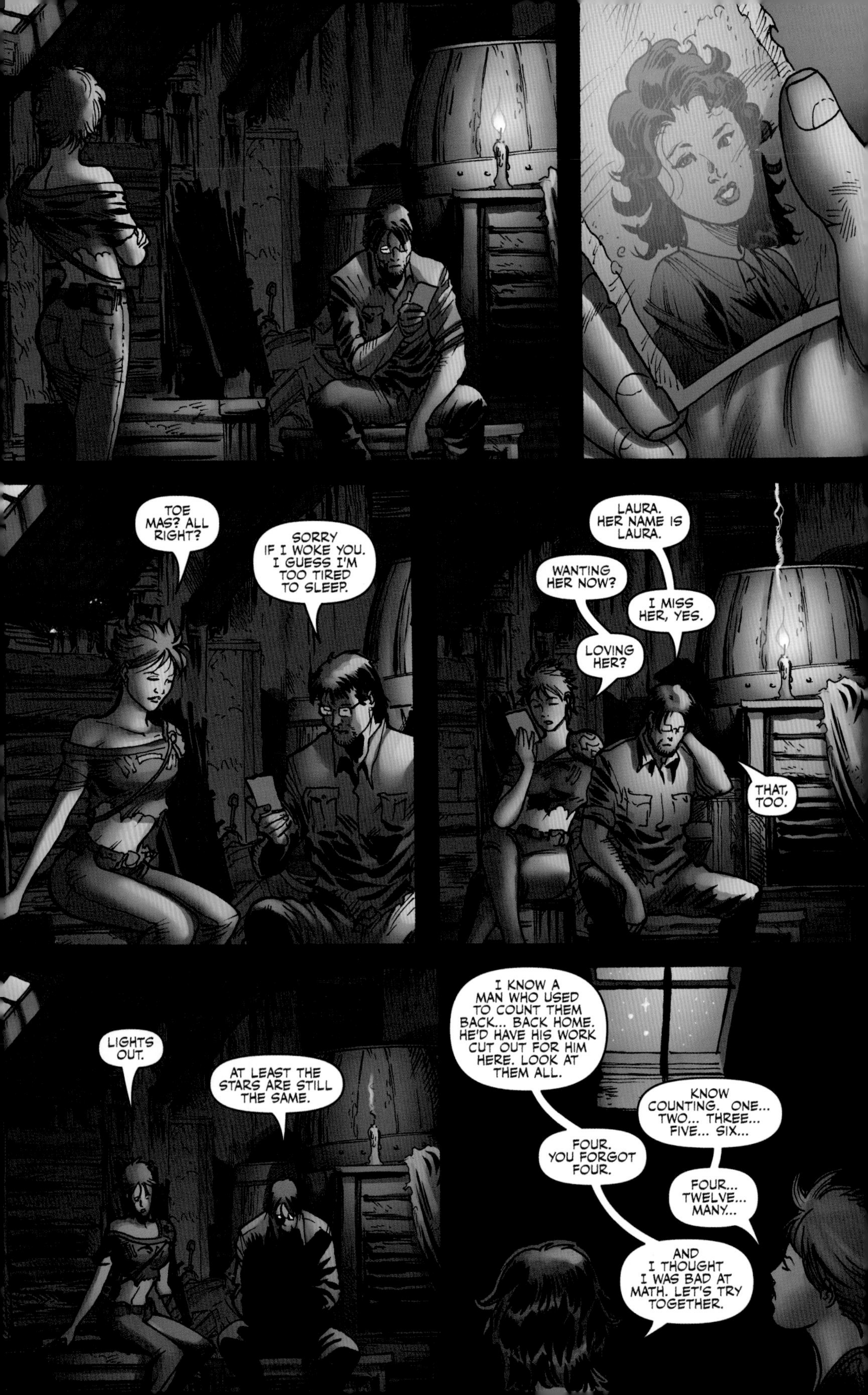
TOE MAS? ALL RIGHT?
SORRY IF I WOKE YOU. I GUESS I'M TOO TIRED TO SLEEP.
LAURA. HER NAME IS LAURA.
WANTING HER NOW?
I MISS HER, YES.
LOVING HER?
THAT, TOO.
LIGHTS OUT.
AT LEAST THE STARS ARE STILL THE SAME.
I KNOW A MAN WHO USED TO COUNT THEM BACK... BACK HOME. HE'D HAVE HIS WORK CUT OUT FOR HIM HERE. LOOK AT THEM ALL.
KNOW COUNTING. ONE... TWO... THREE... FIVE... SIX...
FOUR. YOU FORGOT FOUR.
FOUR... TWELVE... MANY...
AND I THOUGHT I WAS BAD AT MATH. LET'S TRY TOGETHER.

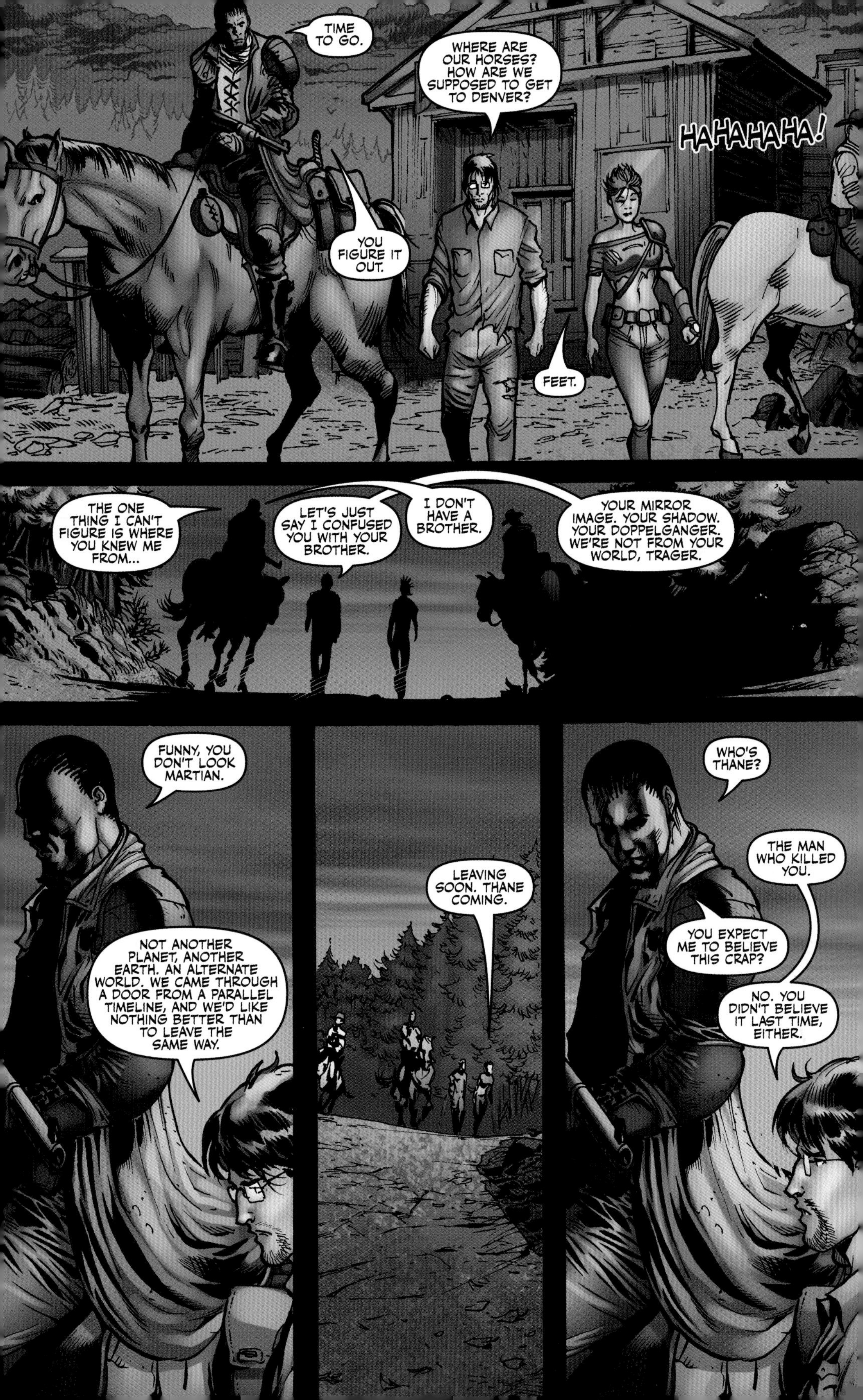
TIME TO GO.
WHERE ARE OUR HORSES? HOW ARE WE SUPPOSED TO GET TO DENVER?
HAHAHAHA!
YOU FIGURE IT OUT.
FEET.
THE ONE THING I CAN'T FIGURE IS WHERE YOU KNEW ME FROM...
LET'S JUST SAY I CONFUSED YOU WITH YOUR BROTHER.
I DON'T HAVE A BROTHER.
YOUR MIRROR IMAGE. YOUR SHADOW. YOUR DOPPELGANGER. WE'RE NOT FROM YOUR WORLD, TRAGER.
FUNNY, YOU DON'T LOOK MARTIAN.
NOT ANOTHER PLANET, ANOTHER EARTH. AN ALTERNATE WORLD. WE CAME THROUGH A DOOR FROM A PARALLEL TIMELINE, AND WE'D LIKE NOTHING BETTER THAN TO LEAVE THE SAME WAY.
LEAVING SOON. THANE COMING.
WHO'S THANE?
THE MAN WHO KILLED YOU.
YOU EXPECT ME TO BELIEVE THIS CRAP?
NO. YOU DIDN'T BELIEVE IT LAST TIME, EITHER.

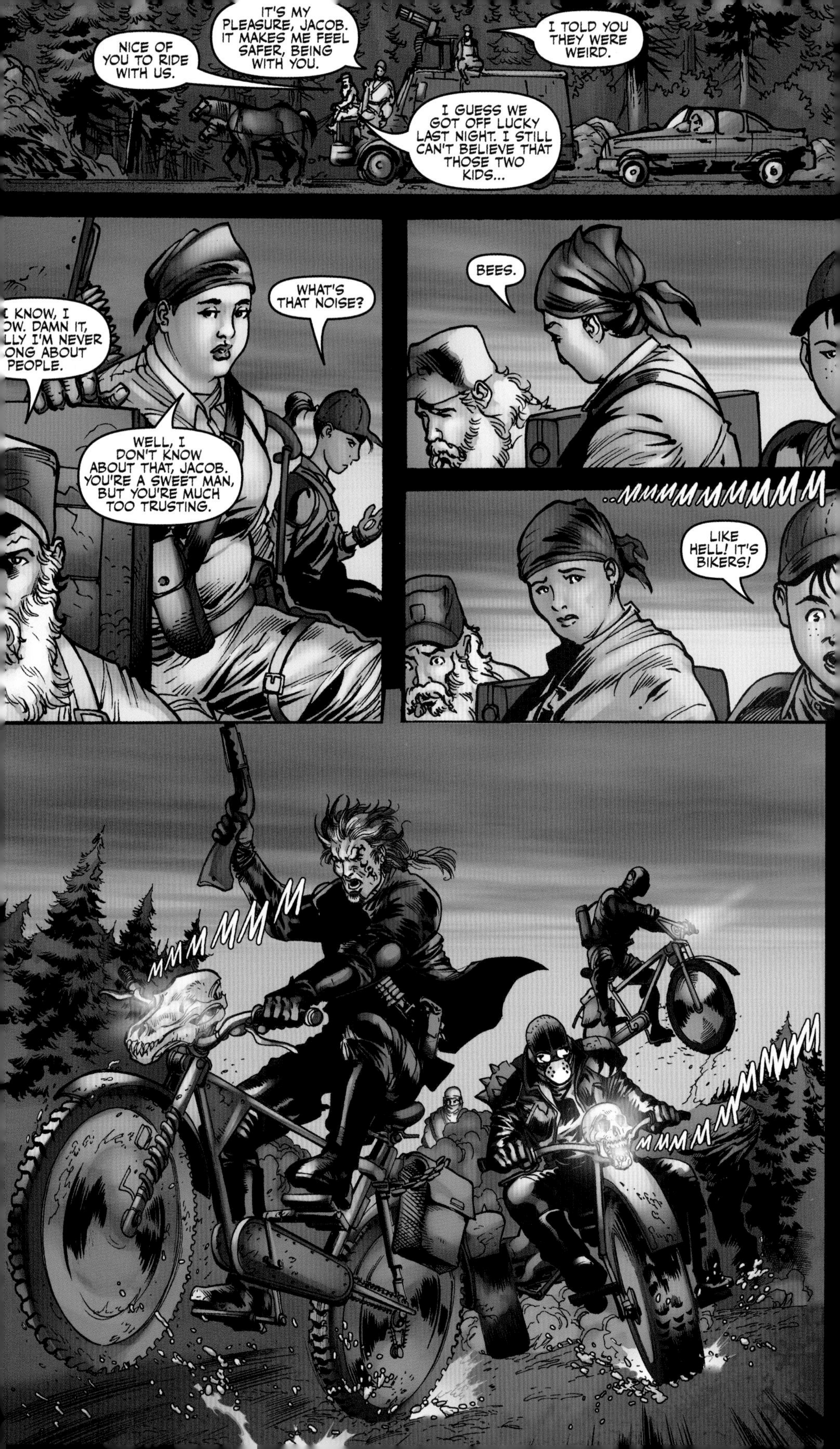
NICE OF YOU TO RIDE WITH US.
IT'S MY PLEASURE, JACOB. IT MAKES ME FEEL SAFER, BEING WITH YOU.
I TOLD YOU THEY WERE WEIRD.
I GUESS WE GOT OFF LUCKY LAST NIGHT. I STILL CAN'T BELIEVE THAT THOSE TWO KIDS...
WELL, I DON'T KNOW ABOUT THAT, JACOB. YOU'RE A SWEET MAN, BUT YOU'RE MUCH TOO TRUSTING.
KNOW, I OW. DAMN IT, LLY I'M NEVER ONG ABOUT PEOPLE.
WHAT'S THAT NOISE?
BEES.
..MMMMMMMMMMM
LIKE HELL! IT'S BIKERS!
MMMMMMM
MMMMMMMMMMM

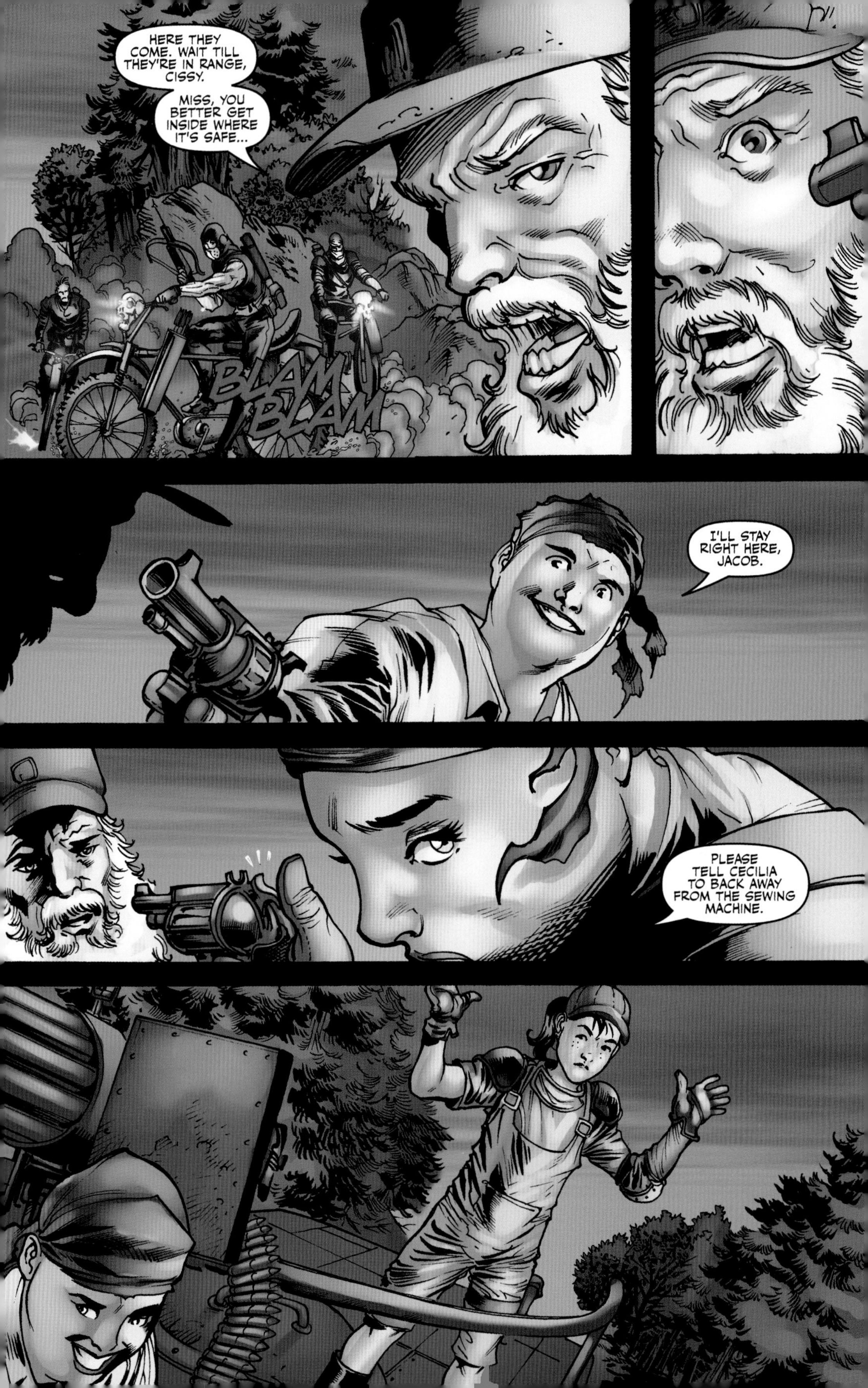
HERE THEY COME. WAIT TILL THEY'RE IN RANGE, CISSY.
MISS, YOU BETTER GET INSIDE WHERE IT'S SAFE...
BLAM BLAM
I'LL STAY RIGHT HERE, JACOB.
PLEASE TELL CECILIA TO BACK AWAY FROM THE SEWING MACHINE.

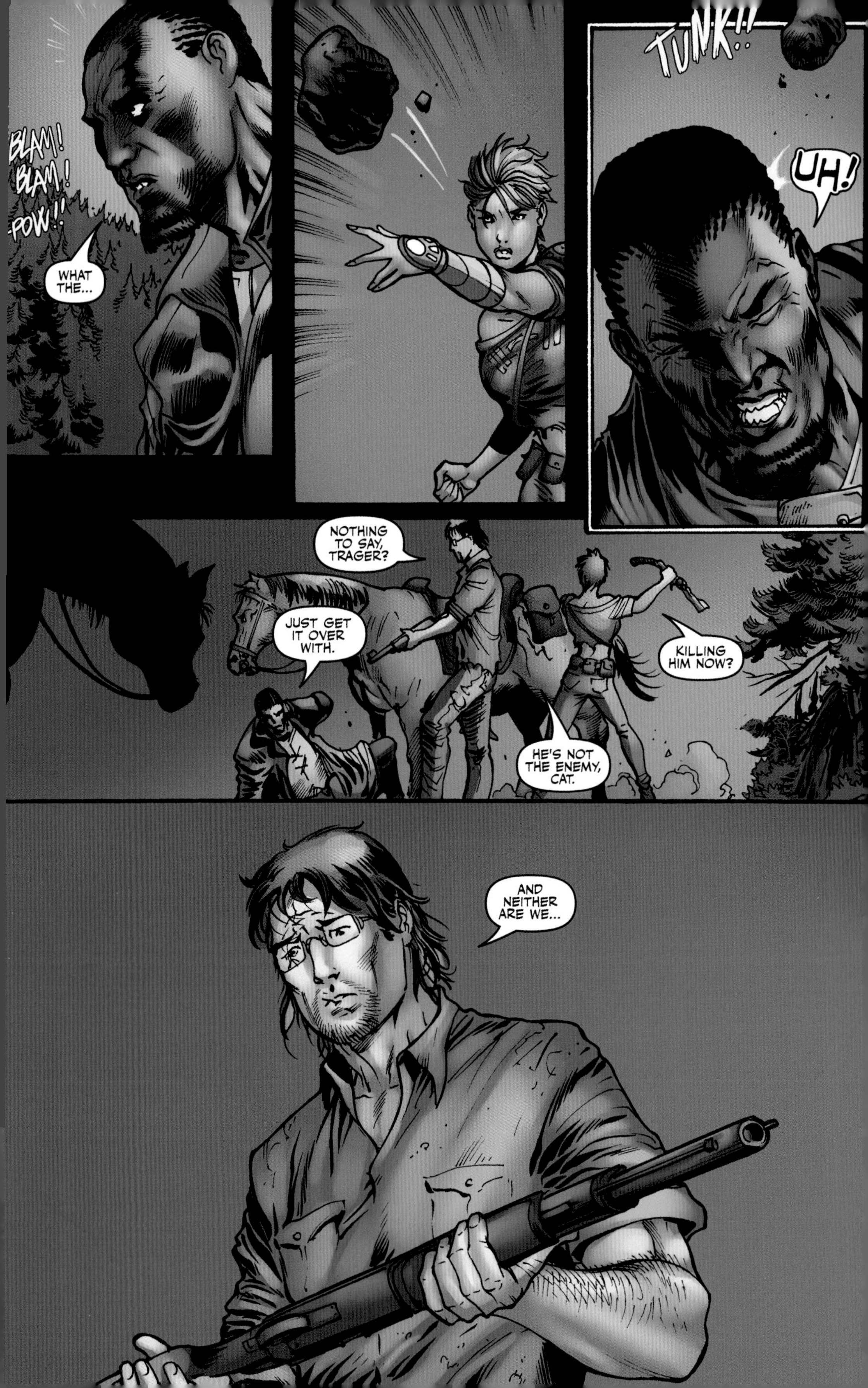
BLAM!
BLAM!
POW!!
WHAT THE...
TUNK!!
UH!
NOTHING TO SAY, TRAGER?
JUST GET IT OVER WITH.
KILLING HIM NOW?
HE'S NOT THE ENEMY, CAT.
AND NEITHER ARE WE...

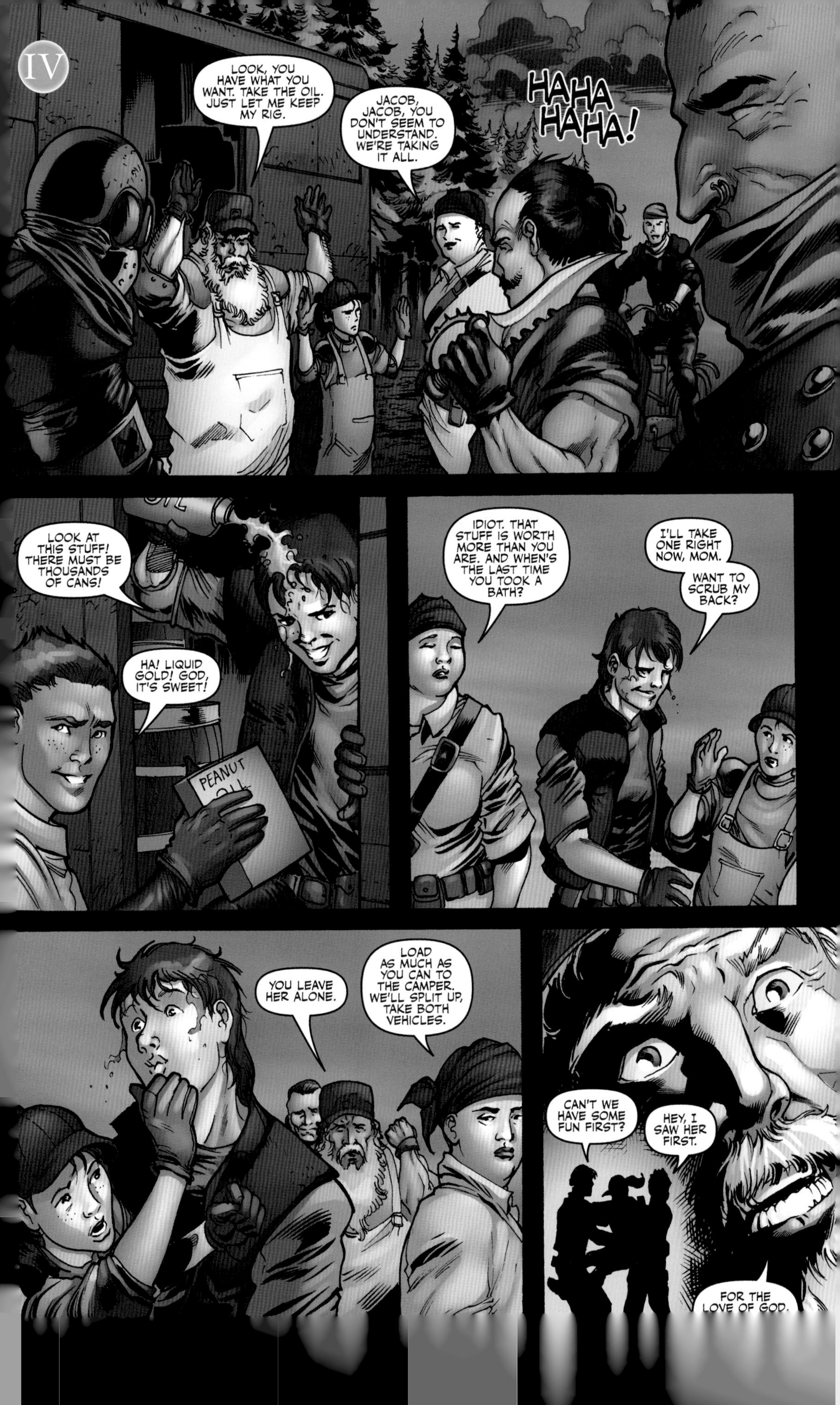
IV
LOOK, YOU HAVE WHAT YOU WANT. TAKE THE OIL. JUST LET ME KEEP MY RIG.
JACOB, JACOB, YOU DON'T SEEM TO UNDERSTAND. WE'RE TAKING IT ALL.
HAHA HAHA!
LOOK AT THIS STUFF! THERE MUST BE THOUSANDS OF CANS!
HA! LIQUID GOLD! GOD, IT'S SWEET!
PEANUT OIL
IDIOT. THAT STUFF IS WORTH MORE THAN YOU ARE. AND WHEN'S THE LAST TIME YOU TOOK A BATH?
I'LL TAKE ONE RIGHT NOW, MOM.
WANT TO SCRUB MY BACK?
YOU LEAVE HER ALONE.
LOAD AS MUCH AS YOU CAN TO THE CAMPER. WE'LL SPLIT UP, TAKE BOTH VEHICLES.
CAN'T WE HAVE SOME FUN FIRST?
HEY, I SAW HER FIRST.
FOR THE LOVE OF GOD.

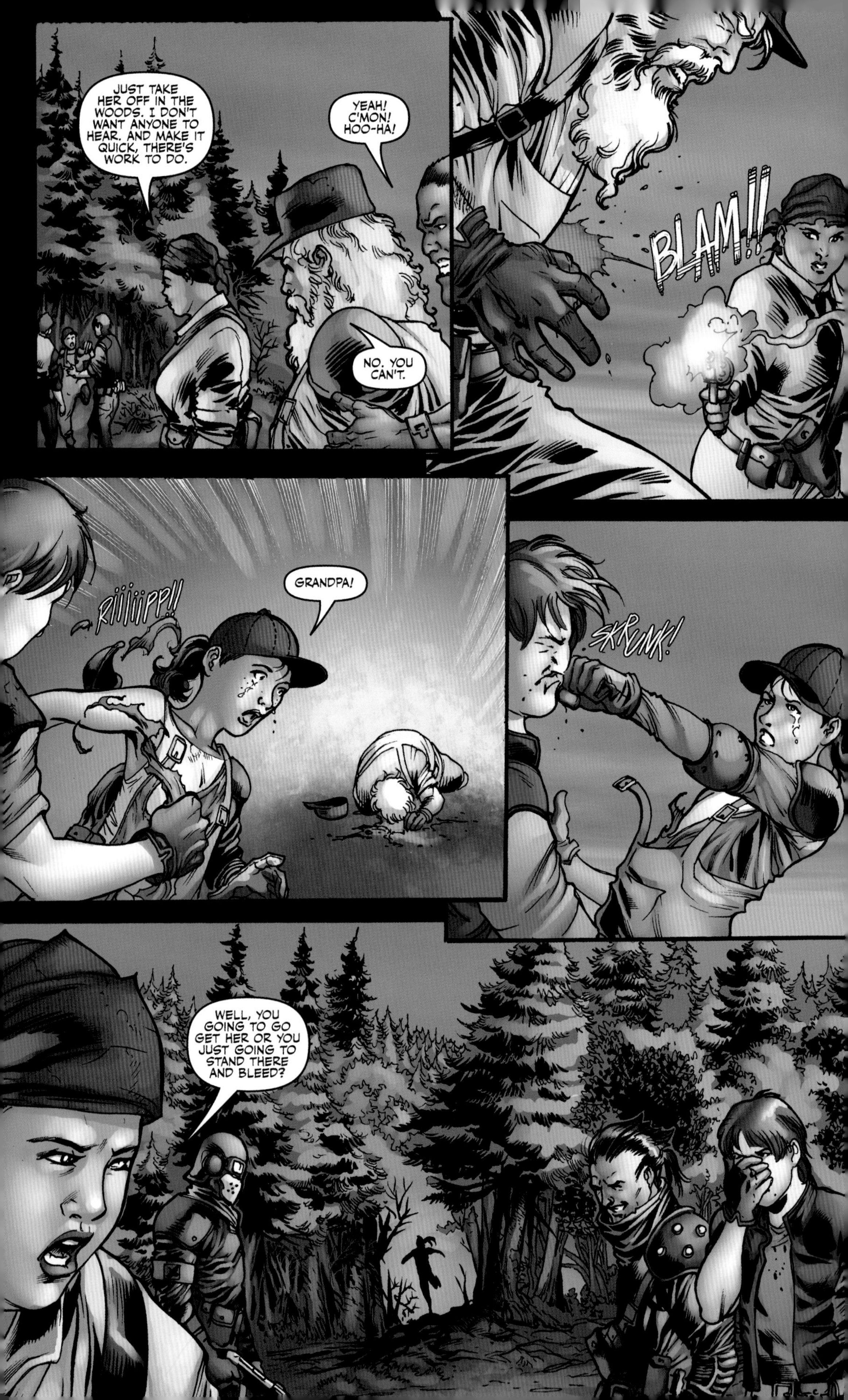
JUST TAKE HER OFF IN THE WOODS. I DON'T WANT ANYONE TO HEAR. AND MAKE IT QUICK, THERE'S WORK TO DO.
YEAH! C'MON! HOO-HA!
NO. YOU CAN'T.
BLAM!!
GRANDPA!
RIIIIIPP!!
SKRUNK!
WELL, YOU GOING TO GO GET HER OR YOU JUST GOING TO STAND THERE AND BLEED?

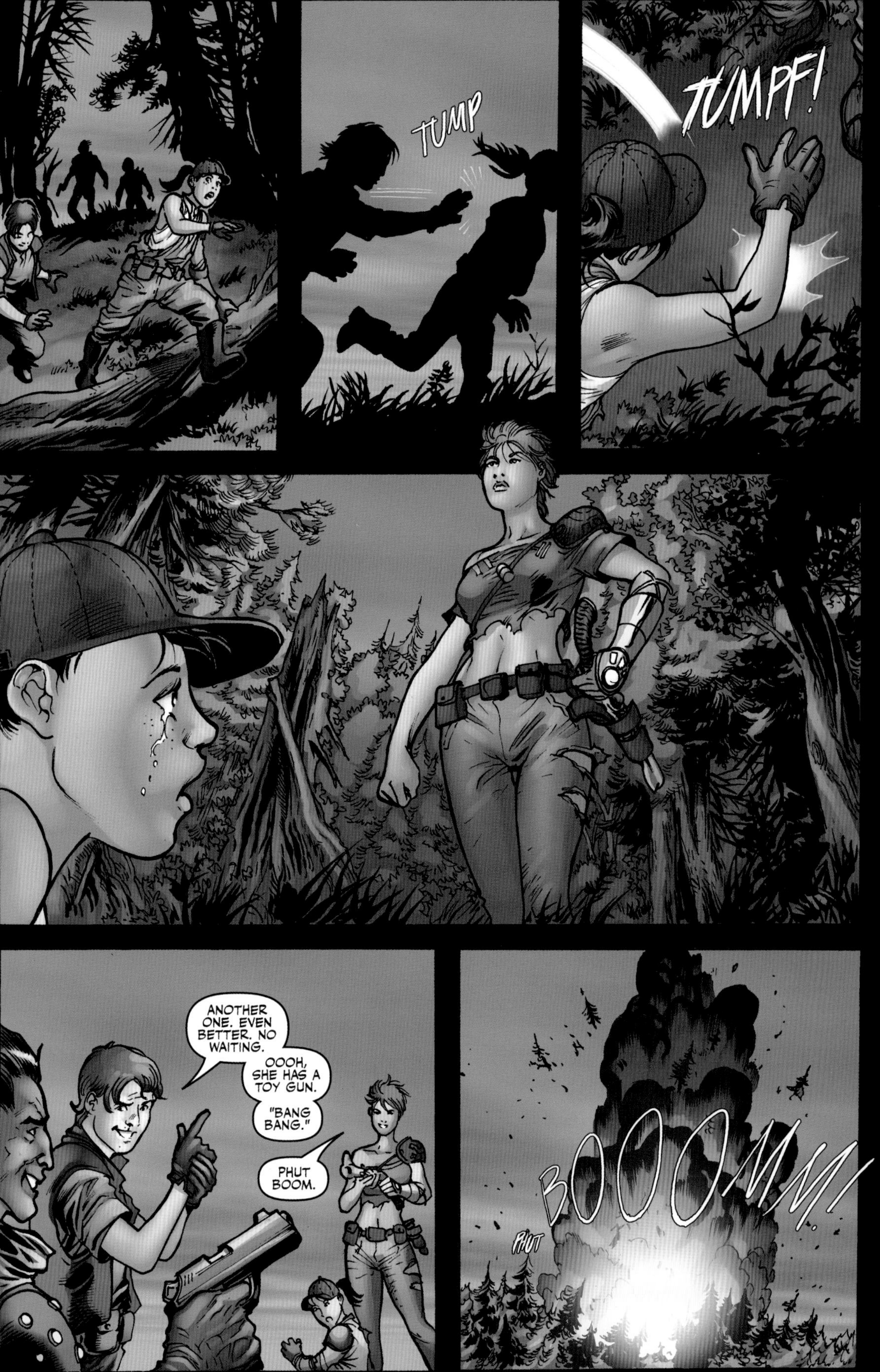
TUMP
TUMPF!
ANOTHER ONE. EVEN BETTER. NO WAITING.
OOOH, SHE HAS A TOY GUN.
"BANG BANG."
PHUT BOOM.
PHUT
BOOOMM!

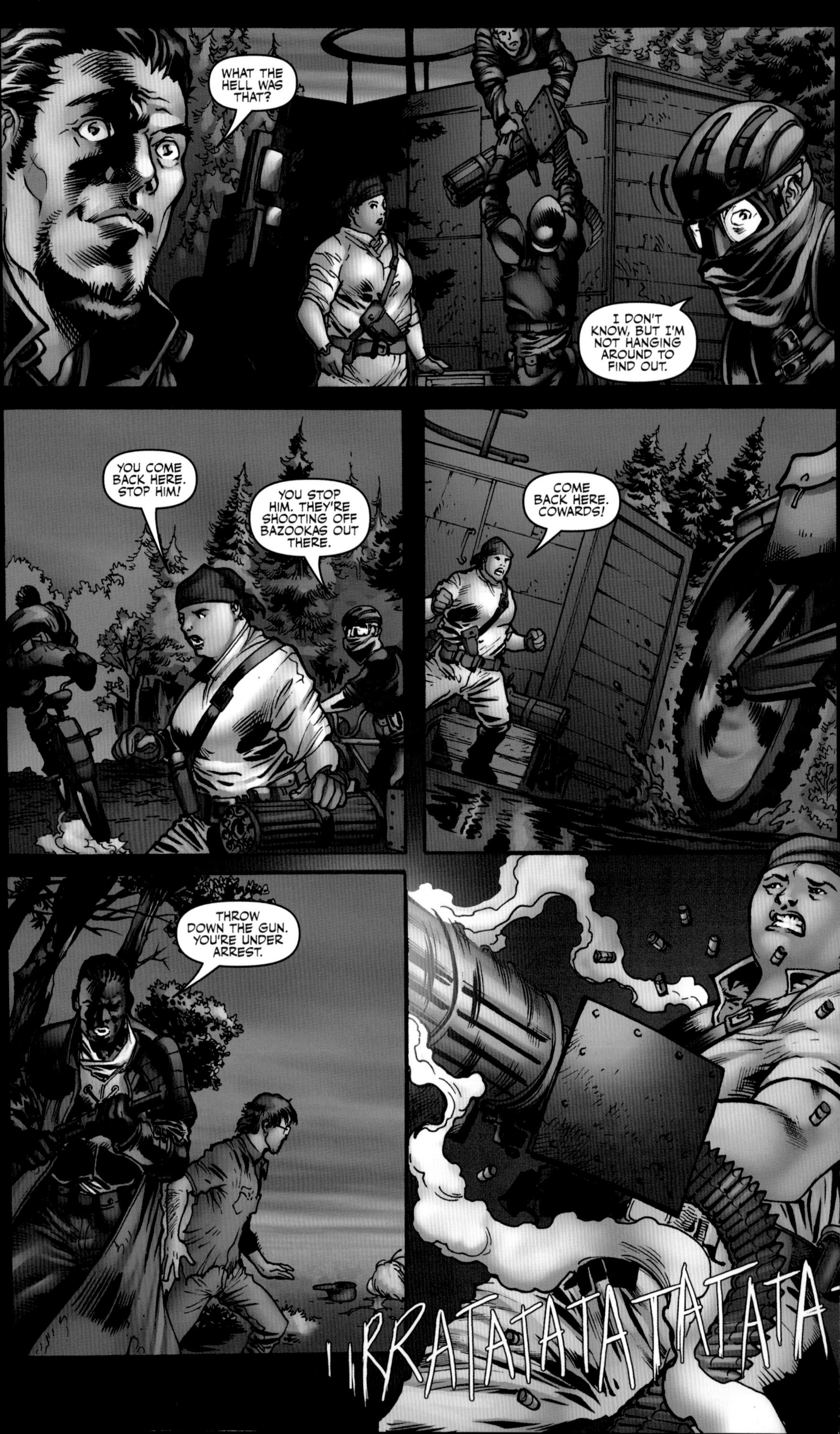
WHAT THE HELL WAS THAT?
I DON'T KNOW, BUT I'M NOT HANGING AROUND TO FIND OUT.
YOU COME BACK HERE. STOP HIM!
YOU STOP HIM. THEY'RE SHOOTING OFF BAZOOKAS OUT THERE.
COME BACK HERE. COWARDS!
THROW DOWN THE GUN. YOU'RE UNDER ARREST.
KRRATATATATATATA-

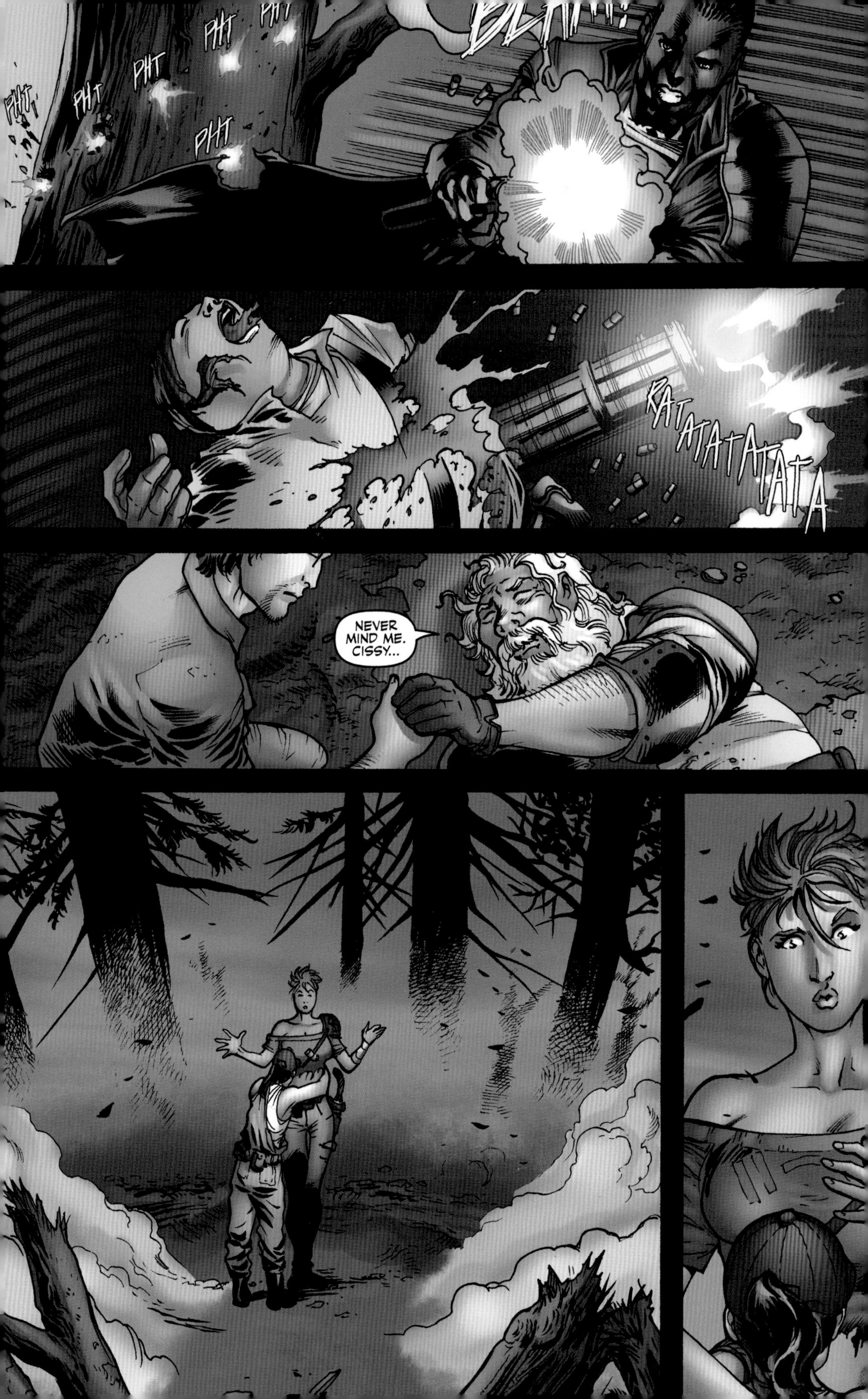
PHT PHT PHT PHT PHT PHT
RATATATATATATATA
NEVER MIND ME. CISSY...

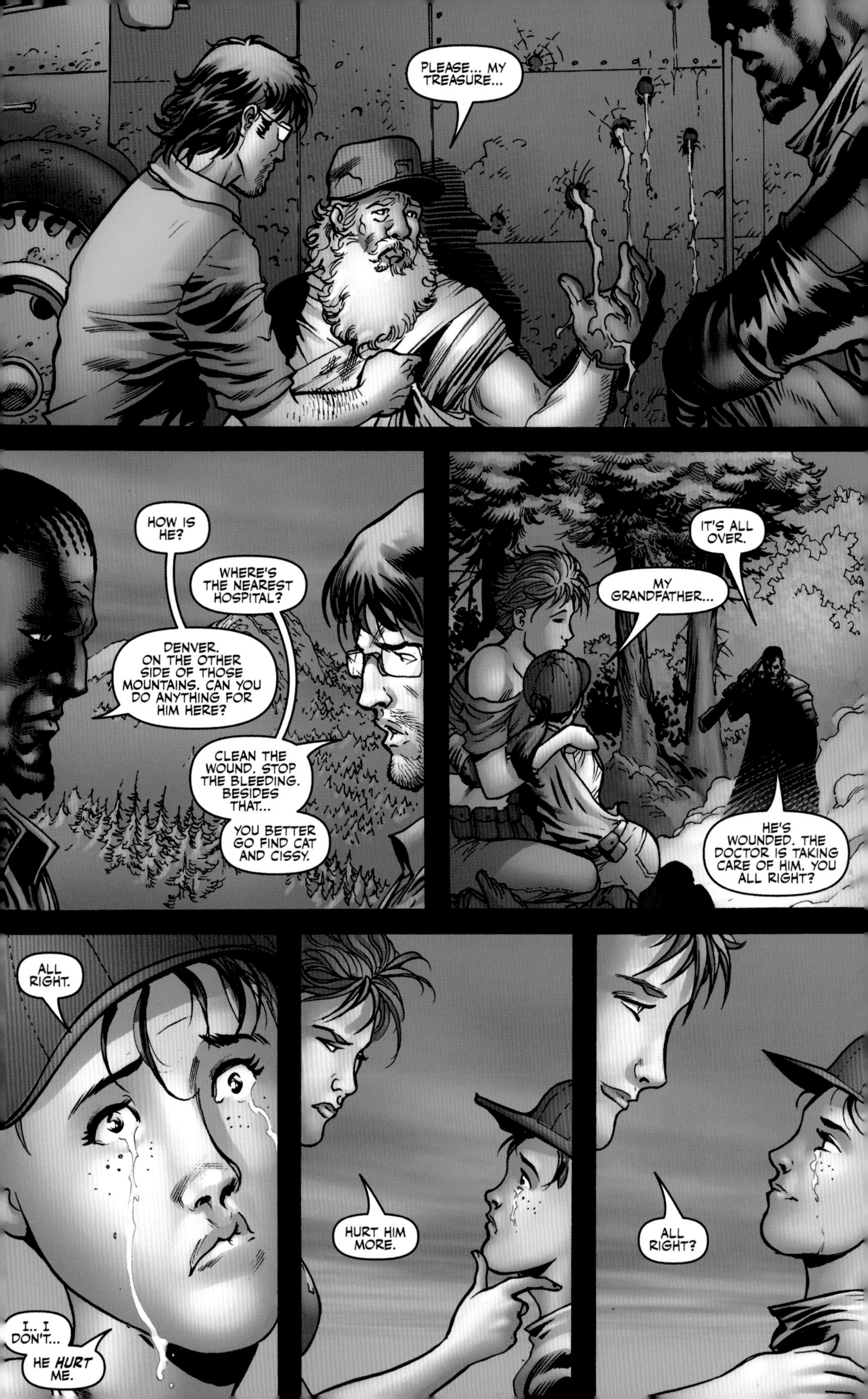
PLEASE... MY TREASURE...
HOW IS HE?
WHERE'S THE NEAREST HOSPITAL?
DENVER. ON THE OTHER SIDE OF THOSE MOUNTAINS. CAN YOU DO ANYTHING FOR HIM HERE?
CLEAN THE WOUND. STOP THE BLEEDING. BESIDES THAT...
YOU BETTER GO FIND CAT AND CISSY.
IT'S ALL OVER.
MY GRANDFATHER...
HE'S WOUNDED. THE DOCTOR IS TAKING CARE OF HIM. YOU ALL RIGHT?
ALL RIGHT.
I.. I DON'T...
HE HURT ME.
HURT HIM MORE.
ALL RIGHT?

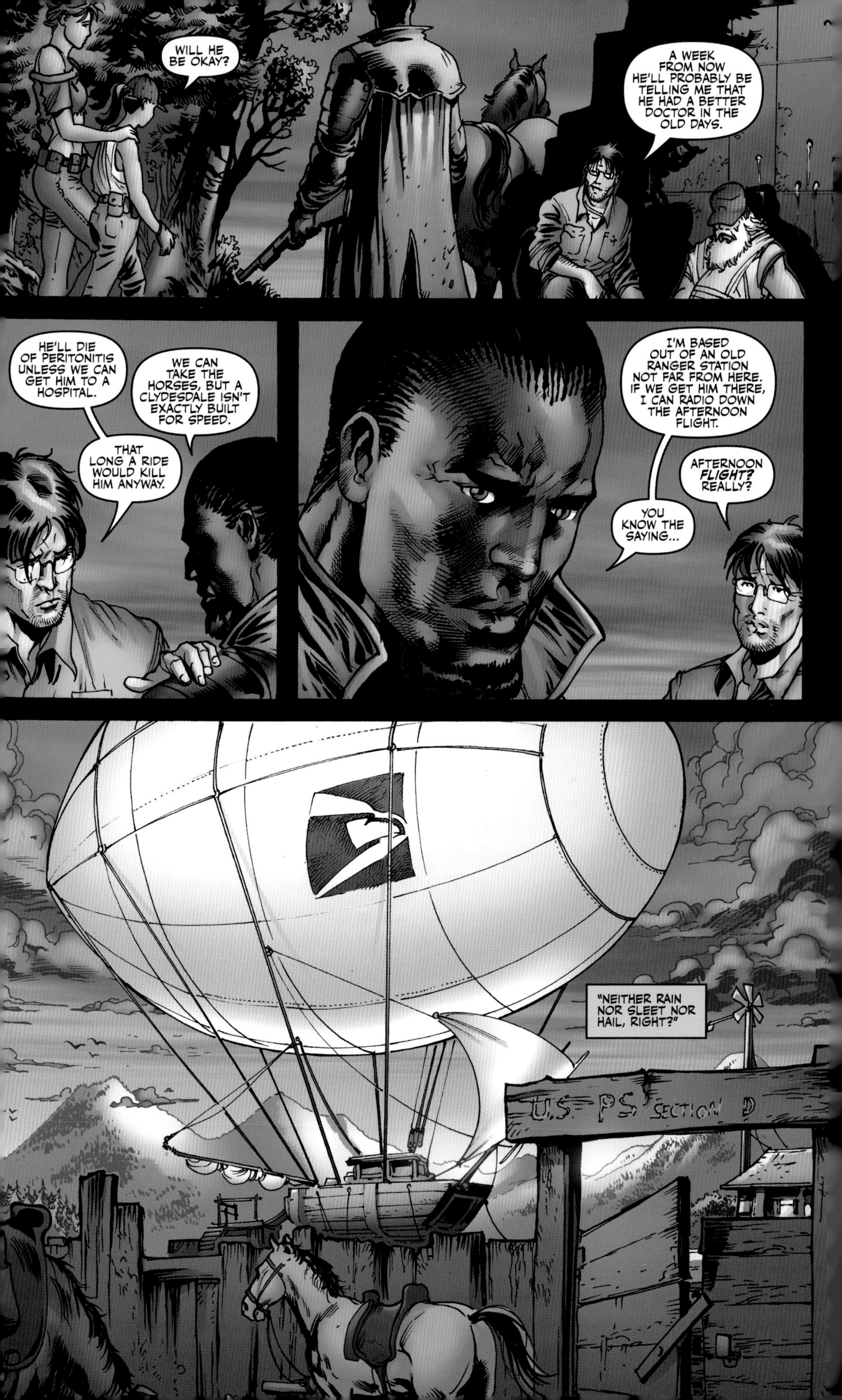
WILL HE BE OKAY?
A WEEK FROM NOW HE'LL PROBABLY BE TELLING ME THAT HE HAD A BETTER DOCTOR IN THE OLD DAYS.
HE'LL DIE OF PERITONITIS UNLESS WE CAN GET HIM TO A HOSPITAL.
WE CAN TAKE THE HORSES, BUT A CLYDESDALE ISN'T EXACTLY BUILT FOR SPEED.
THAT LONG A RIDE WOULD KILL HIM ANYWAY.
I'M BASED OUT OF AN OLD RANGER STATION NOT FAR FROM HERE. IF WE GET HIM THERE, I CAN RADIO DOWN THE AFTERNOON FLIGHT.
AFTERNOON *FLIGHT?* REALLY?
YOU KNOW THE SAYING...
"NEITHER RAIN NOR SLEET NOR HAIL, RIGHT?"
U.S. PS SECTION D

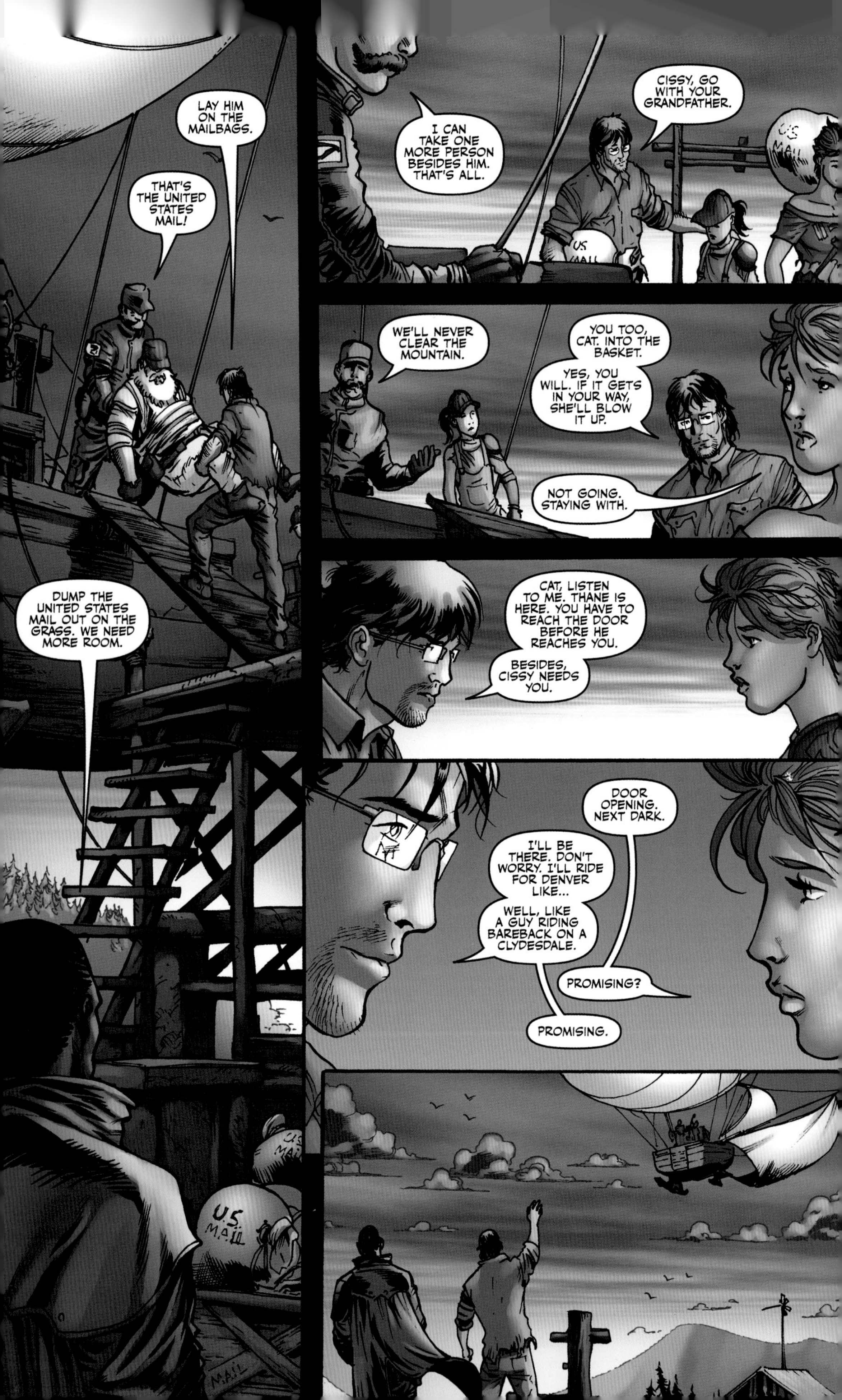

LAY HIM ON THE MAILBAGS.
THAT'S THE UNITED STATES MAIL!
DUMP THE UNITED STATES MAIL OUT ON THE GRASS. WE NEED MORE ROOM.
U.S. MAIL
I CAN TAKE ONE MORE PERSON BESIDES HIM. THAT'S ALL.
CISSY, GO WITH YOUR GRANDFATHER.
WE'LL NEVER CLEAR THE MOUNTAIN.
YOU TOO, CAT. INTO THE BASKET.
YES, YOU WILL. IF IT GETS IN YOUR WAY, SHE'LL BLOW IT UP.
NOT GOING. STAYING WITH.
CAT, LISTEN TO ME. THANE IS HERE. YOU HAVE TO REACH THE DOOR BEFORE HE REACHES YOU.
BESIDES, CISSY NEEDS YOU.
DOOR OPENING. NEXT DARK.
I'LL BE THERE. DON'T WORRY. I'LL RIDE FOR DENVER LIKE...
WELL, LIKE A GUY RIDING BAREBACK ON A CLYDESDALE.
PROMISING?
PROMISING.

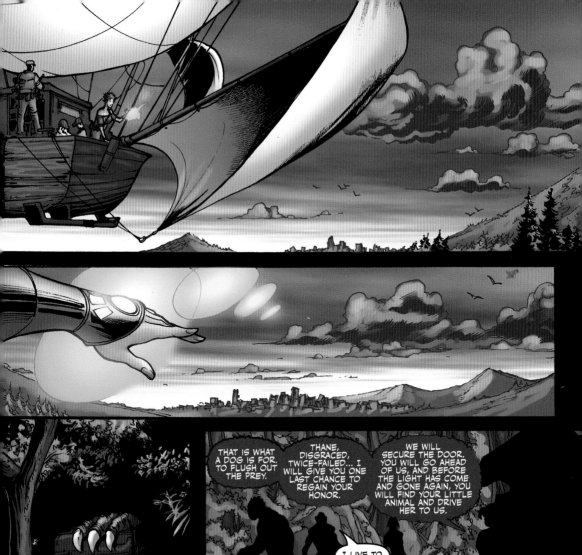

THAT IS WHAT A DOG IS FOR. TO FLUSH OUT THE PREY.

THANE, DISGRACED, TWICE-FAILED... I WILL GIVE YOU ONE LAST CHANCE TO REGAIN YOUR HONOR.

WE WILL SECURE THE DOOR. YOU WILL GO AHEAD OF US, AND BEFORE THE LIGHT HAS COME AND GONE AGAIN, YOU WILL FIND YOUR LITTLE ANIMAL AND DRIVE HER TO US.

I LIVE TO SERVE.

SHE MOVES EAST, ON THE WIND. SHE WILL [B]E AT THE DOOR BEFORE THE DAWNING.

TOO SOON. THE DOOR WILL STILL BE CLOSED. WE MUST BE THERE BEFORE IT OPENS.

DO NOT HARM HER. HER CRIME HAS BEEN GREAT. HER ANGUISH MUST BE GREATER. SHE WILL SERVE MY PLEASURE, NOT YOUR EMPTY HUMAN PRIDE.

SHE MAY [N]OT GO TO [TH]E DOOR. SHE [M]AY HIDE INSTEAD.

TO HEAR IS TO OBEY.

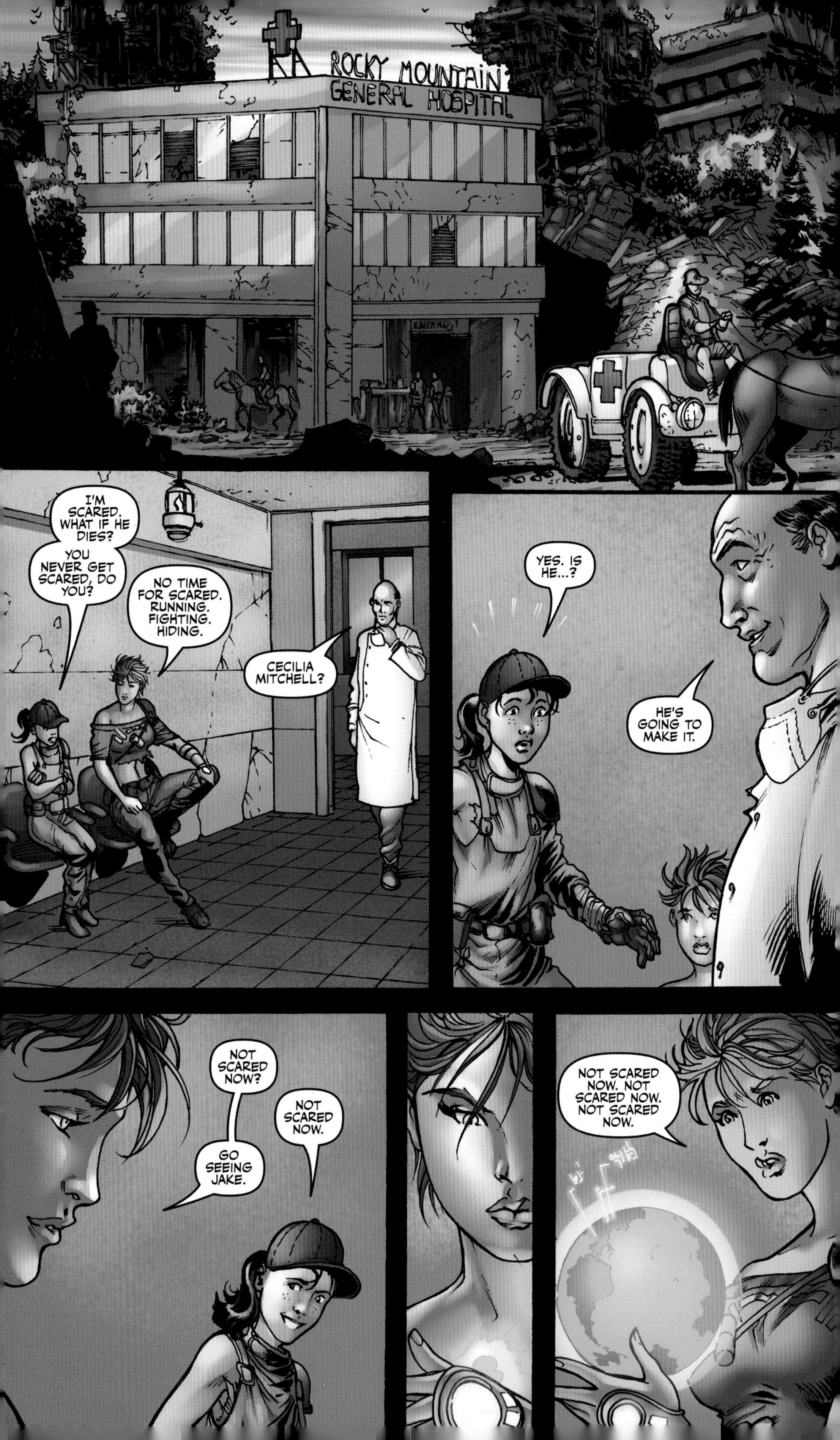
ROCKY MOUNTAIN
GENERAL HOSPITAL
I'M SCARED. WHAT IF HE DIES?
YOU NEVER GET SCARED, DO YOU?
NO TIME FOR SCARED. RUNNING. FIGHTING. HIDING.
CECILIA MITCHELL?
YES. IS HE...?
HE'S GOING TO MAKE IT.
NOT SCARED NOW?
NOT SCARED NOW.
GO SEEING JAKE.
NOT SCARED NOW. NOT SCARED NOW. NOT SCARED NOW.

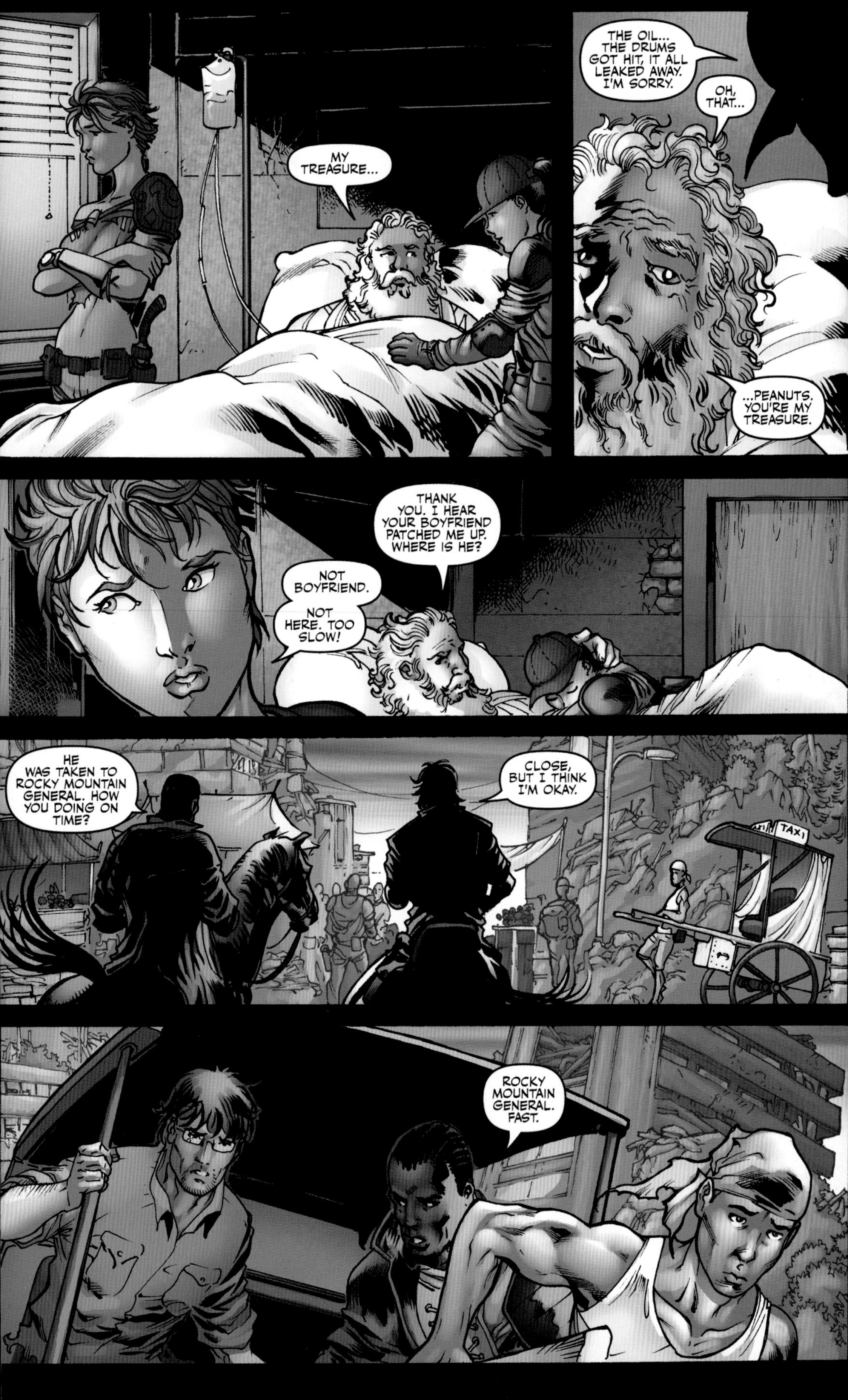
MY TREASURE...
THE OIL... THE DRUMS GOT HIT, IT ALL LEAKED AWAY. I'M SORRY.
OH, THAT...
...PEANUTS. YOU'RE MY TREASURE.
THANK YOU. I HEAR YOUR BOYFRIEND PATCHED ME UP. WHERE IS HE?
NOT BOYFRIEND.
NOT HERE. TOO SLOW!
HE WAS TAKEN TO ROCKY MOUNTAIN GENERAL. HOW YOU DOING ON TIME?
CLOSE, BUT I THINK I'M OKAY.
TAXI
ROCKY MOUNTAIN GENERAL. FAST.

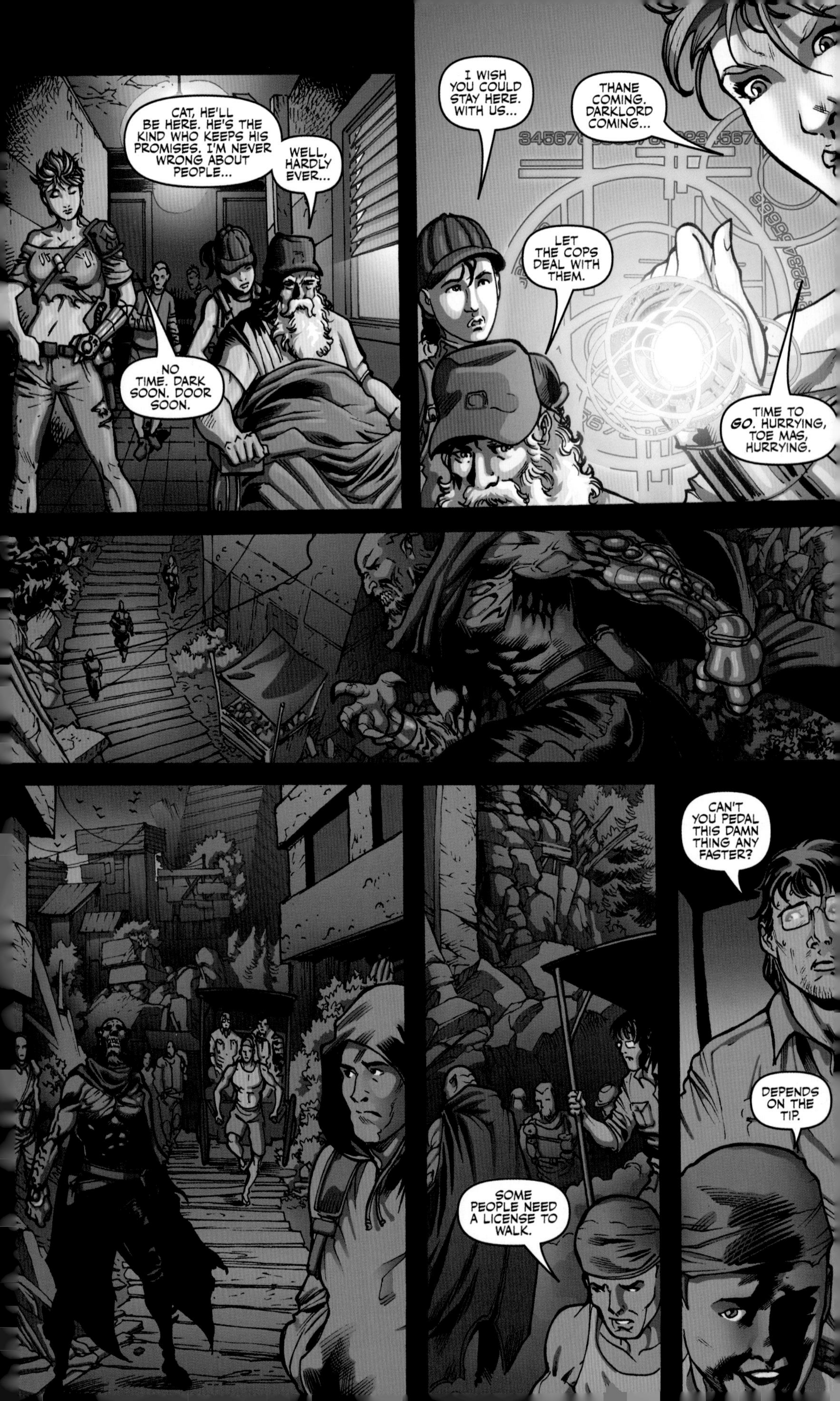

CAT, HE'LL BE HERE. HE'S THE KIND WHO KEEPS HIS PROMISES. I'M NEVER WRONG ABOUT PEOPLE...
WELL, HARDLY EVER...
NO TIME. DARK SOON. DOOR SOON.
I WISH YOU COULD STAY HERE. WITH US...
THANE COMING. DARKLORD COMING...
LET THE COPS DEAL WITH THEM.
TIME TO GO. HURRYING, TOE MAS, HURRYING.
CAN'T YOU PEDAL THIS DAMN THING ANY FASTER?
DEPENDS ON THE TIP.
SOME PEOPLE NEED A LICENSE TO WALK.

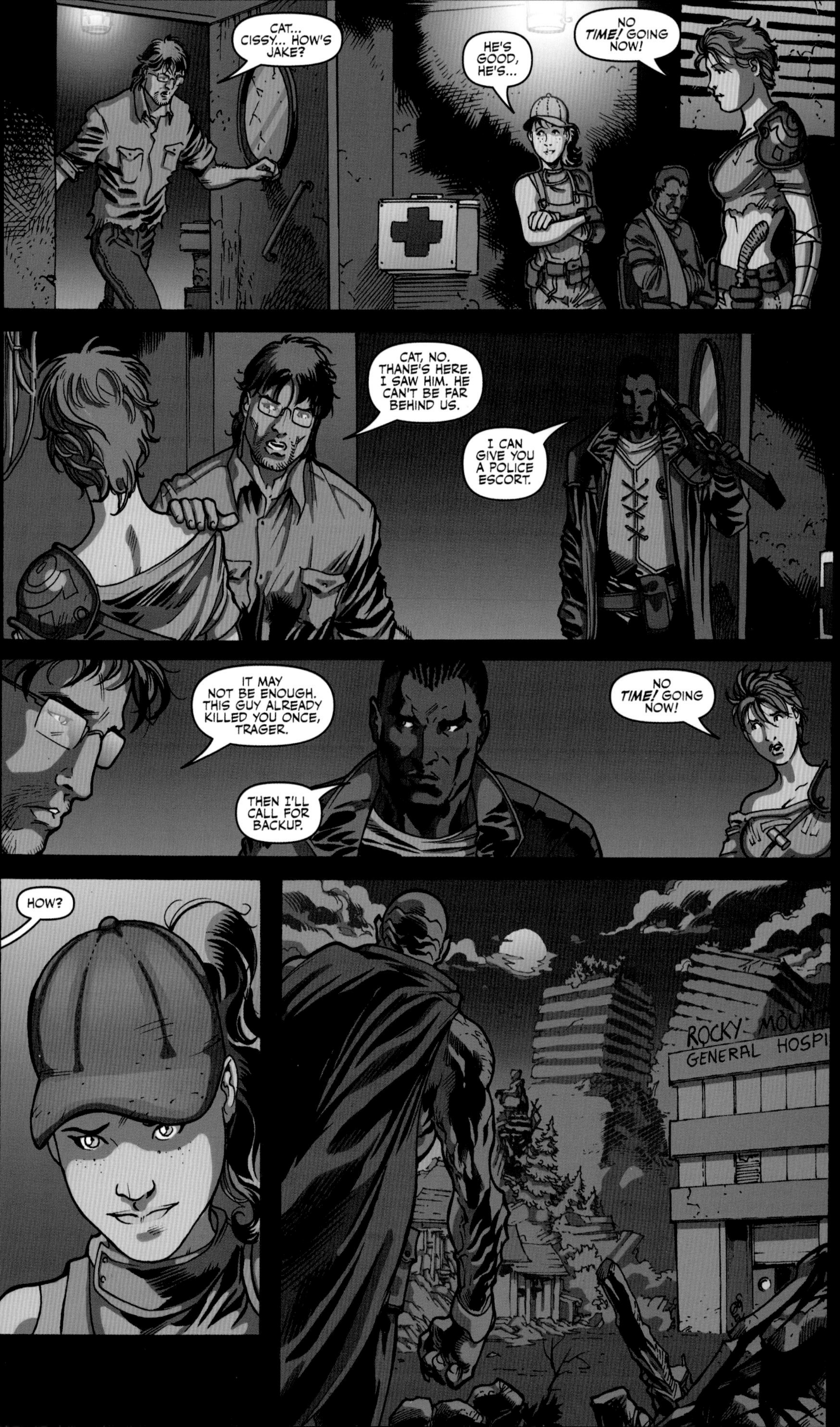
CAT... CISSY... HOW'S JAKE?
HE'S GOOD, HE'S...
NO TIME! GOING NOW!
CAT, NO. THANE'S HERE. I SAW HIM. HE CAN'T BE FAR BEHIND US.
I CAN GIVE YOU A POLICE ESCORT.
IT MAY NOT BE ENOUGH. THIS GUY ALREADY KILLED YOU ONCE, TRAGER.
THEN I'LL CALL FOR BACKUP.
NO TIME! GOING NOW!
HOW?
ROCKY MOUNT
GENERAL HOSPI

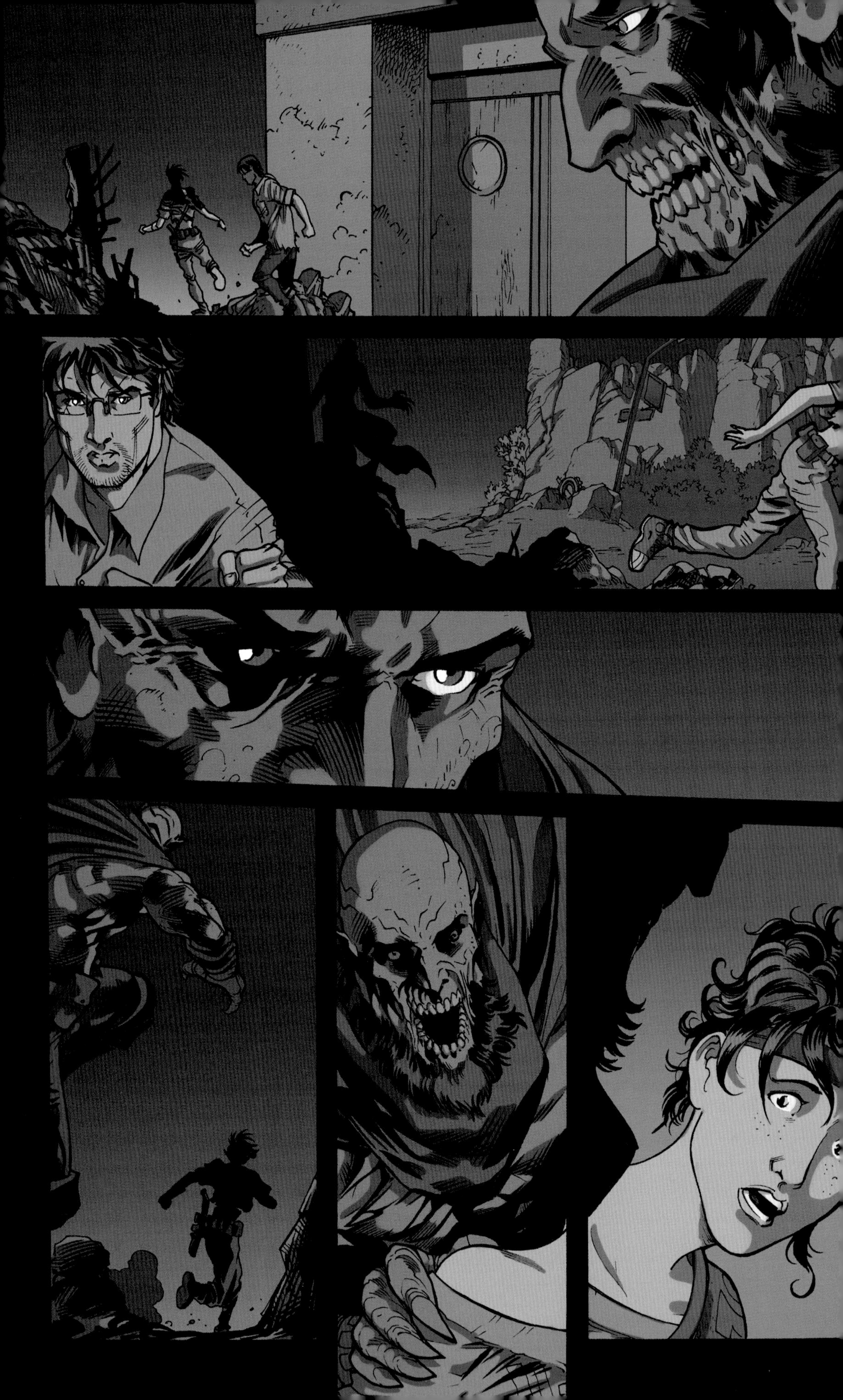

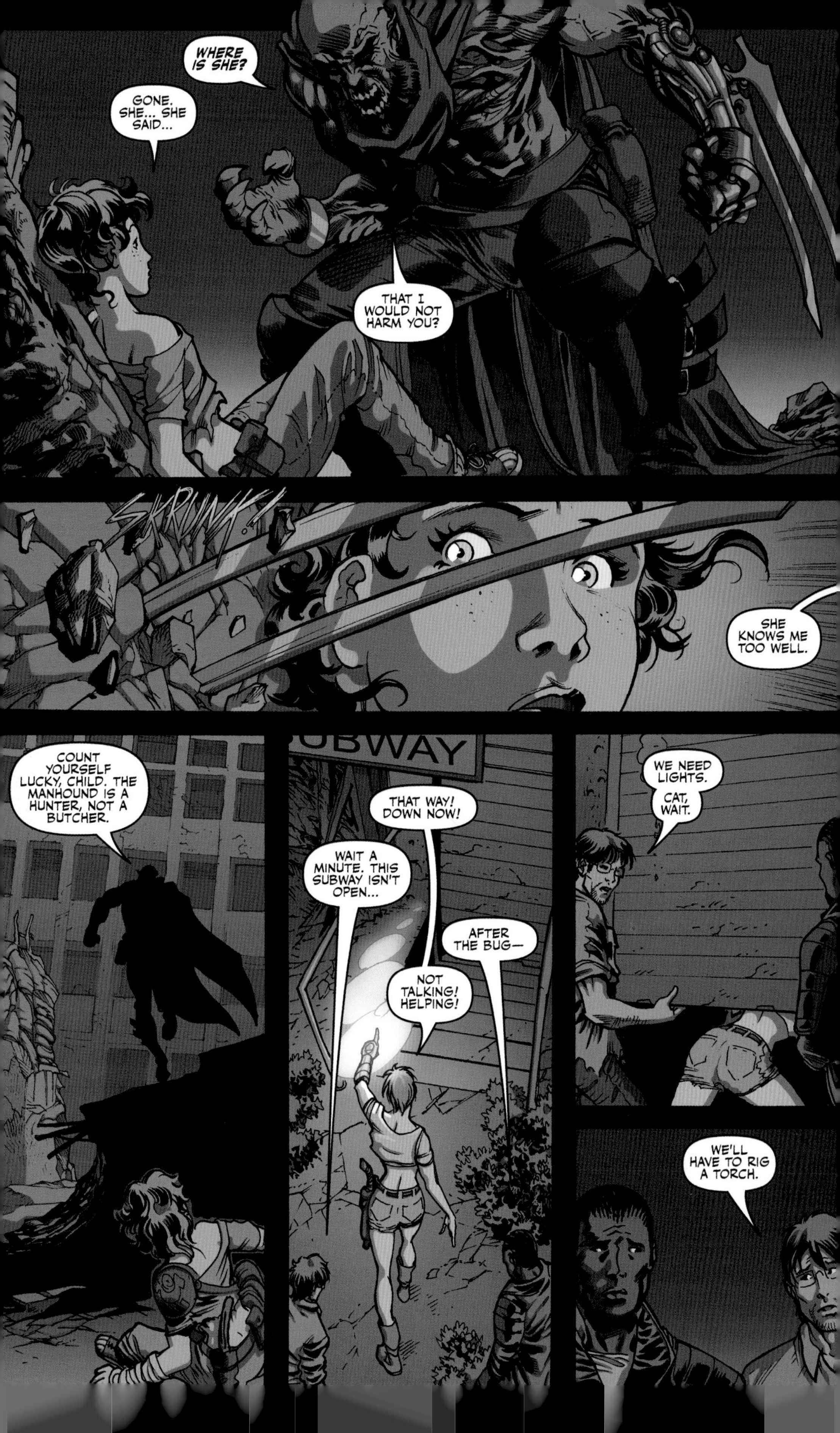
WHERE IS SHE?
GONE. SHE... SHE SAID...
THAT I WOULD NOT HARM YOU?
SKRUNK!
SHE KNOWS ME TOO WELL.
COUNT YOURSELF LUCKY, CHILD. THE MANHOUND IS A HUNTER, NOT A BUTCHER.
UBWAY
THAT WAY! DOWN NOW!
WAIT A MINUTE. THIS SUBWAY ISN'T OPEN...
AFTER THE BUG—
NOT TALKING! HELPING!
WE NEED LIGHTS. CAT, WAIT.
WE'LL HAVE TO RIG A TORCH.

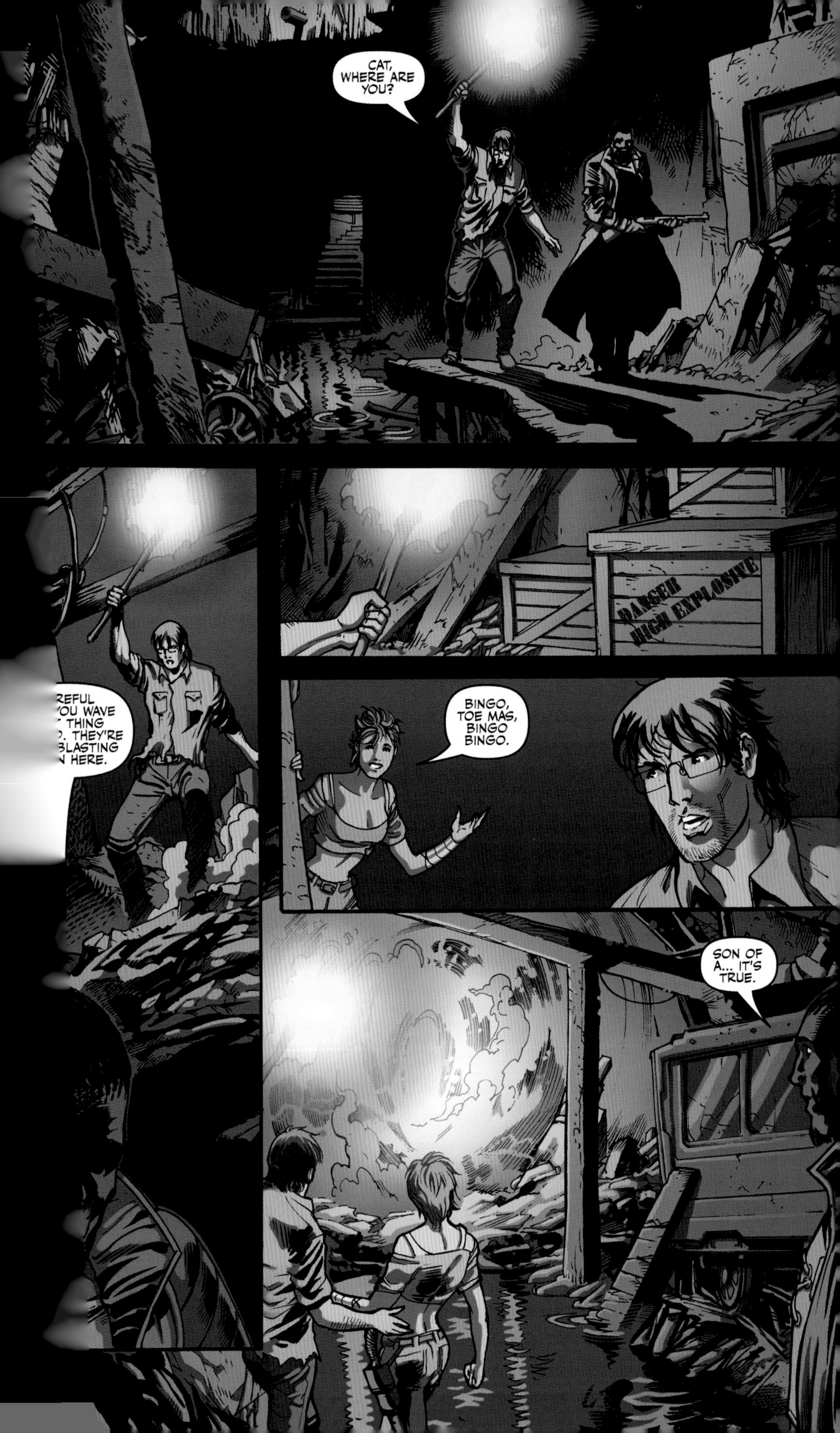
CAT, WHERE ARE YOU?
REFUL YOU WAVE THING D. THEY'RE BLASTING N HERE.
DANGER HIGH EXPLOSIVE
BINGO, TOE MAS, BINGO BINGO.
SON OF A... IT'S TRUE.

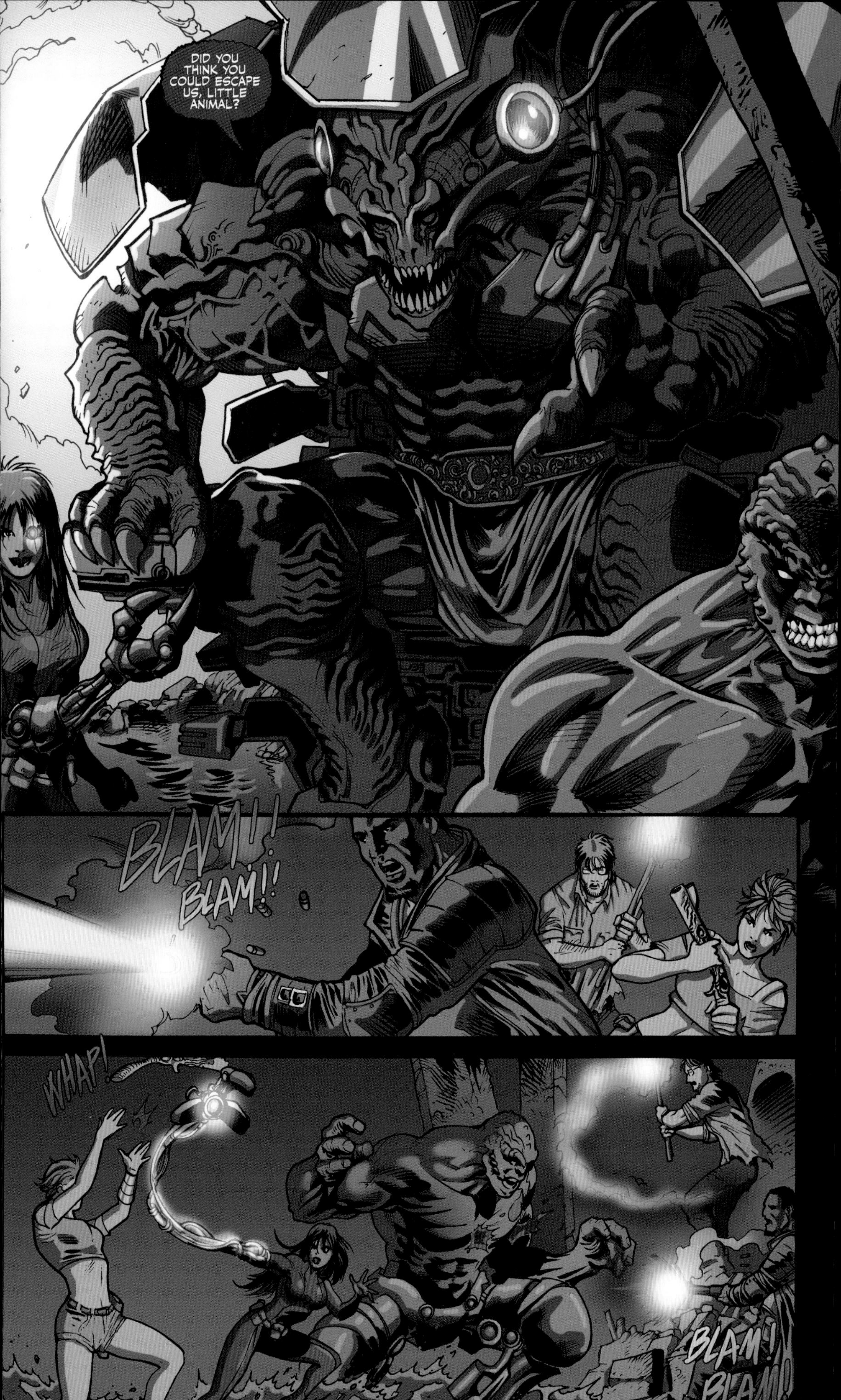
DID YOU THINK YOU COULD ESCAPE US, LITTLE ANIMAL?
BLAM!!
BLAM!!
WHAP!
BLAM!
BLAM!

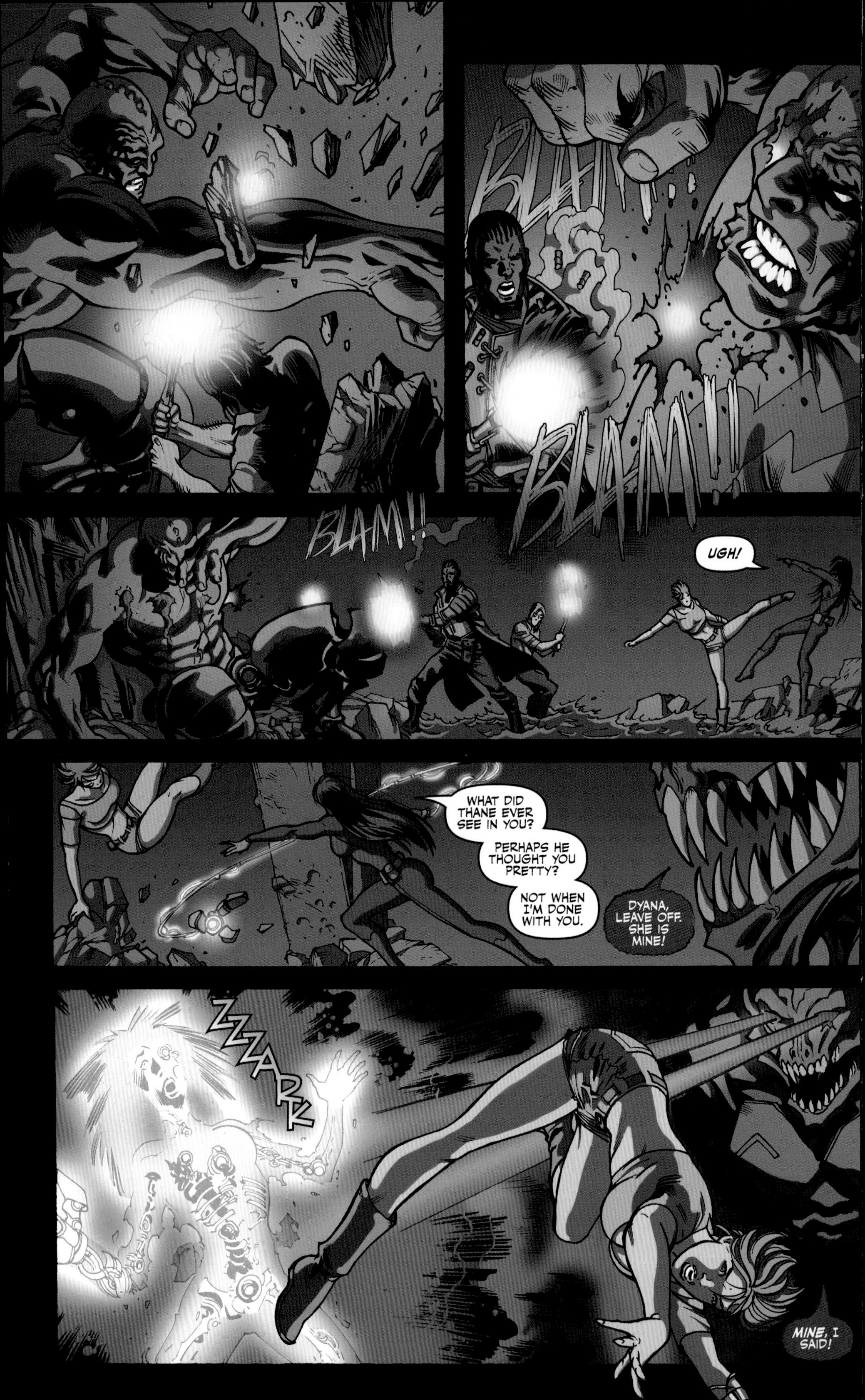
BLAM
BLAM!!
BLAM!!
UGH!
WHAT DID THANE EVER SEE IN YOU?
PERHAPS HE THOUGHT YOU PRETTY?
NOT WHEN I'M DONE WITH YOU.
DYANA, LEAVE OFF. SHE IS MINE!
ZZZAARK
MINE, I SAID!

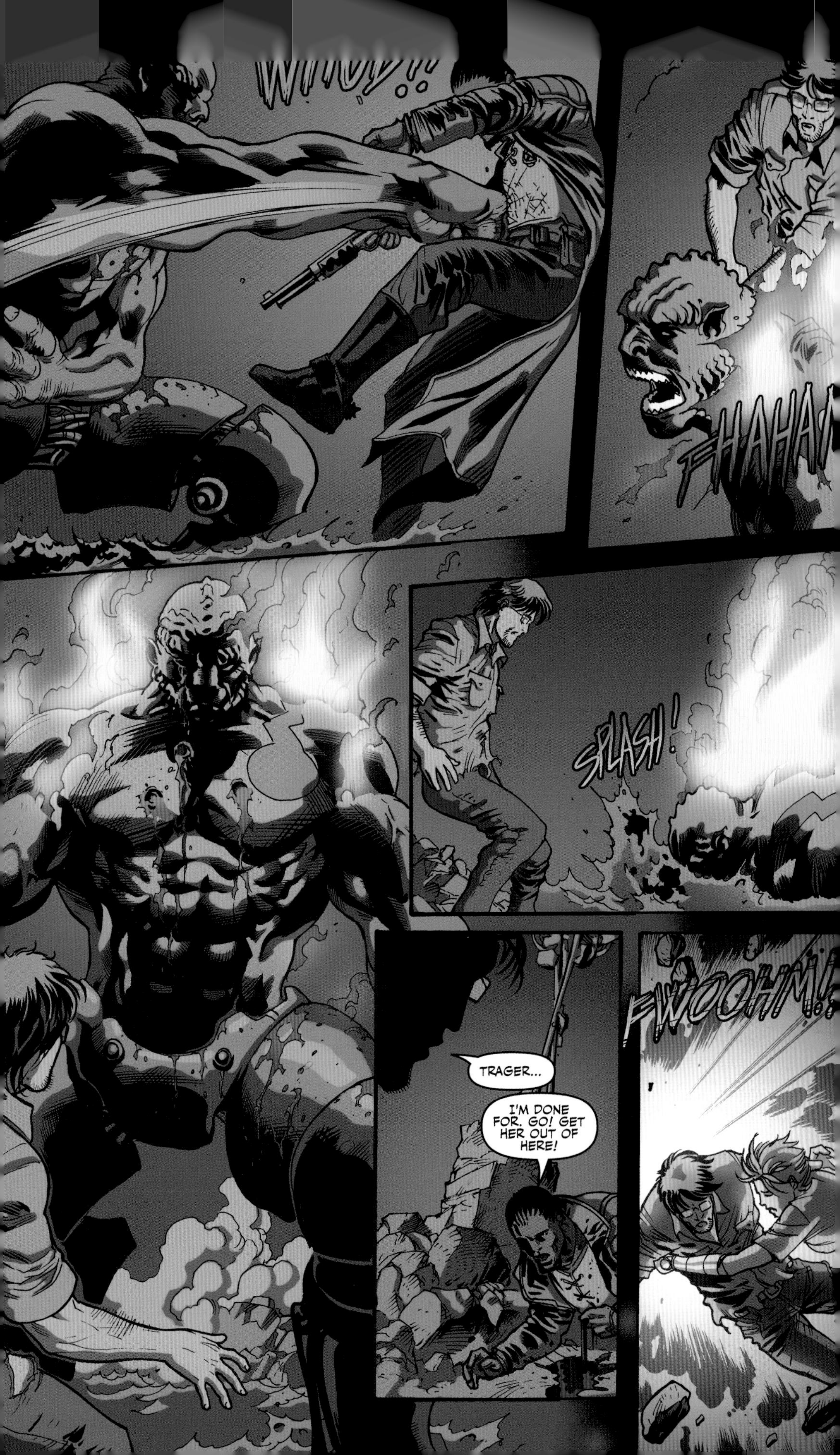
SPLASH!
TRAGER...
I'M DONE FOR. GO! GET HER OUT OF HERE!
FWOOHM!!

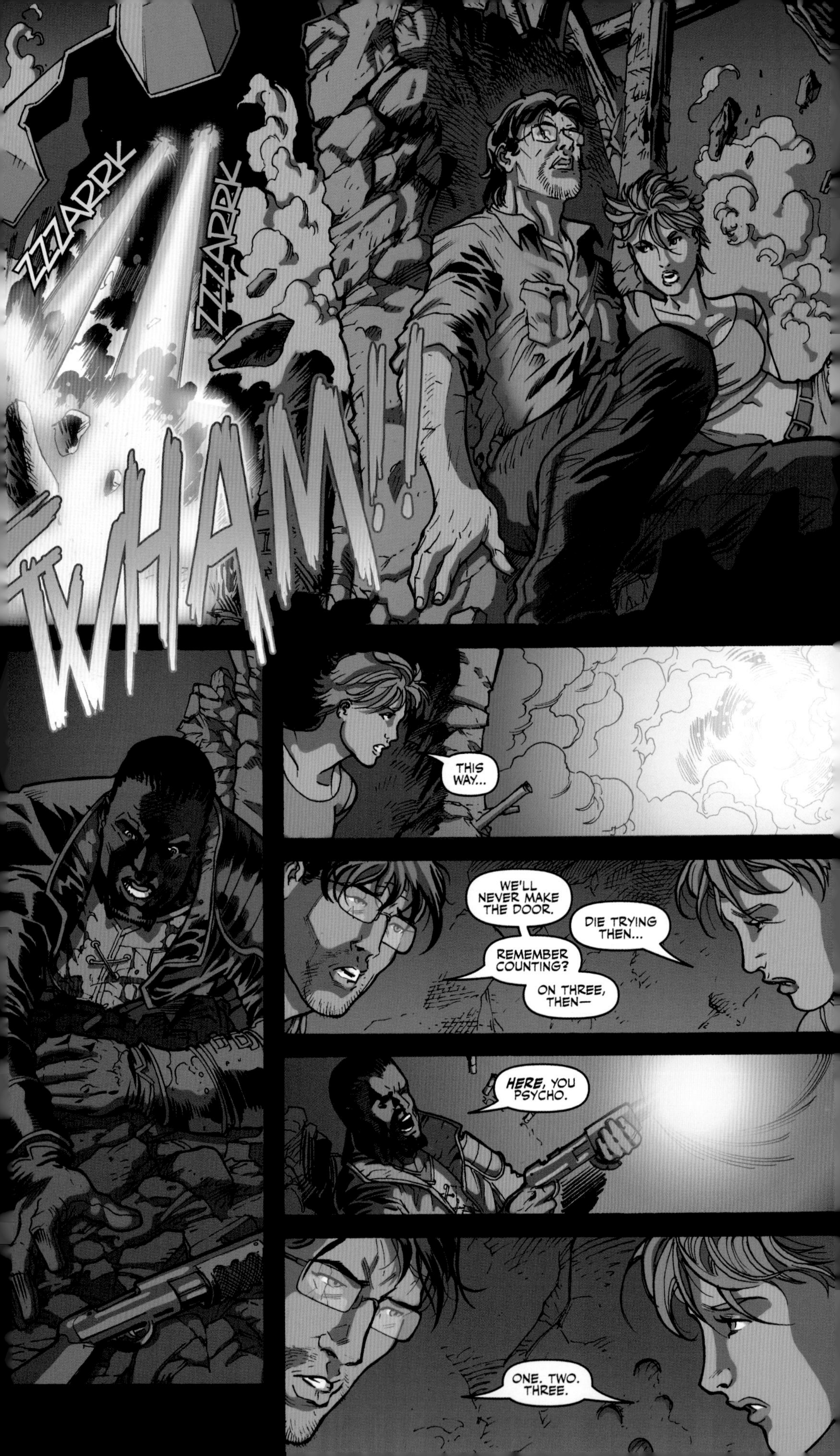
ZZZARRK
ZZZARRK
WHAM!!
THIS WAY...
WE'LL NEVER MAKE THE DOOR.
DIE TRYING THEN...
REMEMBER COUNTING?
ON THREE, THEN—
HERE, YOU PSYCHO.
ONE. TWO. THREE.

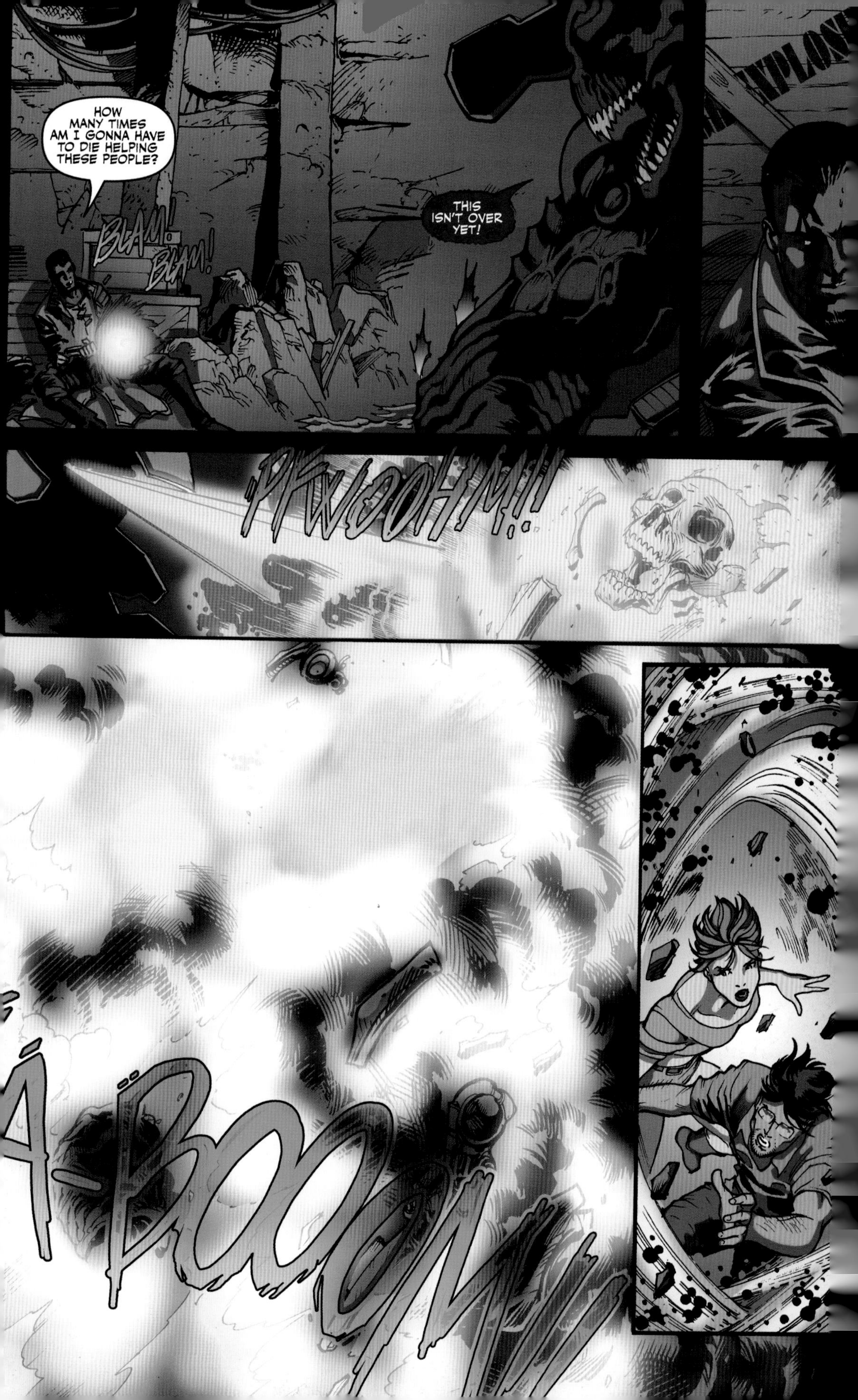
HOW MANY TIMES AM I GONNA HAVE TO DIE HELPING THESE PEOPLE?
BLAM! BLAM!
THIS ISN'T OVER YET!
PFWOOOM!!!

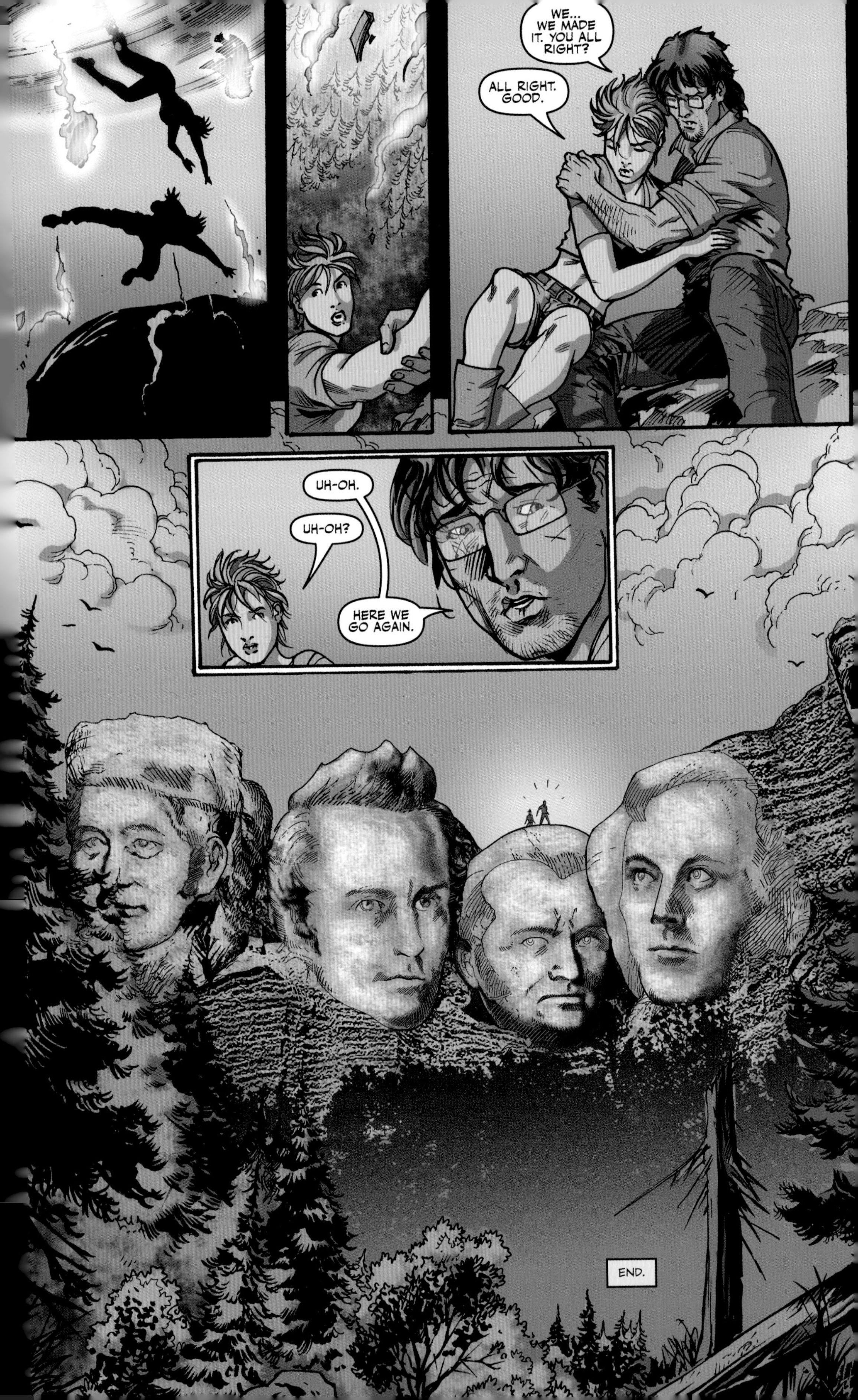
WE... WE MADE IT. YOU ALL RIGHT?
ALL RIGHT. GOOD.
UH-OH.
UH-OH?
HERE WE GO AGAIN.
END.

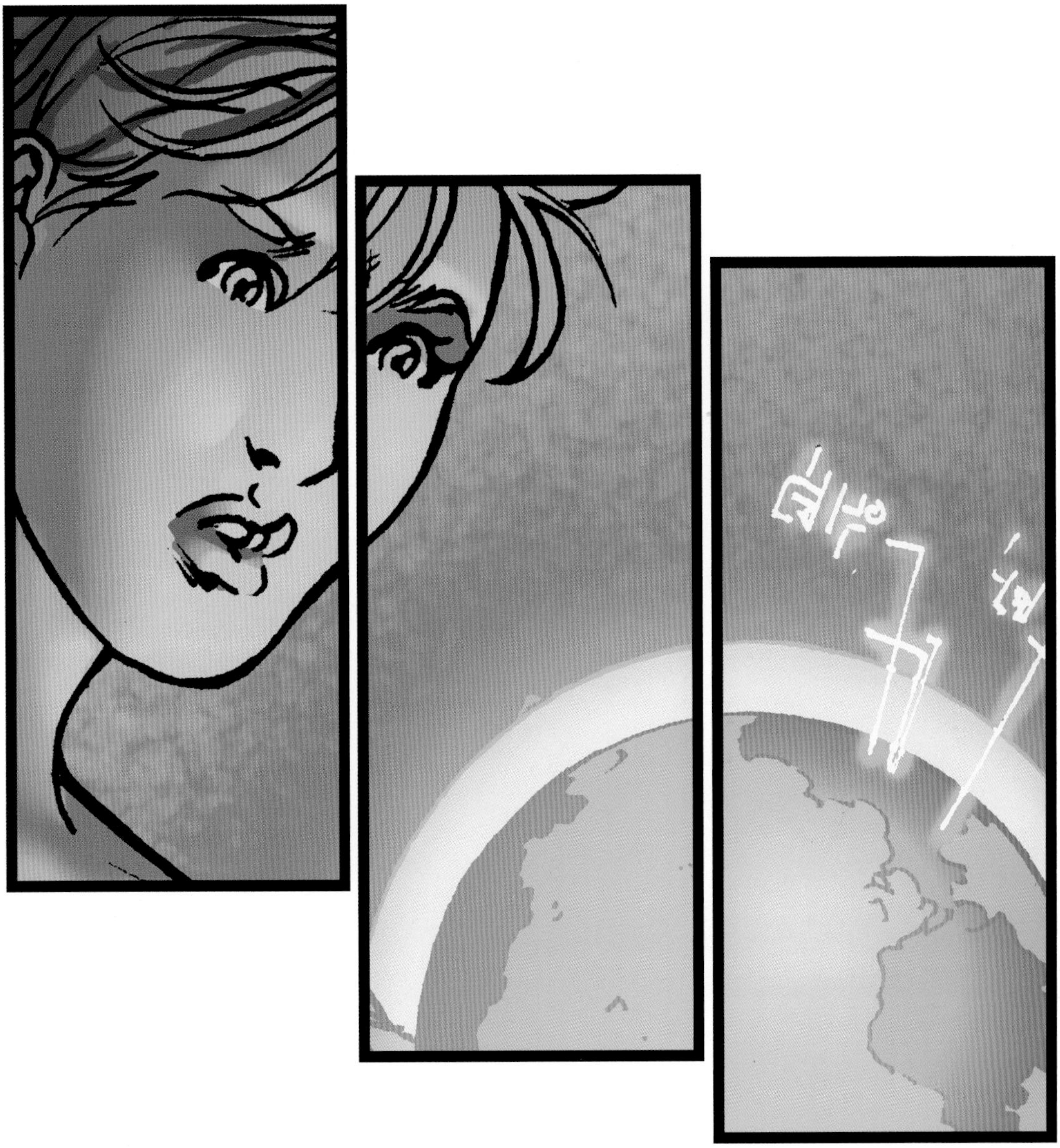

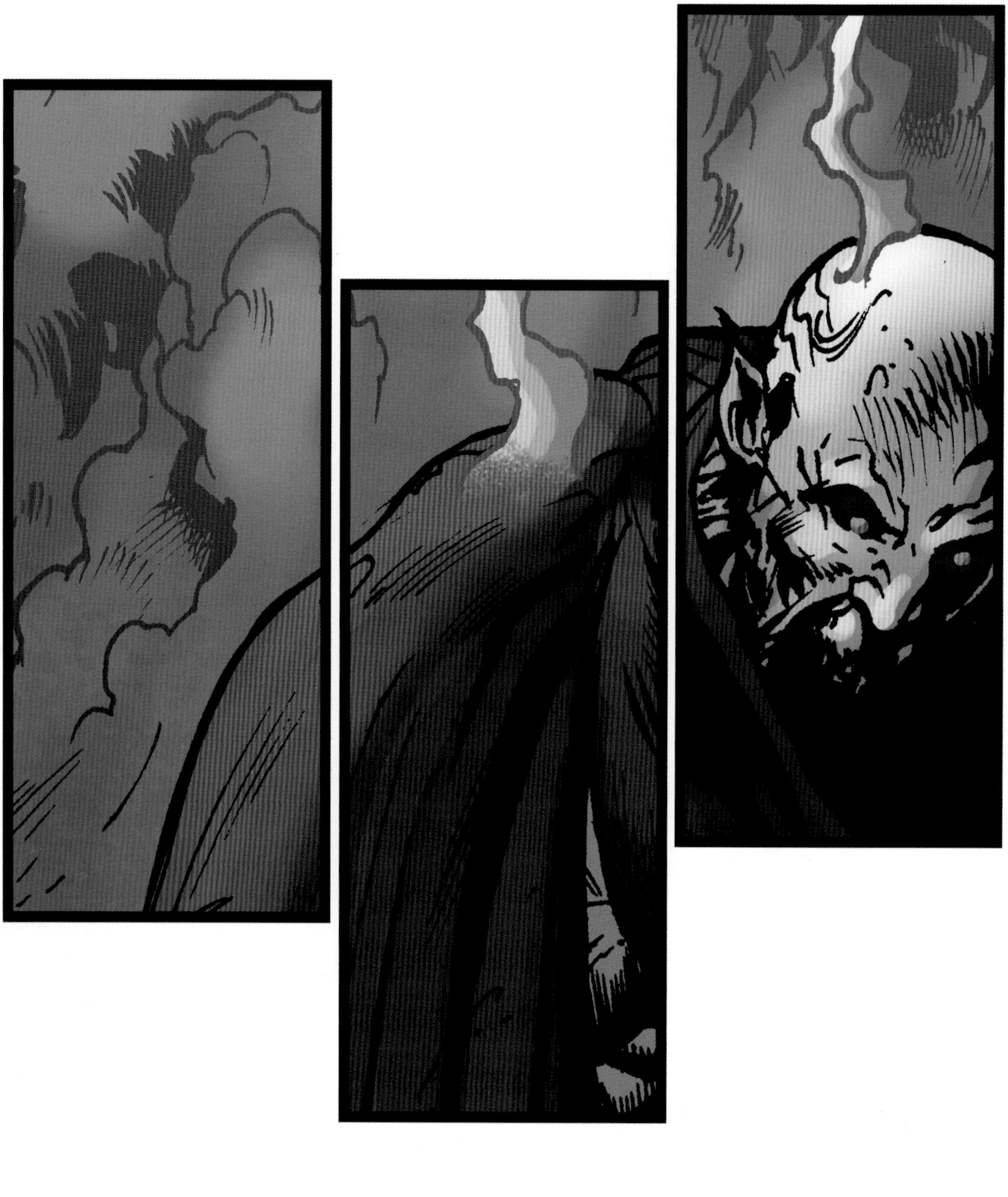

ART GALLERY

Art by Stefano Martino

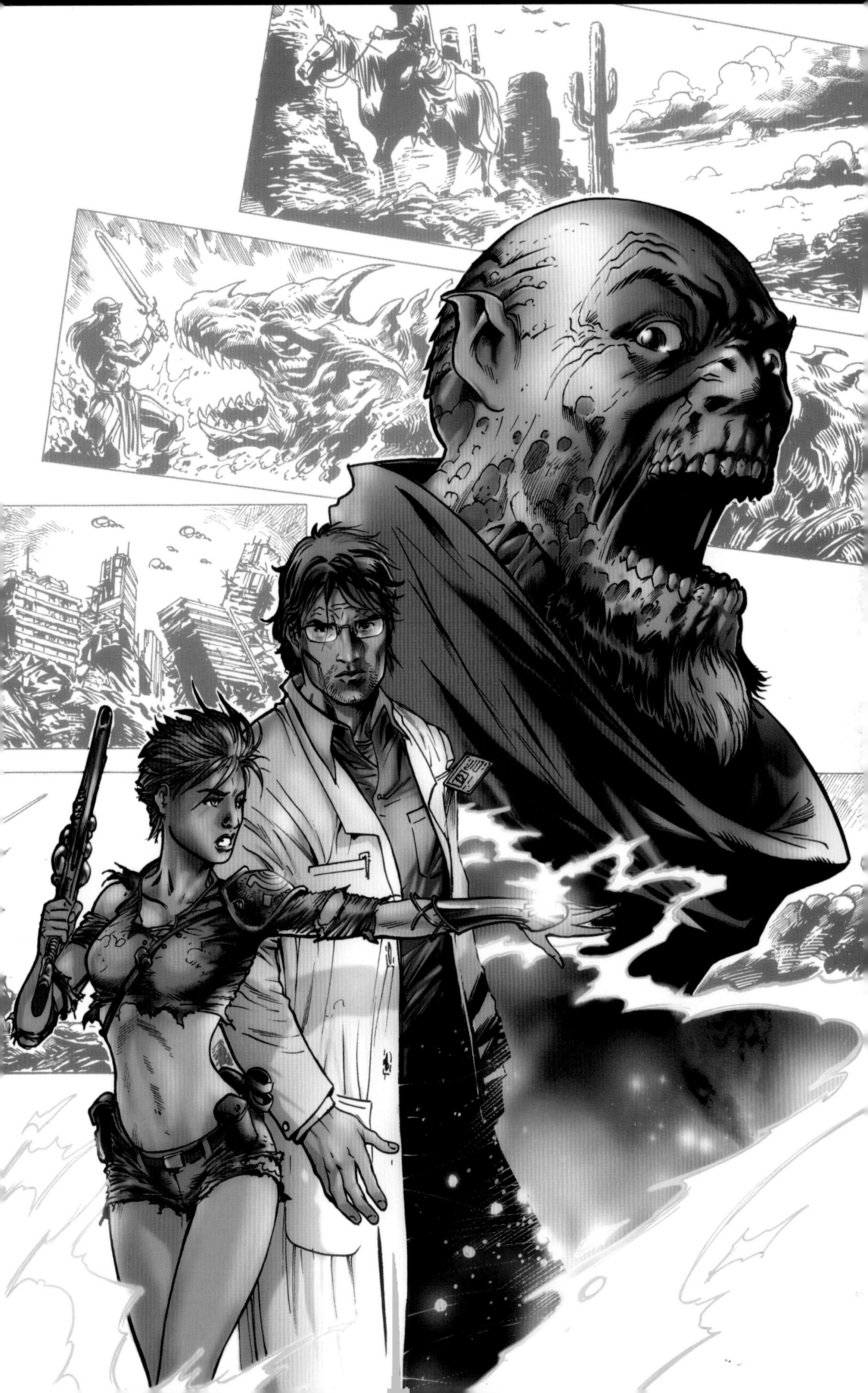

Art by Stefano Martino

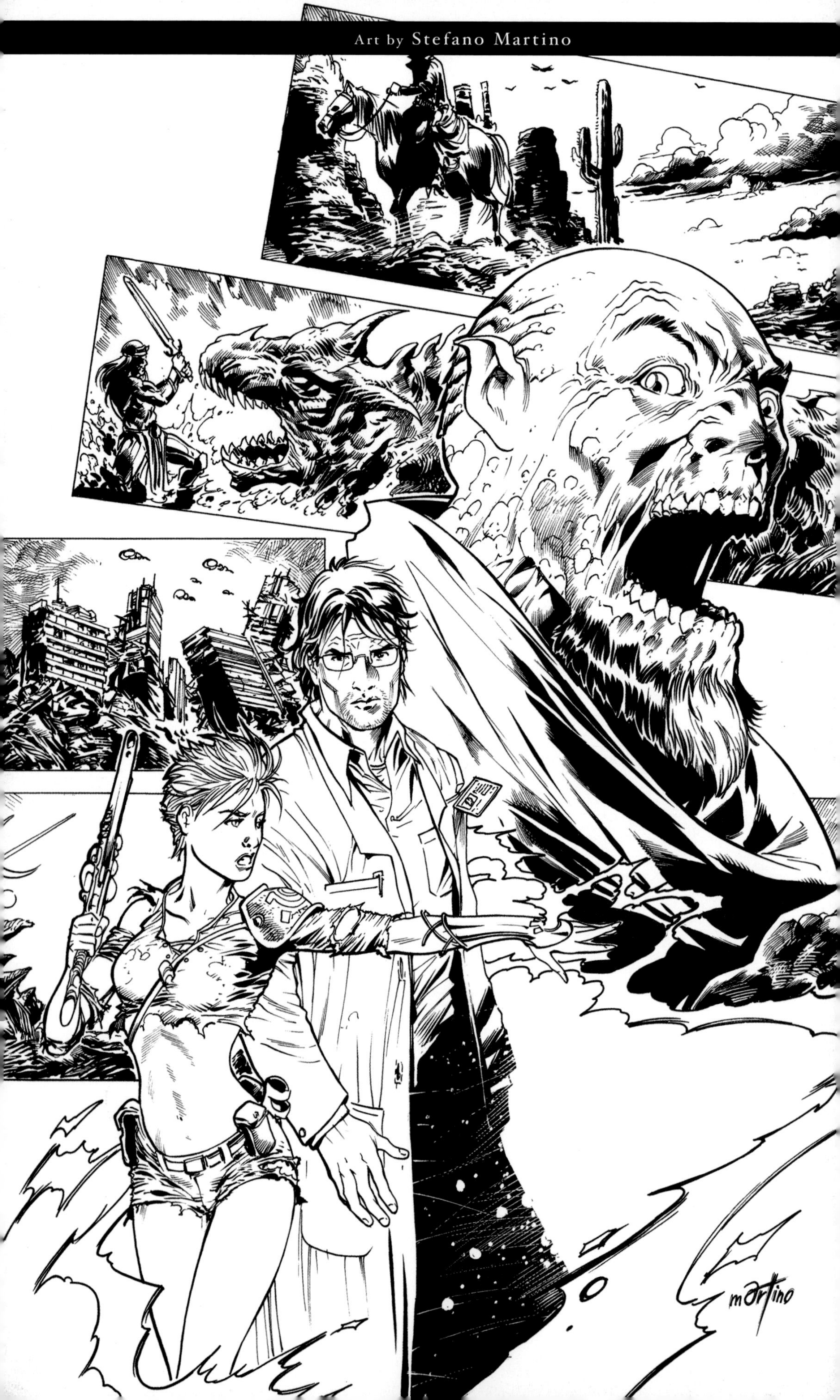
martino

Art by Rebecca Wrigley

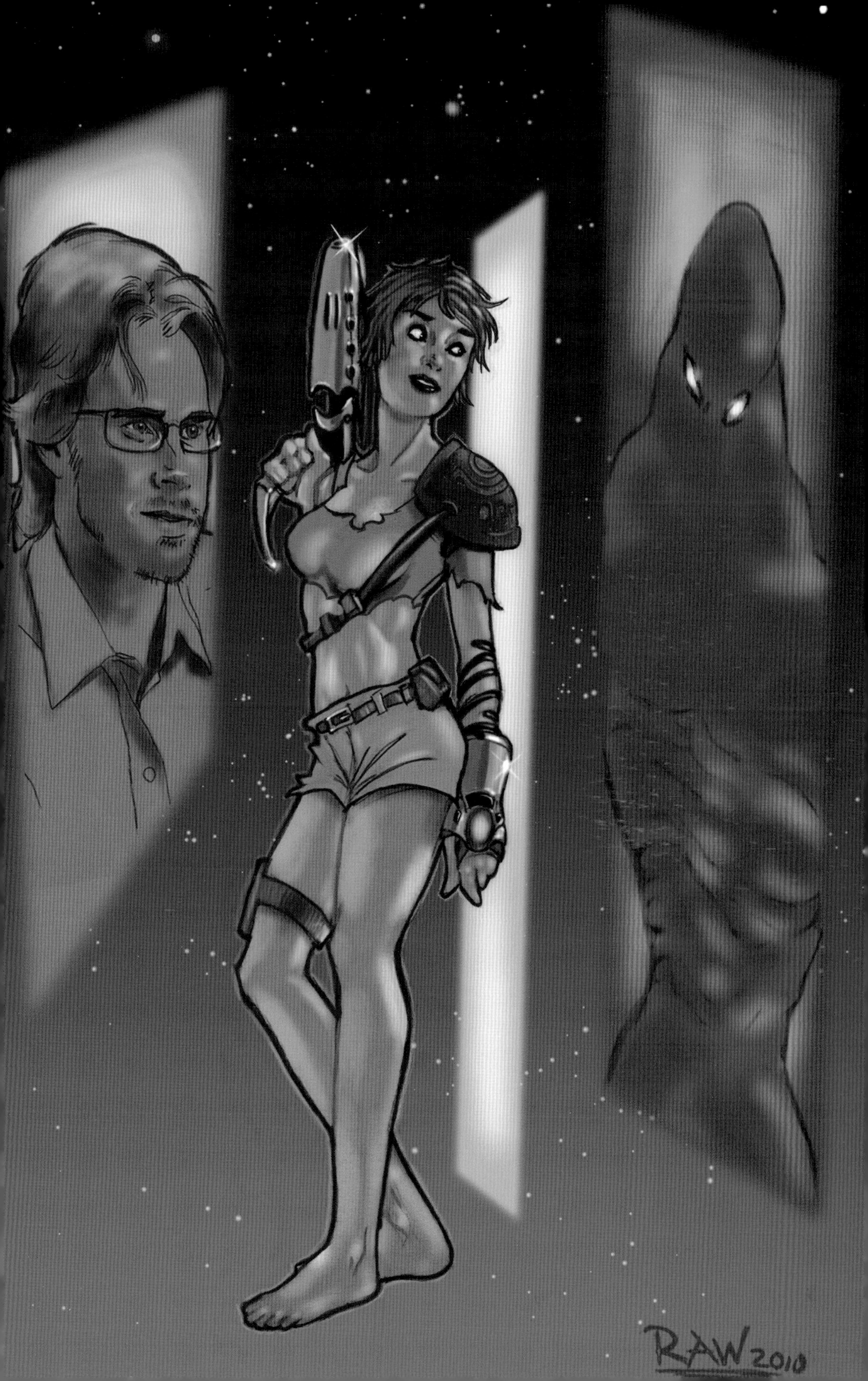
RAW 2010

Art by Stefano Martino

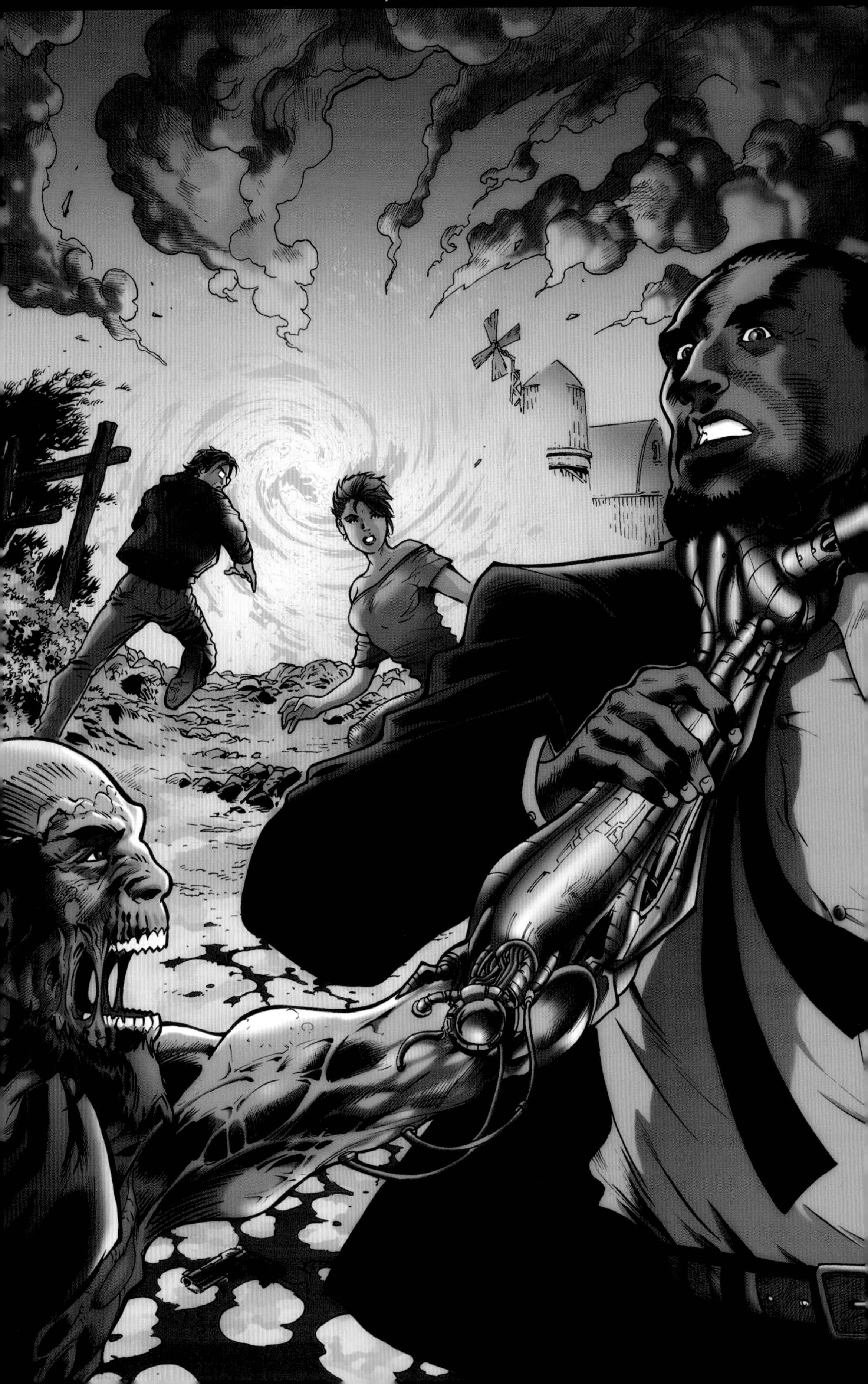

Art by Stefano Martino

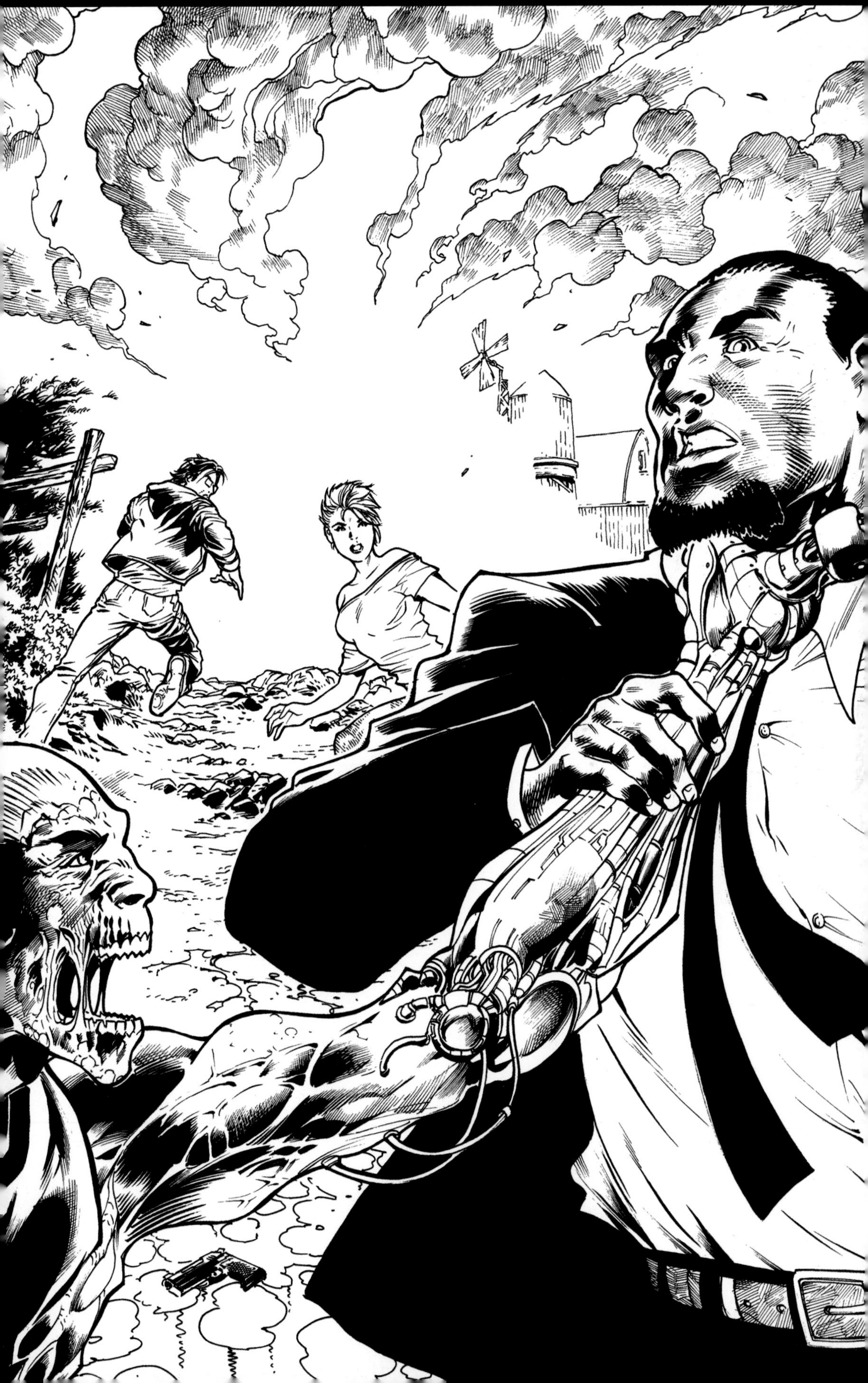

Art by Rebecca Wrigley

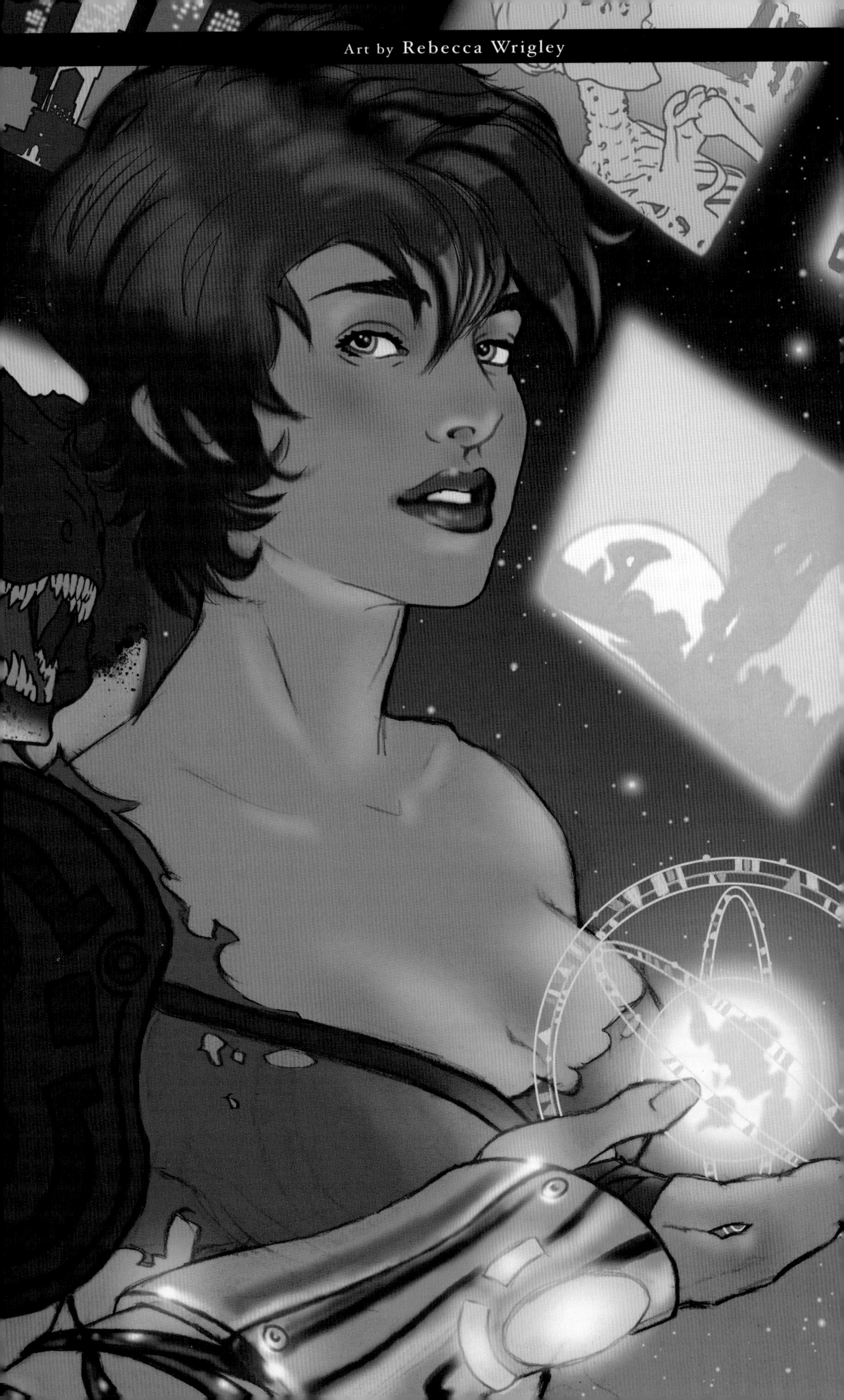

Art by Stefano Martino

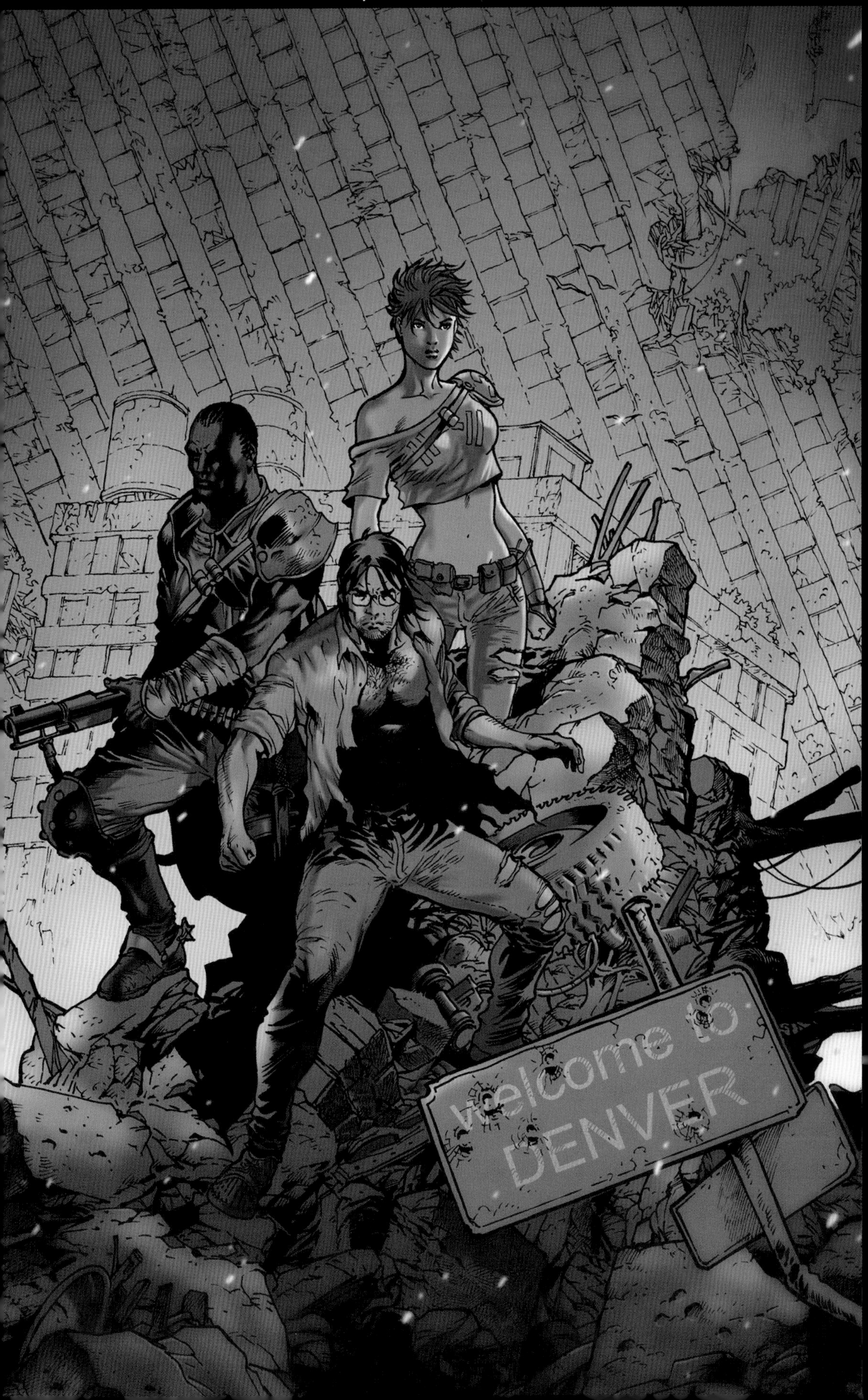
welcome to
DENVER

Art by Stefano Martino

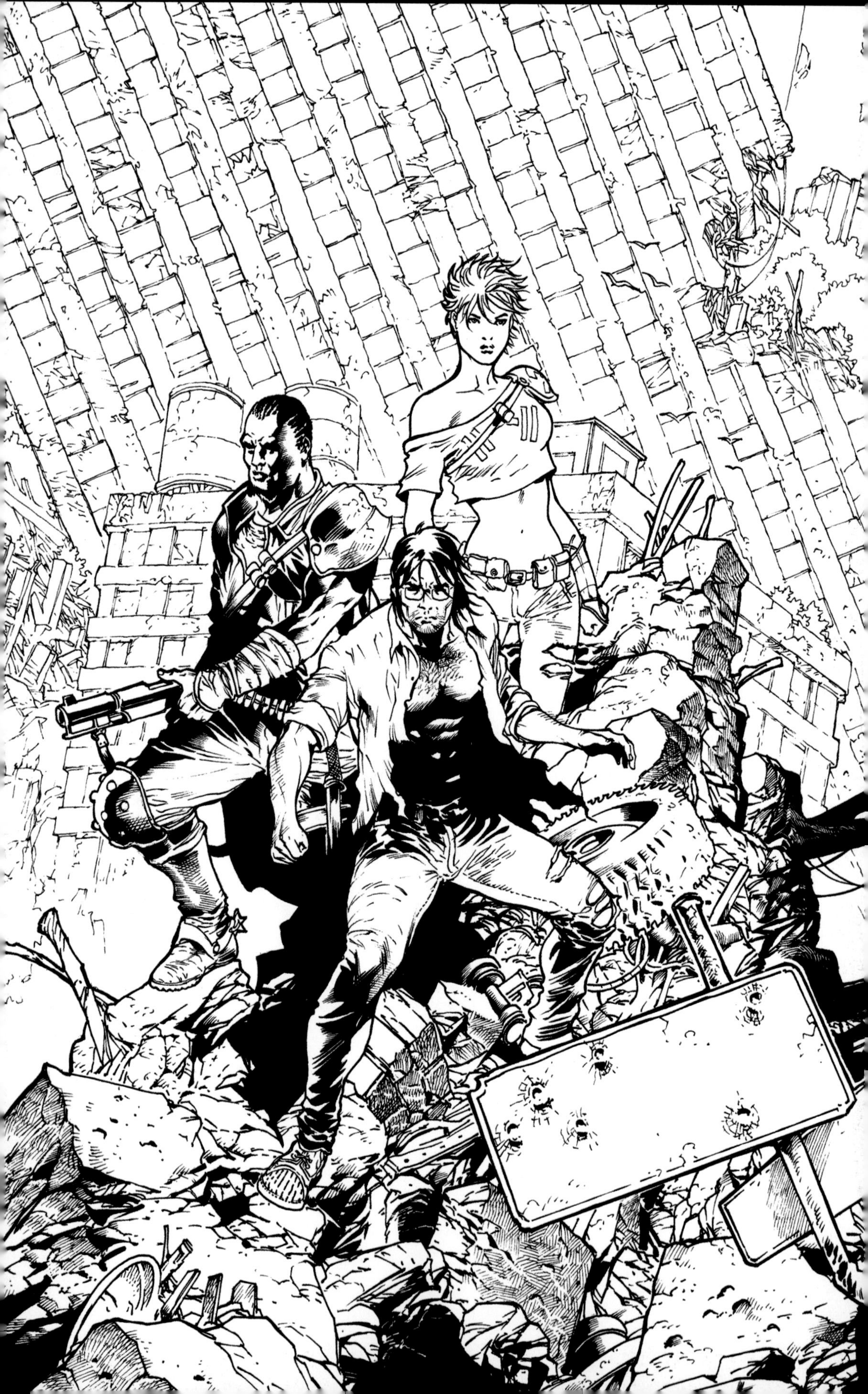

Art by Rebecca Wrigley

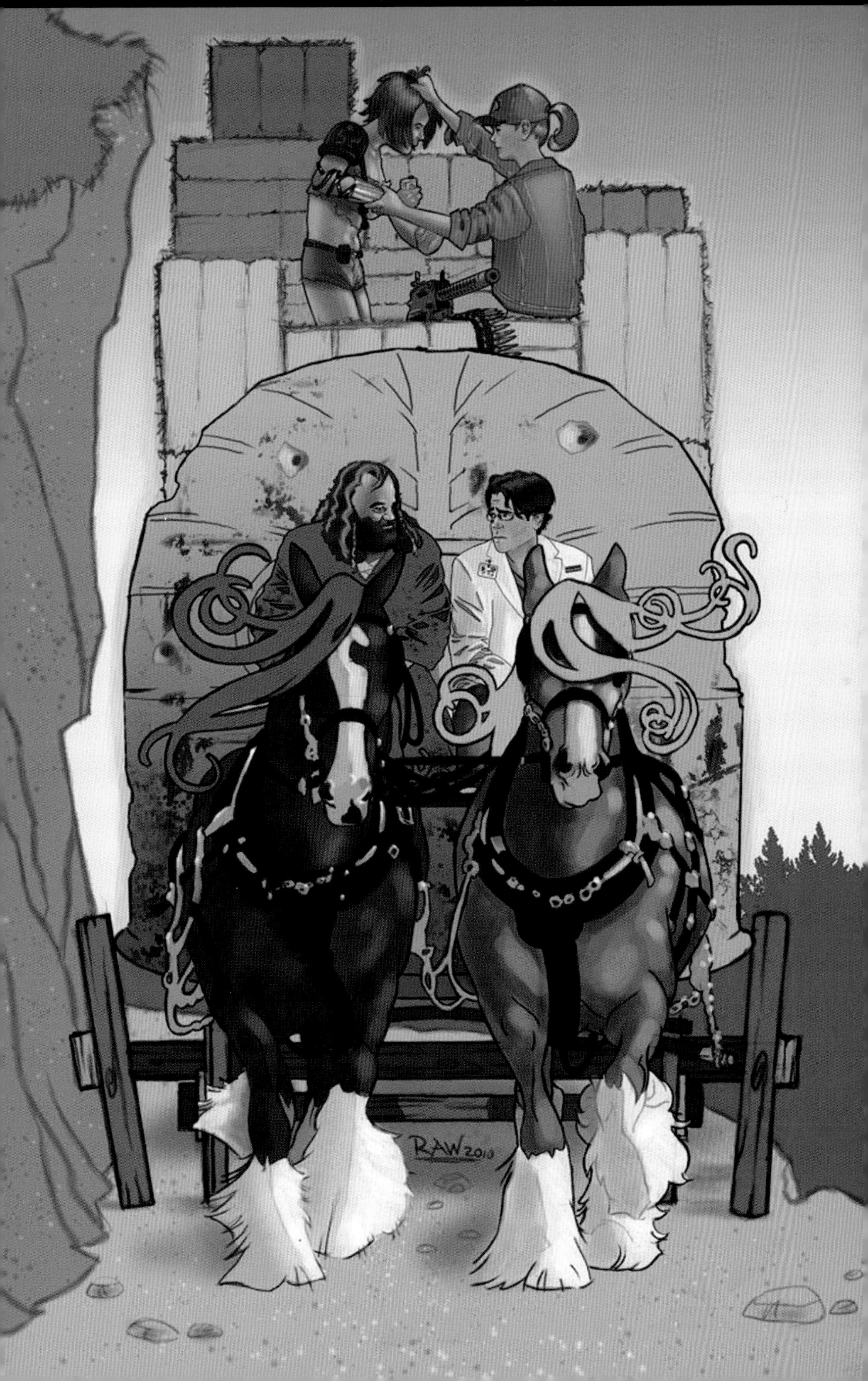
RAW 2010

Art by Stefano Martino

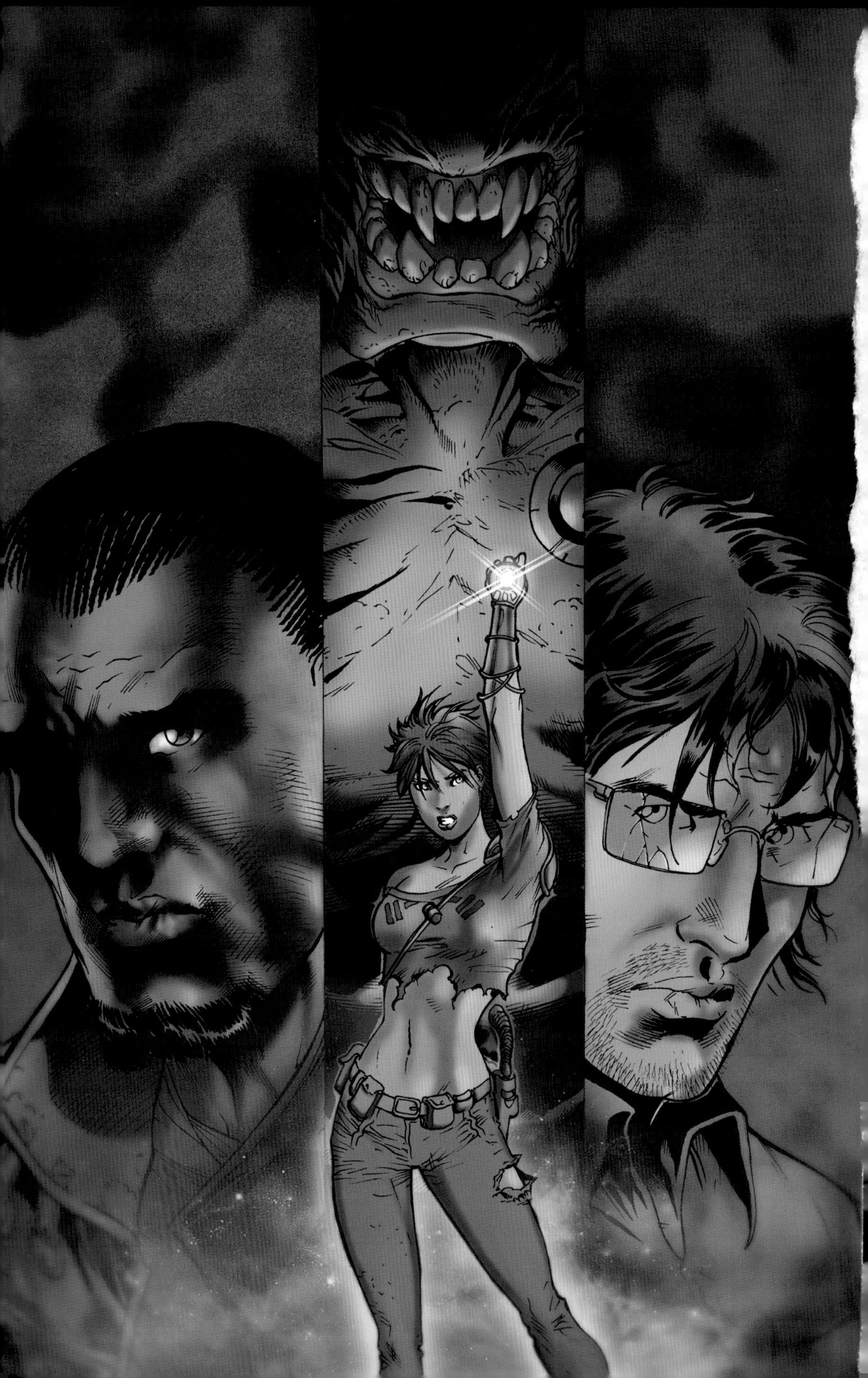